IMAGES
of America

VINELAND

HARPER'S WEEKLY.

SATURDAY, JANUARY 16, 1864.

Lands. To all Wanting Farm.

LANDS.—TO ALL WANTING FARMS.—Large an thriving settlement, mild and healthful climate, 30 mile south of Philadelphia by railroad. Rich soil, produce large crops, which can now be seen growing. Twenty an fifty acre tracts, at from $15 to $20 per acre, payabl within four years. Good business opening for MANUFAC TURERS and others, churches, schools, and good society. I is now the most improving place East or West. Hundred are settling and building. The beauty with which th place is laid out is unsurpassed. Letters answered. Pa pers containing reports and giving full information wi be sent free. Address CHAS. K. LANDIS, Vineland Pos Office, Cumberland County, New Jersey.

From Report of Solon Robinson, Agricultural Editor o the Tribune:—It is one of the most extensive fertile tracts in an almost level position and suitable condition fo pleasant farming that we know of this side of the Wes ern prairies.

"TO ALL WANTING FARMS," 1864. Through advertisements like this one, Charles K. Landis promoted Vineland and its attractions in newspapers across the country and in periodicals such as *Harper's Weekly*. In the advertisement pictured above, Landis speaks of Vineland as having a "beauty . . . unsurpassed," and proudly cites a report in the *New York Tribune* identifying Vineland's soils to be among the most fertile "this side of the Western prairies."

ON THE COVER: Vineland celebrates Memorial Day, 1889. This photograph captures the vitality of a moment in time in which children, dressed in all their finery, and mothers with their baby carriages, prepare to line up for their participation in the parade. Symbolic of the American spirit of the time, this freeze-frame captures the patriotism and progress of its citizenry as it gathers on its main street, Landis Avenue.

IMAGES
of America

VINELAND

Vineland Historical and Antiquarian Society

ARCADIA
PUBLISHING

ISBN 978-0-7385-7395-3

Published by Arcadia Publishing
Charleston, South Carolina

Printed in the United States of America

Library of Congress Control Number: 2010930264

For all general information, please contact Arcadia Publishing:
Telephone 843-853-2070
Fax 843-853-0044
E-mail sales@arcadiapublishing.com
For customer service and orders:
Toll-Free 1-888-313-2665

Visit us on the Internet at www.arcadiapublishing.com

Contents

Acknowledgments		6
Introduction		7
1.	Beginnings of Vineland	9
2.	Early Growth	23
3.	Vineland's Firsts	33
4.	Early Vineland Industry	47
5.	Government in Vineland	67
6.	Entertainment in Vineland	77
7.	Vineland Schools	93
8.	Vineland Churches	103
9.	Vineland Homes and Vinelanders	111

ACKNOWLEDGMENTS

The Vineland Historical and Antiquarian Society is proud to present this book, one made possible by the enthusiasm, dedication, and hard work of a number of individuals. Each made important contributions, whether in selecting and scanning images, researching and writing descriptive and informative captions, or otherwise. They include former society trustee Dr. John Gruccio, trustee Nancy Steelman, life member John Carr, as well as Kathleen Harbold and Lauren Valentine.

Special thanks to two society trustees, Lois Genovese and Roger Scull, who each made a number of meaningful contributions to the production of this book. Drawing upon the knowledge gained from their research for this book, they developed an entertaining and informative presentation that they have given and intend to continue to give to various groups and at various venues throughout Vineland.

Special thanks also to Erin M. Rocha, our editor at Arcadia Publishing, whose assistance, guidance, and support have been invaluable throughout.

Our expressions of appreciation would not be complete without acknowledgment of those most responsible for creating and preserving a record of Vineland's earliest days, without which this book would not have been possible: Charles K. Landis, whose manuscripts and business records have long been a part of the collections of the society; Levi D. Johnson, pioneer Vineland photographer whose November 1865 large-format photographs serve as the first visual documentary record of Vineland; Francis P. Crocker and William Taylor, publishers of Vineland's first two newspapers, which served as the earliest printed records of Vineland's formative years; and Frank DeWette Andrews, whose stewardship of the society in the first four decades of the 20th century was instrumental in the construction of the society's building and museum and in the archiving, cataloging, and preservation of its collections. Appreciation goes also to the members and trustees of the society who have come before us, who recognized the importance of collecting and preserving the rich history of our community.

All images in this book are from originals in the collections of the Vineland Historical and Antiquarian Society. For more information on the Vineland Historical and Antiquarian Society visit www.vinelandhistory.org or email VinelandHistory@gmail.com.

—Frank P. Amari Jr., Esq.
President, Board of Trustees
Vineland Historical and Antiquarian Society

Introduction

As Vineland prepares to celebrate its 150th anniversary, presented here as an introduction are excerpts from *The Settlement of Vineland*, an essay by Charles K. Landis published in *Fraser's London Magazine*, January 1875, and from *Address on the History of Vineland* by Joseph A. Conwell, 1913. Collectively they present the spirit with which Vineland was begun, developed, and prospered:

The Settlement of Vineland

In the year 1861, being about twenty-eight years of age, and full of hope and courage, I conceived the idea of starting a settlement upon virgin land, near the great seaboard markets of America. I decided upon this location in order to afford the widest and most certain scope for individual success, alike on account of the markets and of the opportunities for skilled labor in farming, gardening and mechanics. I selected a tract of about thirty thousand acres, or about forty-eight square miles, in the wildest part of New Jersey, on a railroad which had just been completed, but did very little business. On this land I had no resources but the soil itself; the large timber had all been cut off years before, to supply the New York and Philadelphia markets; there was no coal, no iron, and no great navigable stream—nothing to help by way of commercial speculation. Besides, at that time there was no tide of emigration pouring into New Jersey—it all went West. Before my time, small tracts of land would not be sold to strangers, and emigration to that section was discouraged.

I knew, therefore, I had no chance help to depend upon, such as ordinarily allures people to new places, but that whatever was won had to be created by industry; yet I believed that if this could be attracted, and then placed in the most favorable condition for its development and increase, all the disadvantages would be overcome. It was necessary for me to create such a state of things that, when the people were brought together from the commencement, and during the progress of the Settlement, and after it had become a populous settlement, these people should prosper as a mass, and be contented. My own profits depended upon this. If the people did not individually prosper, the Settlement would cease to increase or spread, land would not sell, and the result would be a financial failure. I therefore had to deliberate carefully upon all possible things which would benefit the settler directly or indirectly, develop industry, protect it—make the improvements of one man, in usefulness and beauty, redound to the benefit of each neighboring man, make families contented by giving them religious and educational privileges, supply them with information as to the best things to cultivate, and how to do it, secure to them facilities for transporting their goods to market at the lowest possible prices, keep down all local trade monopolies, which would take money from the people without an adequate return. In short, selling land to them was but the beginning of the business; without their prosperity the sale of land would soon stop, before a fifth of my immense purchase could be taken up.

It was in the centre of this place, upon a mile square of land, that I proposed to build a city which should be filled with manufactories, shops and stores for mercantile purposes, schools and halls for public recreation, also churches of various denominations, and private residences, and around this square mile of city, as far as the boundaries of the land would reach, with farms, gardens, orchards and vineyards . . . The broad design of the Settlement was that it should be agricultural, manufacturing, commercial, and educational—one object could not well prosper without the others.

—Charles K. Landis

The Opportunity of a Wilderness

When Charles K. Landis drove the now famous stake in the wilderness on the 8th of August, 1861, he established not only a landmark, but a great historical starting point. This area was then a vast wilderness. It was such a wilderness that the conductor refused to stop the railroad train at the prospective city, and instead put Mr. Landis off near what is now Newfield, forcing him to walk five miles to drive his fancy city-centered stake. It was such a wilderness that the government refused to recognize Vineland as a post office until Mr. Landis gave security for the expense incurred. Yet Mr. Landis had the faith and courage and grit to walk over this wilderness for weeks and months, and employ men to survey and lay out roads and avenues, and pull stumps and haul dirt. He advertised town lots and farms until he had not only spent all of his own resources, but had eventually gone into debt over three hundred thousand dollars to improve and beautify the prospective enterprise.

The early struggles and experiences of the founder of Vineland, while in some way may seem like the work of a dreamer, were the true unfoldment of a long-sighted, orderly, systematic plan. His determination was to build a model community free, if possible, from the objections he had seen elsewhere, and possessing those characteristics which experience has proved to best insure beautiful and healthful surroundings and the prosperity, happiness and general well-being of the people. With his life dedicated to this proposition, he, through the public press and other methods, and in the most widespread manner, invited the world to come and make Vineland a model community.

And in all candor he placed before prospective settlers an unusual opportunity. Here was offered what we all more or less crave—the chance to begin afresh and, to a marked degree, live life over again. To those of the north was offered a milder climate. Those in the crowded cities here found fresh air and plenty of room. To those in ill health or weary of monotony was a new hope. Here were good prospects for the ambitious and an equal opportunity to all. The proposition appealed to men and women of intellect, energy and character, and they came from every direction and were received with cordial welcome. No matter from whence it came, all blood was new blood on reaching the primitive and inspiring atmosphere of Vineland.

While at the end of the first year there were only about six settlers, yet at the end of 1862, the second year, about eighty persons attended Mr. Landis' first annual reception. His reception at the end of the third year was attended by over one thousand persons. The attendance at the end of the fourth year was two thousand, and about one thousand partook of supper. His reception at the end of the fifth year was attended by more than three thousand. At this time the population of the tract was fifty-five hundred. In 1867, when Vineland was six years old, it was a community of about eight thousand population, containing churches of all the leading denominations, fourteen schoolhouses and twelve hundred pupils. Not only had churches been organized at this time, but the Historical and Antiquarian Society, the Floral Society, and the various social and secret societies had been organized.

The resources and initiative instinct of Vineland's pioneers were almost without limit. They had come from the four corners of the earth. Each man—and many women—was a distinct individual. While not one of them had been born here, their loyalty and interest had all the intensity and enthusiasm of a second birth.

Among Vineland's early settlers were merchants, manufacturers, inventors, educators, physicians, reformers, editors, financiers, authors—men of affairs—who had both failed and succeeded elsewhere and who had come here to secure a change, to gain health, to retire or to find congenial climate or to hustle for success amidst new surroundings. There were men and women of talent—musicians, singers, artists, actors or adepts in other professions—accustomed to public life and not matter what the occasion, whether a school meeting, political caucus, farmers club, literary or theatrical entertainment, it was more like the work of leaders and professionals than amateurs.

The men and women who settled this wilderness and built the churches and school houses and made it the success that it is have gone to their reward. Vineland is their moment. To possess a heritage so associated with noble efforts and high achievements is our good fortune.

—Joseph A. Conwell

One

Beginnings of Vineland

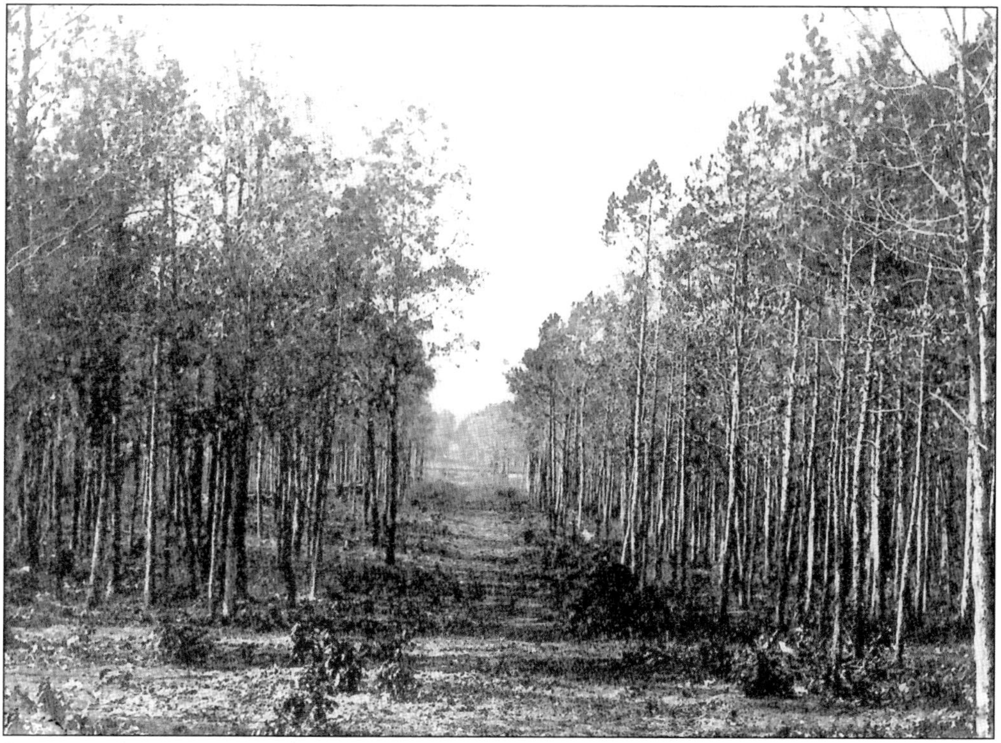

Into the Woods, 1865. This 1865 photograph records the carving out of a road in pinelands to become Pear Street, east of Sixth Street. On creating the first roads in Vineland, Charles K. Landis would later recall: "At that time the country was a dense wilderness of forest trees and thick under-growth, but with a clay and sandy loam soil, well adapted to the cultivation of fruits and the cereals. You could wander in any direction for days without meeting a human creature, and a silence reigned of that particular kind of which the ear is only sensible in a dense wilderness." (Photograph by Union Gallery of Vineland.)

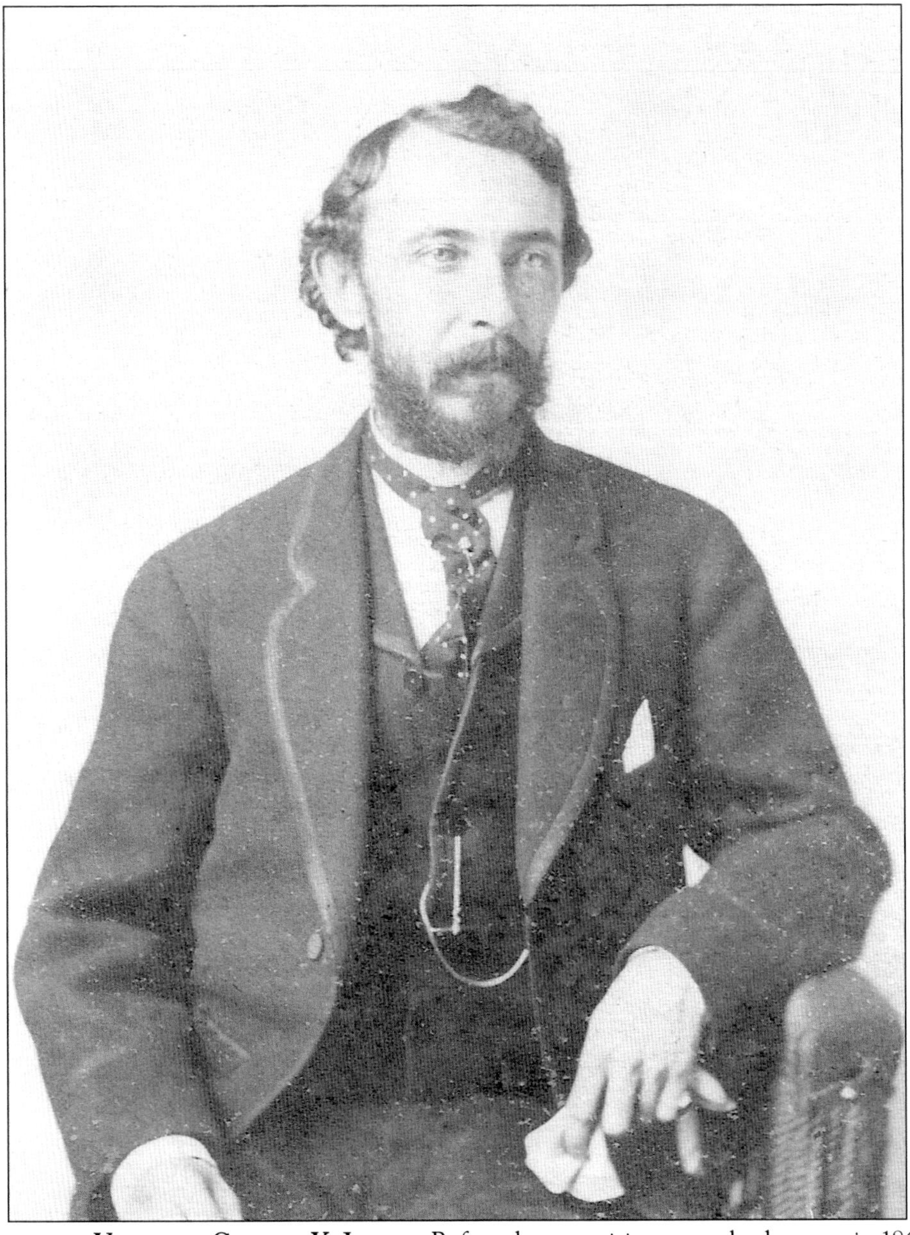

FOUNDER OF VINELAND, CHARLES K. LANDIS. Referred to as a visionary and a dreamer, in 1861 at the age of 28, Landis embarked on his master plan for a perfect community that would exemplify 19th-century utopian ideals and the age of industry at its most significant. In an 1867 statement before the Jury of the Paris Exposition, Landis stated: "In founding the colony, which I have called 'Vineland,' I carefully considered the principles of general policy, which would most increase the material prosperity, and moral welfare of the colonists . . . and produce from that population the greatest amount of industry and the highest order of intellectual improvement." As a lawyer from Philadelphia, Landis's interaction with the social problems of the city and the rise of industry led him to firmly believe that a new community should cater to the needs of its citizens socially, financially, and intellectually. Landis believed that the enforcement of temperance would support these ideals.

FARMS FOR SALE IN

VINELAND.

FARM & FRUIT LANDS

In a Mild and Healthful Climate,

34 MILES SOUTH OF PHILADELPHIA, BY RAILROAD, IN NEW JERSEY, ON THE SAME LINE OF LATITUDE AS BALTIMORE, MARYLAND.

The soil is rich and productive, varying from a clay to a sandy loam, suitable for Wheat, Grass, Corn Tobacco, Fruits and Vegetables.

This is a Great Fruit Country.

One Thousand Vineyards and Orchards

have been planted out by experienced fruit growers. Grapes, Peaches, Pears, &c., producing immense profits. Vineland is already

One of the most Beautiful Places in the United States.

The entire territory, consisting of fifty square miles of land, is laid out upon a general system of improvements.

THE LAND IS SOLD ONLY TO ACTUAL SETTLERS,

with provisions for public adornment. The place, on account of its great beauty, as well as other advantages, has become the resort of people of taste. It has increased nine thousand people within the past four years

CHURCHES, STORES, SCHOOLS, ACADEMIES, SOCIETIES OF ART AND LEARNING,

and other elements of refinement and culture, have been introduced. Hundreds of people are constantly settling. Several hundred houses are being constructed, and it is estimated that five hundred will be built during the season.

Price of Farm Land, Twenty Acre Lots and upward, $25 per Acre.

FIVE AND TEN ACRE, AND VILLAGE LOTS FOR SALE.

Fruit and Vegetables ripen earlier in this district than in any other locality North of Norfolk, Virginia. Improved places for sale. Openings for all kinds of business; lumber yards, manufactories, foundries, stores, and the like. For persons who desire mild winters, a healthful climate, and a good soil, in a country beautifully improved, abounding in fruits, and possessing all other social privileges, in the heart of civilization, it is worthy of a visit.

Letters answered and the "*Vineland Rural*," a paper giving full information, and containing reports of Solon Robinson, sent to applicants.

Address

CHAS. K. LANDIS, Proprietor,

VINELAND, Cumberland County, New Jersey.

[*From Report of Solon Robinson, Agricultural Editor of The Tribune*:]

"It is one of the most extensive fertile tracts, in an almost level position, and suitable condition for pleasant farming, that we know of this side of the Western Prairies."

Vineland Weekly Print.

Promoting Vineland. As the advertisement states, Vineland was a community for growth and immediate development, but not for speculation. Charles K. Landis advertised heavily throughout the United States and promoted Vineland as a "model town of the world." To prospective buyers, Landis stipulated that purchasers build and live on the land within a year. Many parcels of land were turn-key purchases containing a dwelling, planted fruit trees, and fruit-bearing plants.

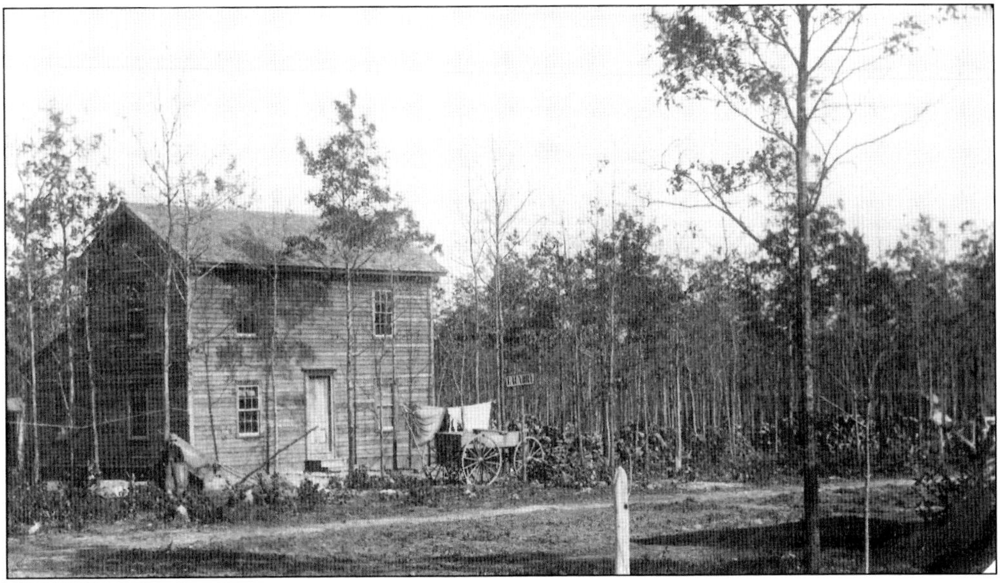

A Laundry, 1865. This 1865 photograph of a laundry at the corner of Sixth and Plum Streets captures the transformation of a once uninhabitable land into a newly born, pioneer-like setting of a new town. The sign above the wagon reads "Laundry," a service offered by the owner of this home, perhaps to the men who worked to clear the land. (Photograph by Union Gallery of Vineland.)

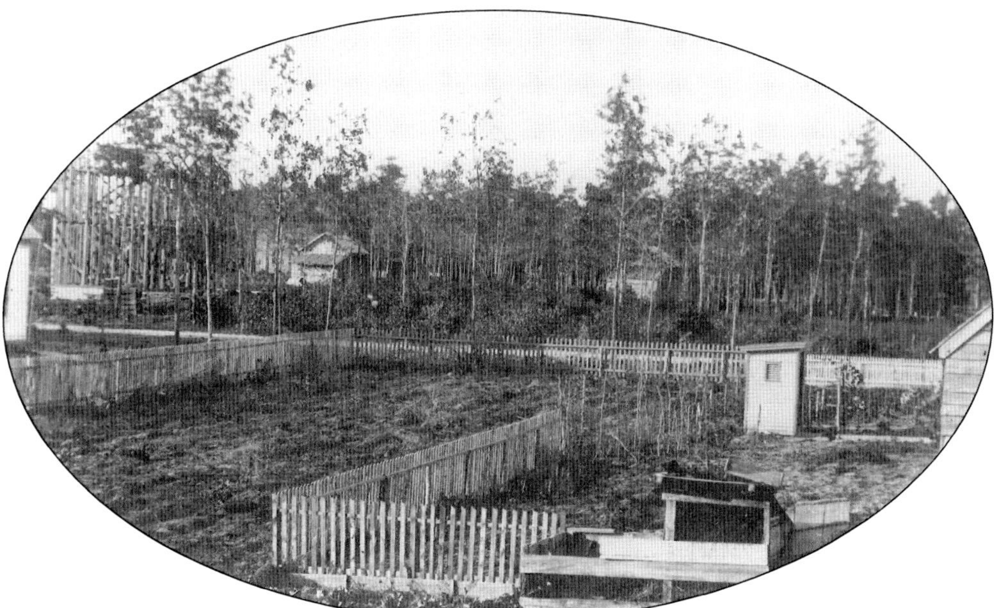

Improved Lots, 1865. Careful surveying of land established clear boundaries and allowed for precise development within the heart of the new city. In this photograph of lands north of Landis Avenue between Sixth and Seventh Streets, a new house is under construction at the far left, and an "earth closet," invented in Vineland to produce fertilizer for farming, is seen at the far right.

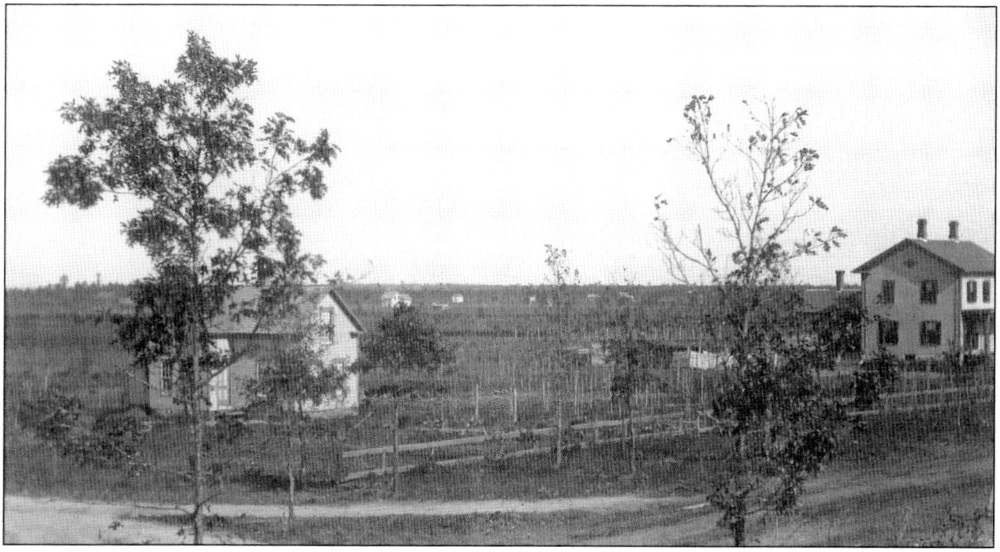

Landis and East, 1865. The picture above shows the northeast corner of Landis and East Avenues as it was improved by houses and rows of grape vines. The picture below shows Landis Avenue looking west from East Avenue, its broad avenue a dirt road bounded by young shade trees. (Photograph by Union Gallery of Vineland.)

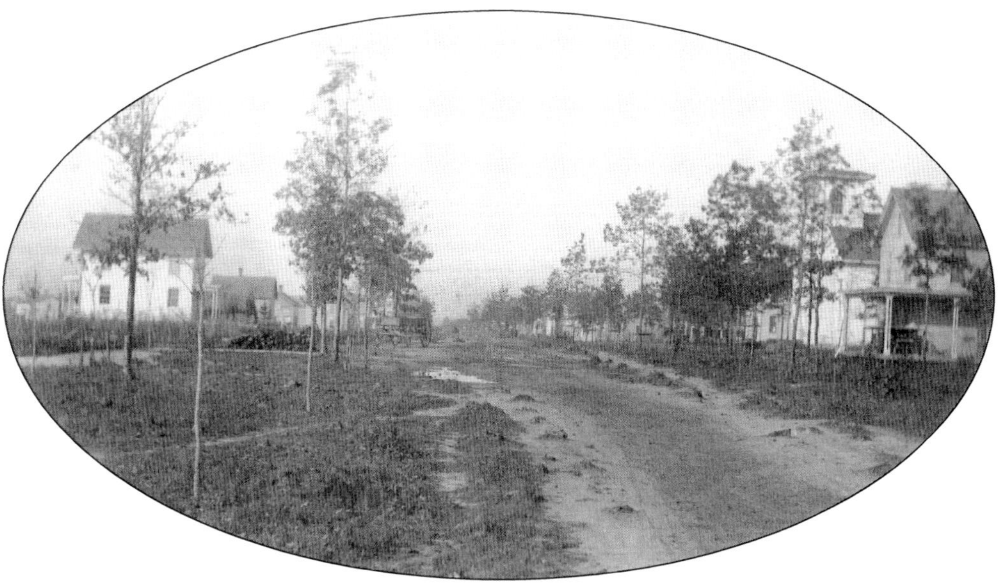

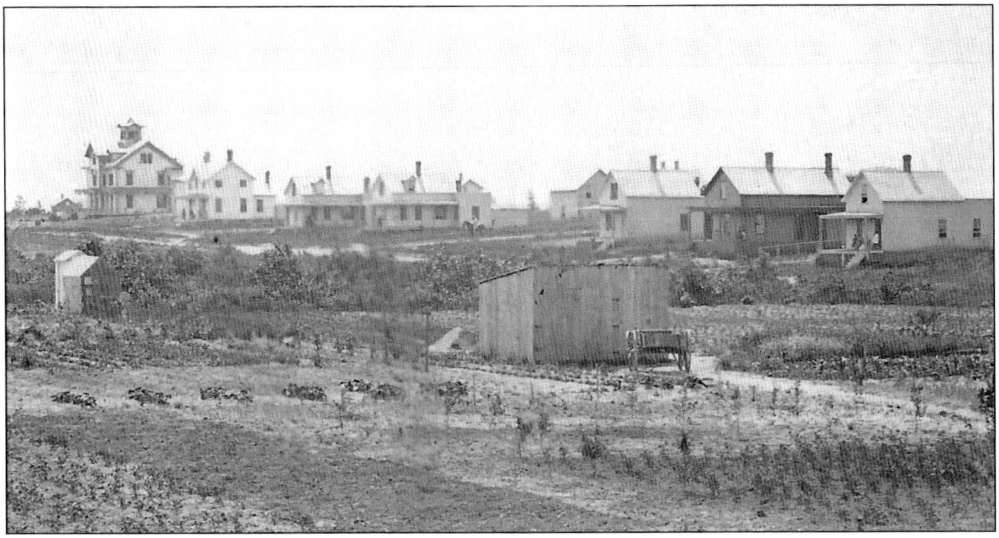

As Advertised, c. 1870. This picture exemplifies a typical promotion for real estate sales in Vineland. The following is an advertisement from about 1869: "House and two Lots, $1900. House 20x24, five finished rooms. Good well. Carriage shop 24x28. All the land is trees, apple, pear and cherry trees, currant bushes, etc." To a new buyer, an offer with many improvements already in place was very desirable. (Photograph by Union Gallery of Vineland.)

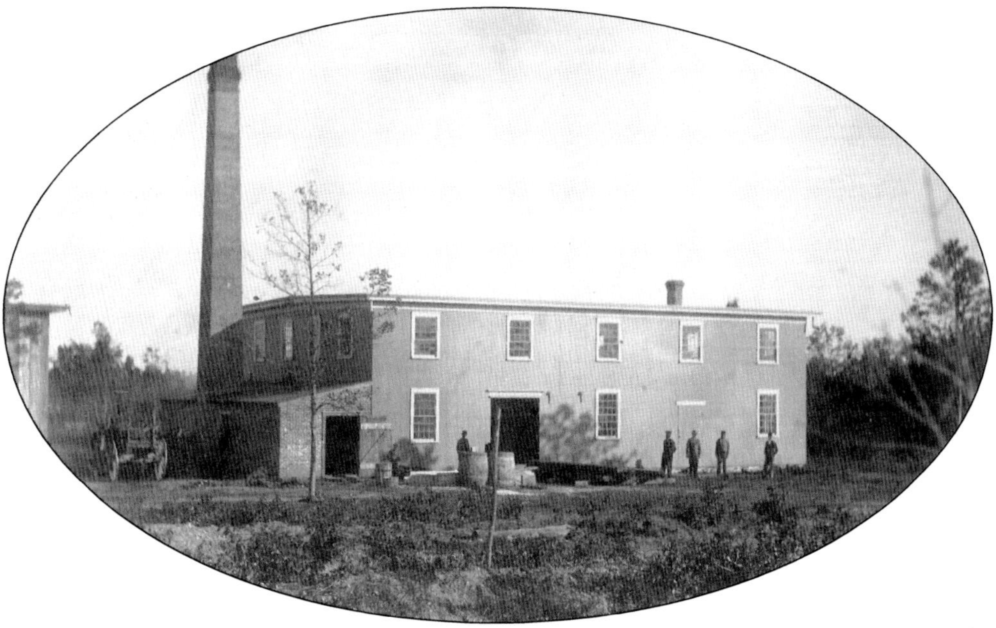

Paine and Mabbett's Sash Factory, 1865. In 1865, Truman Mabbett built this factory on the corner of Boulevard and Almond Street. The factory was used to make window and door sashes. Mabbett and his partner operated the business until 1870, when it was sold. One year later, the building was purchased by the Kimball and Prince Lumber Company, which continued to operate at that location for many years. (Photograph by Union Gallery of Vineland.)

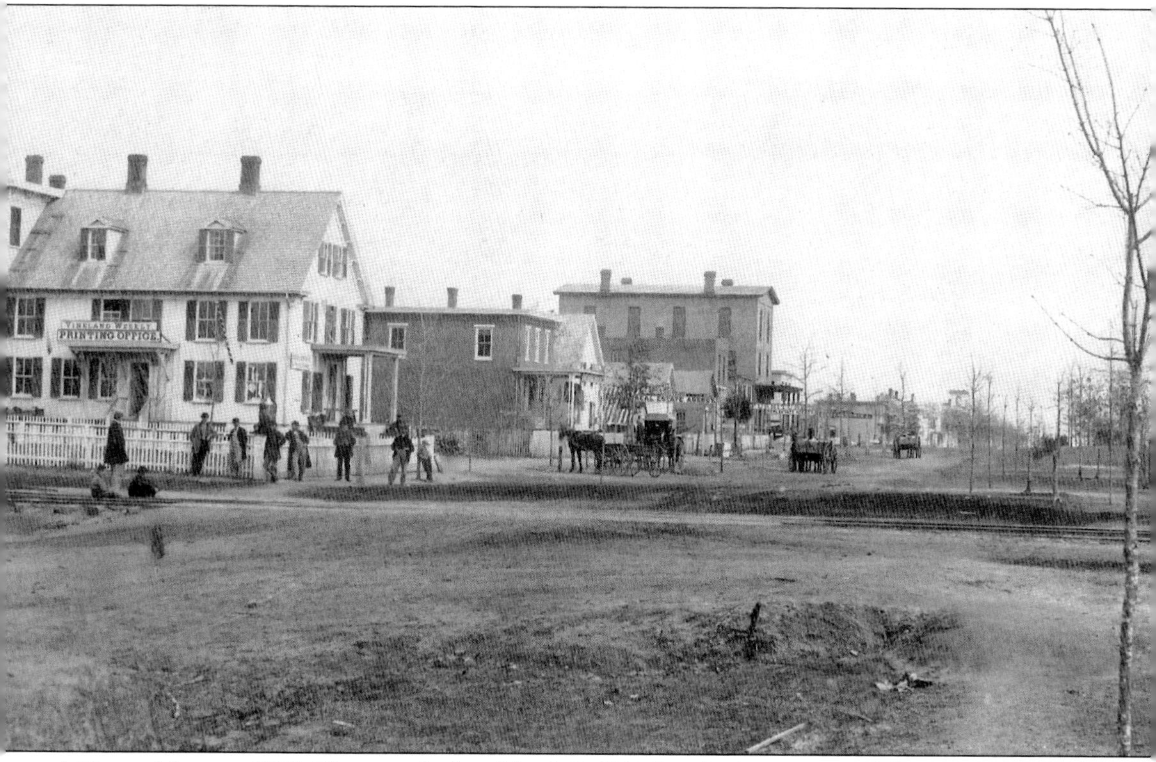

A DAY IN MARCH, 1866. Photographed on March 3, 1866, Landis Avenue east of the train station shows business as usual as spring approaches. On that day, the *Vineland Weekly* newspaper posted, "The pleasant weather for the last few days has brought out the spring birds . . . our people have commenced plowing, and some are planting early vegetables." The railroad tracks are shown crossing in front of the *Vineland Weekly* printing office. This may have been the first view of Vineland that a visitor or settler saw when departing the train. (Photograph by Union Gallery of Vineland.)

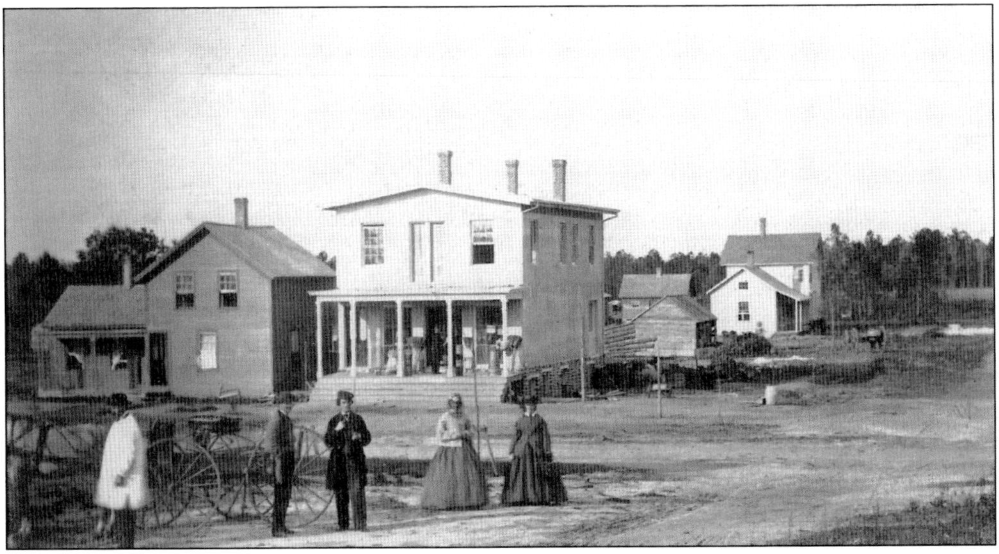

EARLY DOWNTOWN, 1865. This view of Landis Avenue and Fourth Street exemplifies a typical downtown block with its two-story architecture and distinct street boundaries. Within four years of its founding, Vineland's developing downtown began to reflect Landis's intention that residential and commercial development meet the needs of its new settlers. (Photograph by Union Gallery of Vineland.)

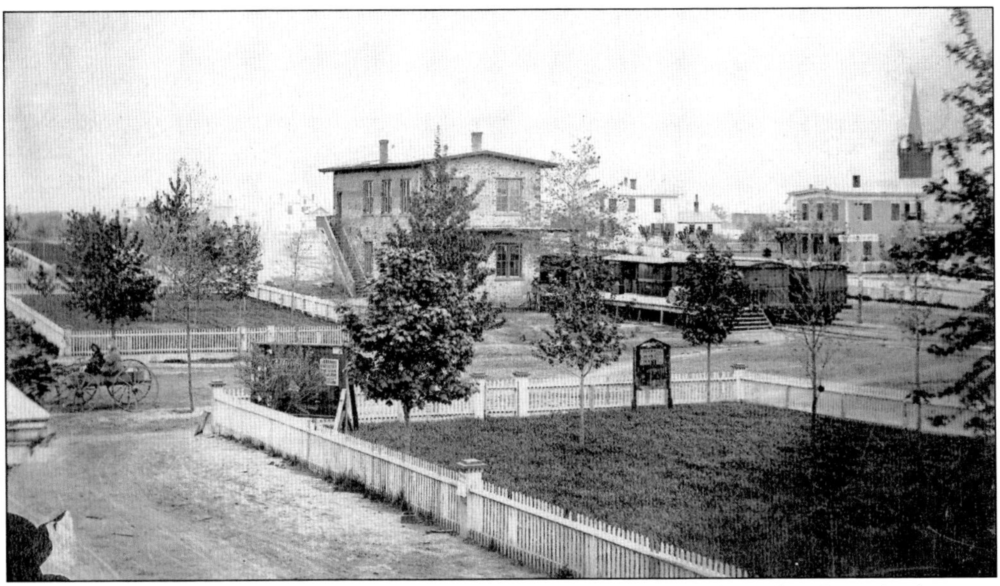

TRAIN STOP, C. 1870. This picture shows the intersection of the Boulevard and Landis Avenue. The large stone building in the middle is the railroad station built by Charles K. Landis, with the second floor being used as Union Hall, a free venue for community meetings and events. Billboards with advertisements and notices are shown displayed across the street.

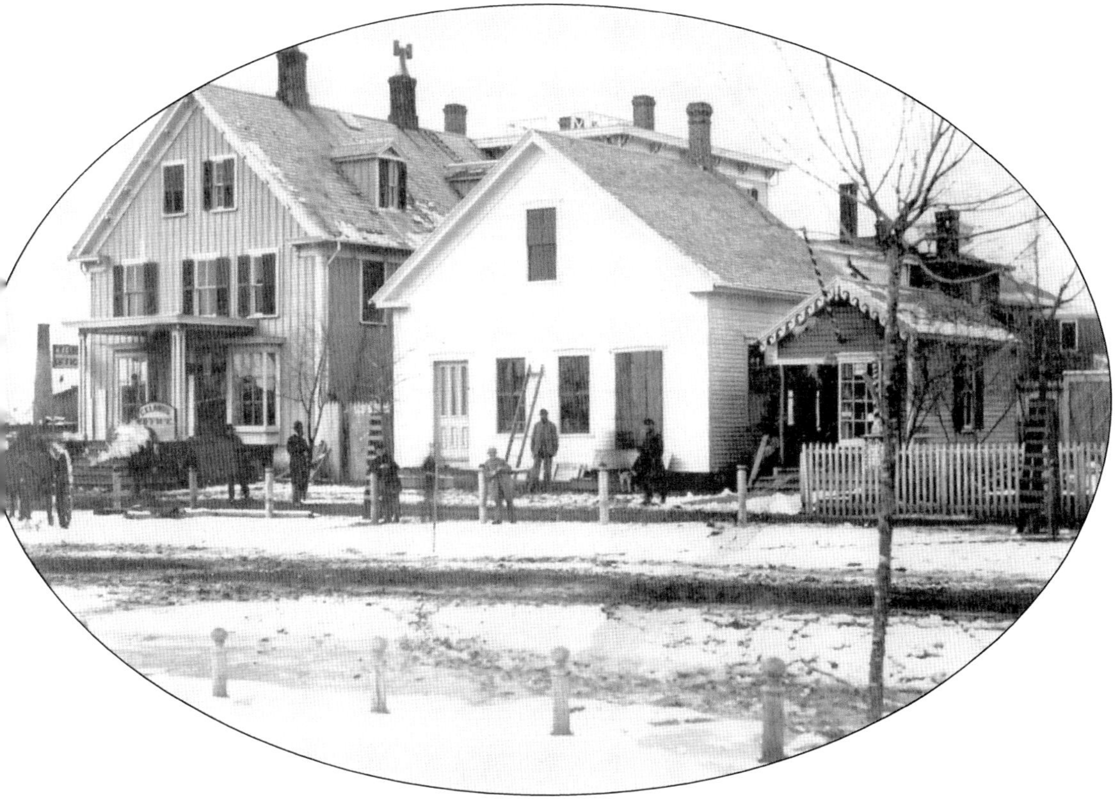

Office of Charles K. Landis, 1865. This picture shows the northeast corner of Landis Avenue and the Boulevard. Landis's office is shown on the far left. It was attached to the Hotel Vineland, which is not shown in this picture but whose roof can be seen behind his office building. When visitors got off the train in Vineland, Landis's agents directed them immediately to his office. (Photograph by Union Gallery of Vineland.)

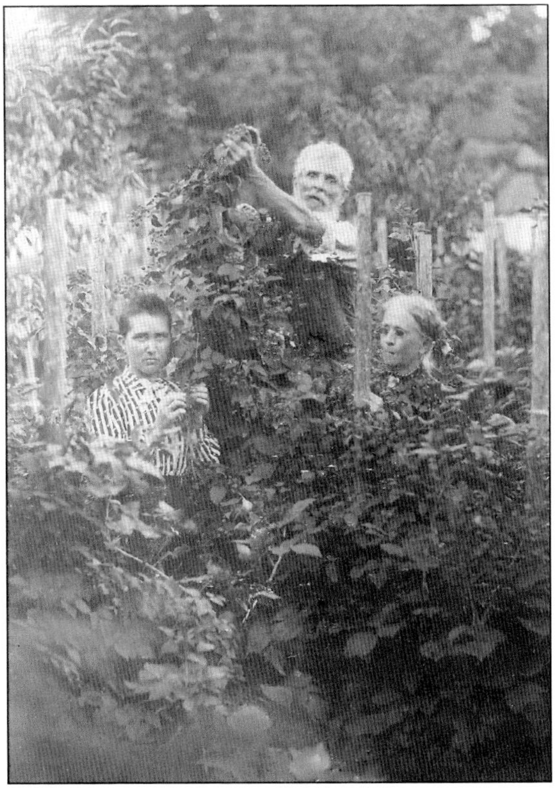

Vines! "Young vines produce beautiful fruit, but old vines produce the richest." (*Vineland Weekly*, June 20, 1868). The local newspapers frequently published articles offering advice on agriculture and news of the latest improvements in farming, complementary to Charles K. Landis's proud promotion of Vineland's soil and climate for the growing of fruit, especially those from the vine. In fact, Landis had named the town "Vineland" because he had intended to make it a vine country. In the photograph at left, Thomas B. Steele and his family are seen among their grapes.

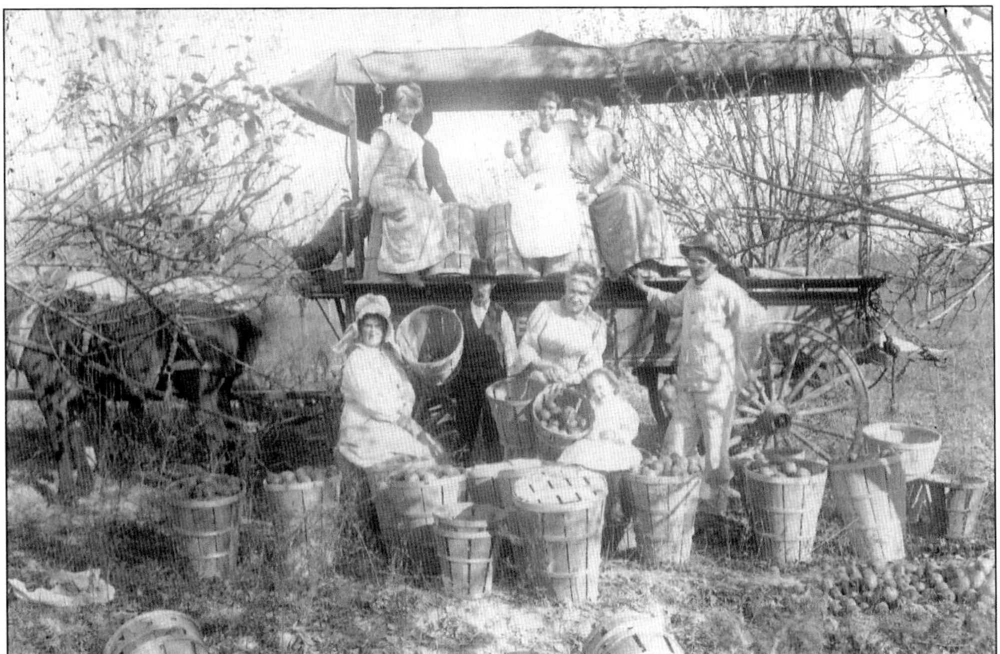

Surrounded by Farms, c. 1875. This picture shows the fruit of the labor of the Hall family, shown seated around their crops. Charles K. Landis's vision for Vineland was that the industrial center of the town would be encircled by an agricultural and fruit-growing colony.

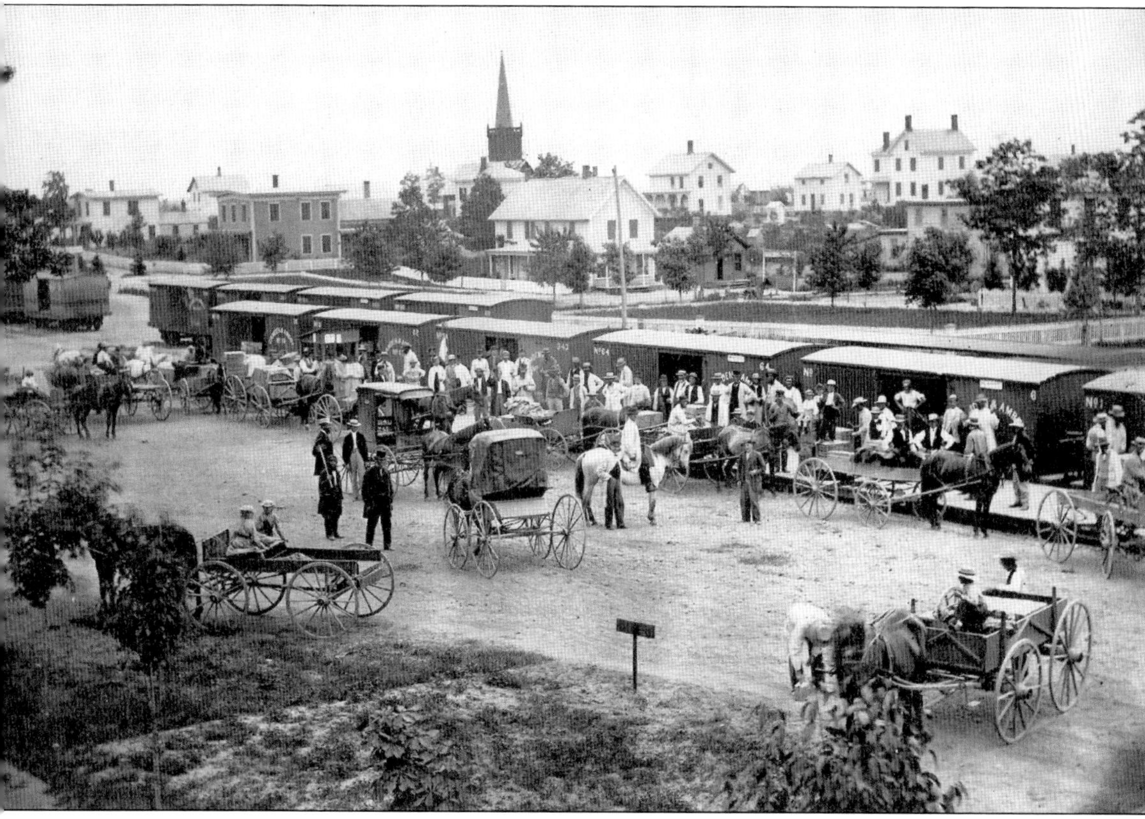

SHIPPING STRAWBERRIES, 1868. The average daily shipment at the height of the strawberry season in May and June 1868 was around 24,000 quarts of strawberries. Newspaper accounts were kept on a regular basis and listed only those shipments from the railway station pictured in the center of the borough of Vineland. Accounts do not show shipments from South or North Vineland, which were also significant. The major markets to which Vinelanders shipped their goods were Philadelphia and New York City. (Photograph by Union Gallery of Vineland.)

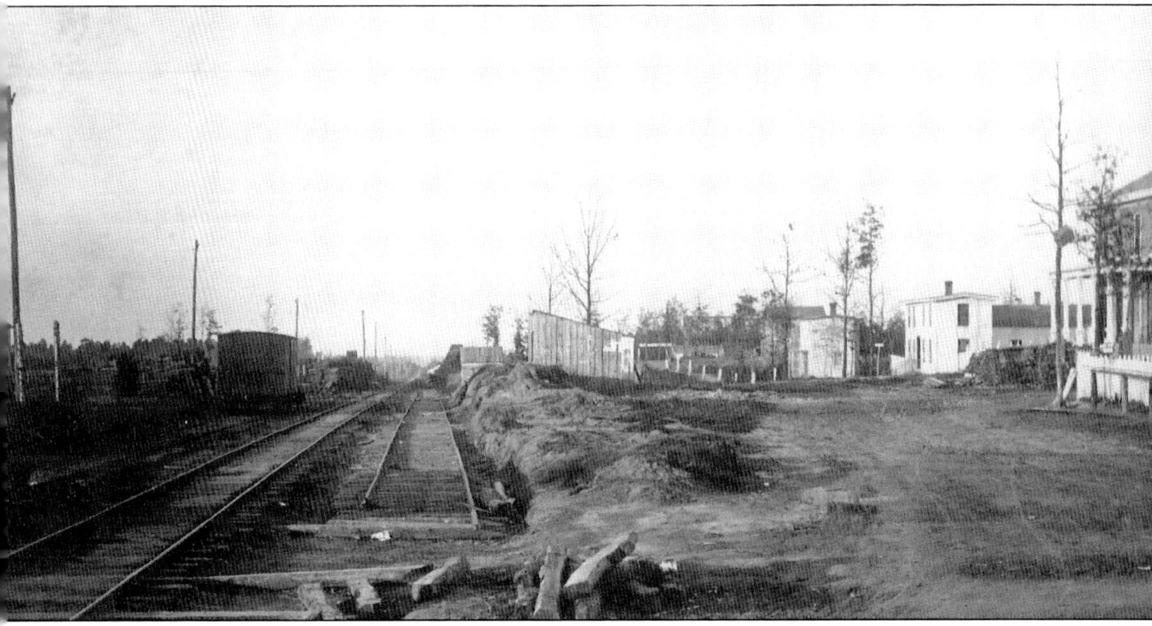

RAIL LINES AT THE BOULEVARD. This photograph from November 15, 1865, shows railway tracks being laid north along the Boulevard, taken from the train station at that location. The people of Vineland considered it critical to the future prosperity of the town that direct railroad communication with New York be established. In 1867, a number of local businessmen were granted a charter to establish a railroad, and most of the shares of stock were purchased by Vinelanders. After completion of the line, the railroad was unable to meet expenses and subsequently was sold in 1873 to Jay Gould for $10,000. It eventually became part of the Central Railroad of New Jersey. (Photograph by Union Gallery of Vineland.)

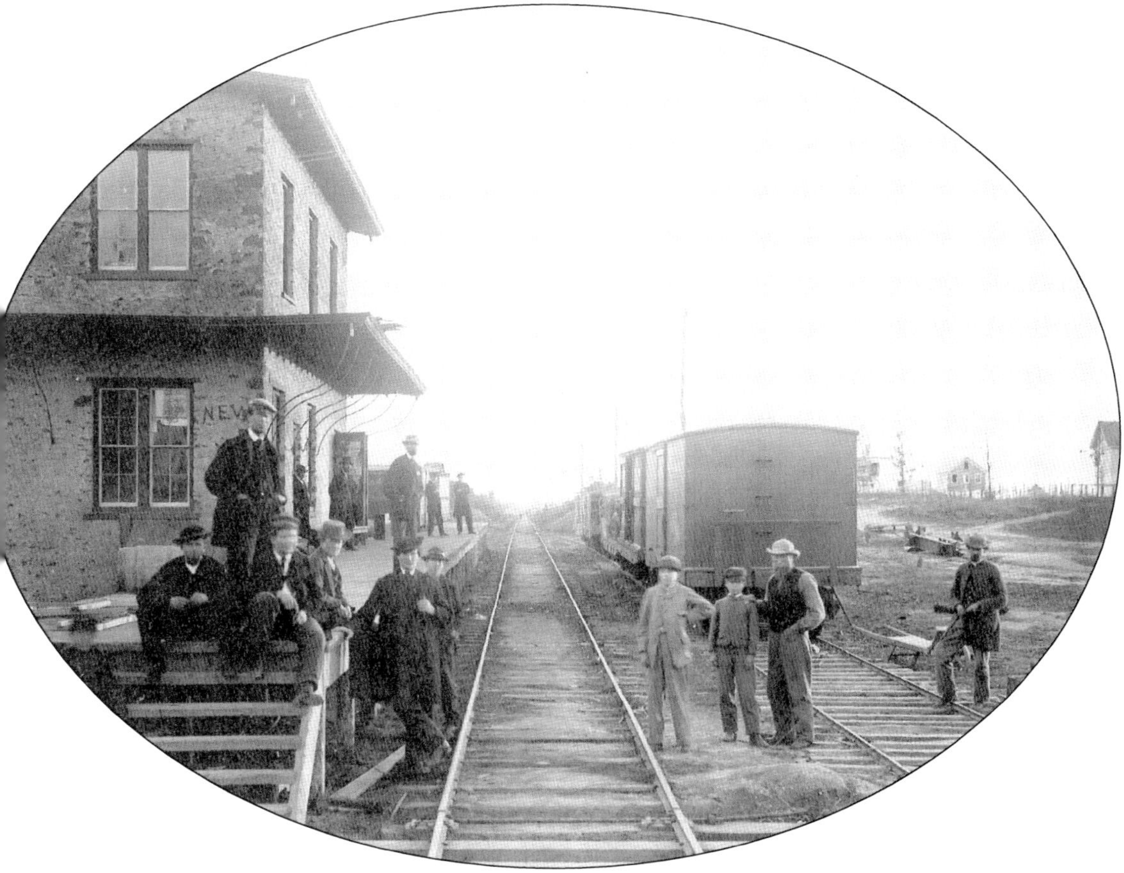

VINELAND RAILROAD STATION, 1865. In 1864, Charles K. Landis replaced the original platform station with the above two-storied stone building. He leased the second floor as a room to be used for public meetings under the name of Union Hall. Landis took responsibility for lighting and heating the room, which became a popular community venue for political meetings, church services, and entertainment. In 1884, that building was replaced with a more accommodating building. The newer brick station contained large waiting rooms with many windows and a long, covered walkway. (Photograph by Union Gallery of Vineland.)

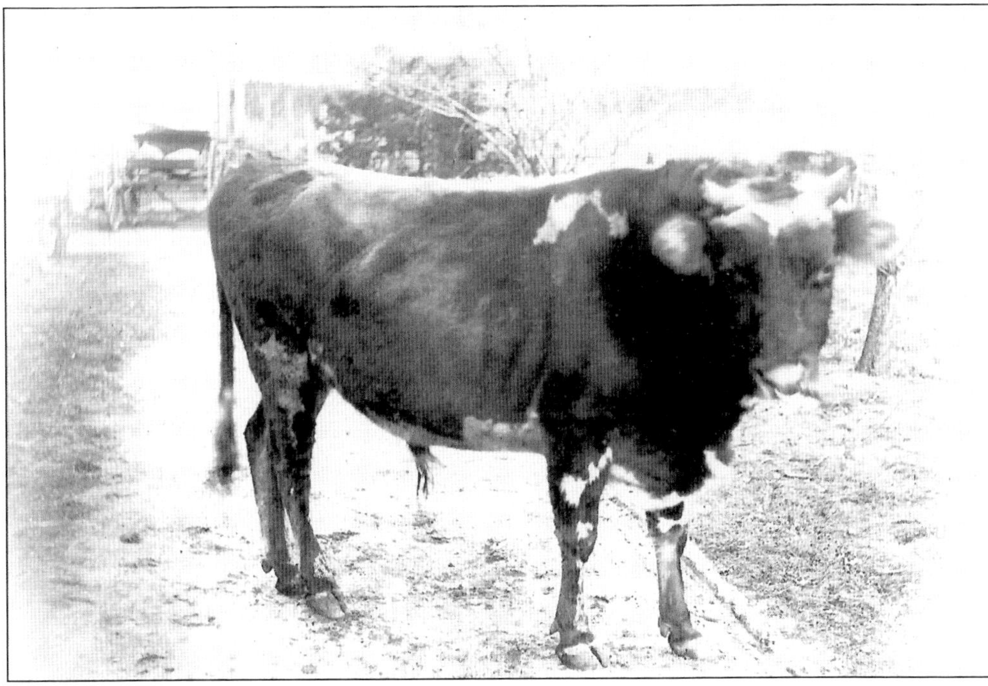

Sir Francis III. This bull belonged to Joseph Neale, a Vineland wagon maker and wheelwright, and stands as a reminder of Vineland's "Bovine War." In 1863, a struggle between cattle owners and neighboring farmers led to the formation of the Cattle League, which sought to prevent cattle from destroying crops. Soon after the league's unsuccessful negotiations with the cattle owners, hundreds of the animals were found dead in the surrounding woods. A bone believed to be from the animal killed is on display at the Vineland Historical and Antiquarian Society.

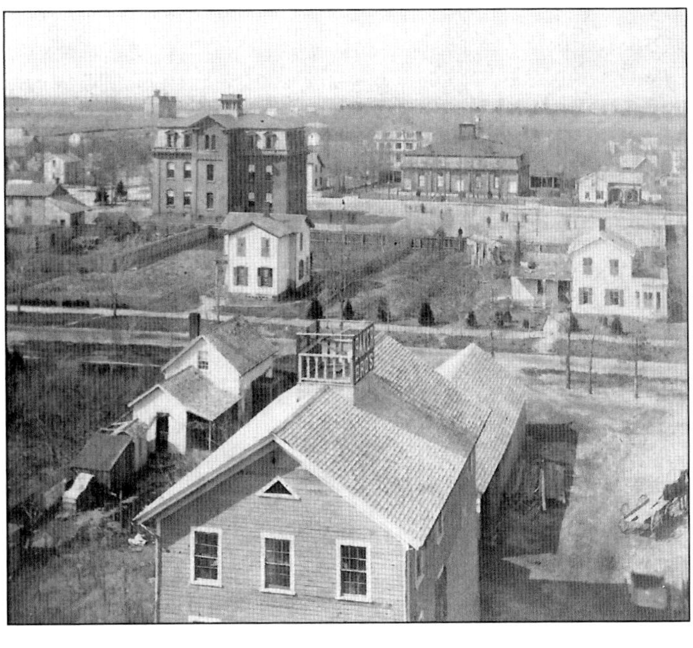

A City Begins to Take Shape. This 1870s photograph shows both Cosmopolitan Hall and the town's first high school, two of the most culturally significant buildings in Vineland's early development. In 1874, Pres. Ulysses S. Grant visited Vineland to dedicate the opening of the high school, the three-story brick building in the background at left. Cosmopolitan Hall, its name reflecting the vision of the city's residents, is the large building to the right of the school.

Two

GROWTH IN VINELAND

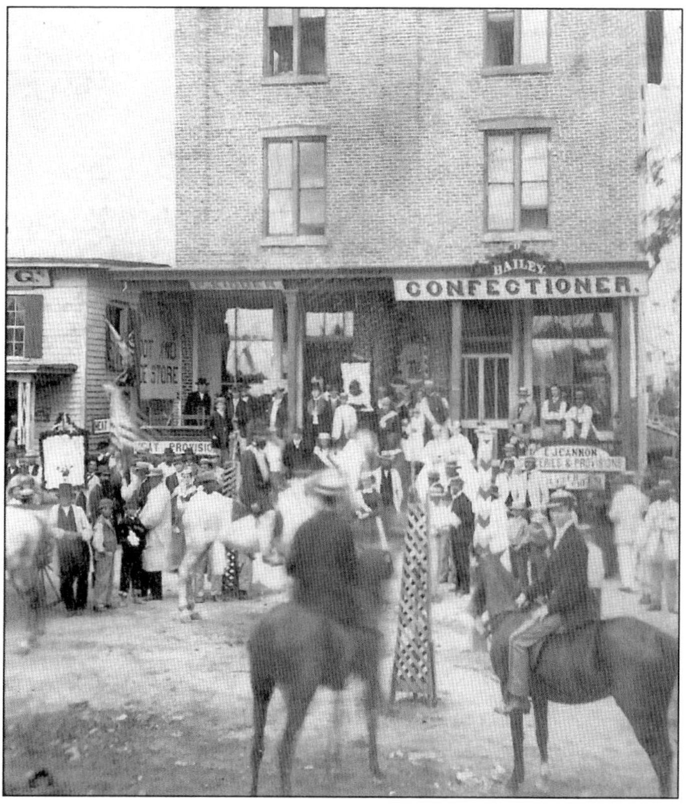

DOWNTOWN. Vineland photographer L. D. Johnson captured the ebb and flow of daily life in Vineland's downtown in the 1860s and 1870s. In this late-1860s photograph, men, women, and children are each drawn to special interests: the Bailey Confectioner; P. Kidder's Boot and Shoe Store; and E. J. Cannon's Groceries and Provisions.

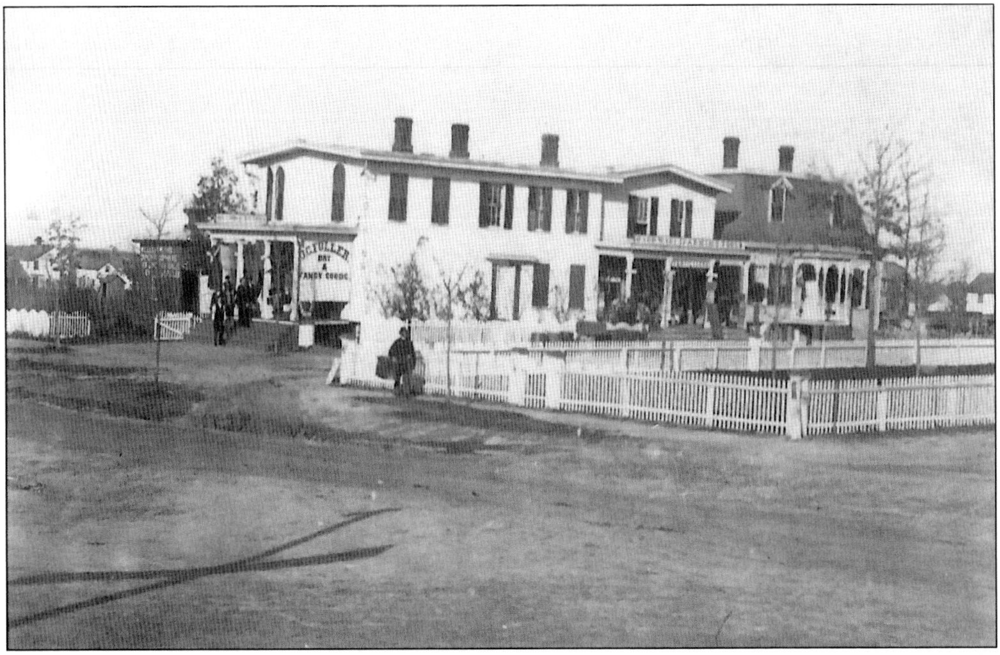

SHOPS AND SERVICES, C. 1870. These *c.* 1870 photographs by L. D. Johnson show Vineland's development within the first 10 years of its founding. Most essentials for daily life were current and readily available. The image above shows the southeast corner of Almond Street and the Boulevard, where, at J. C. Fuller's Dry and Fancy Goods, hardware, fertilizer, and farming tools could also be had. The picture below shows Landis Avenue in front of the New York Cash Store. Hitching posts can be seen along the avenue.

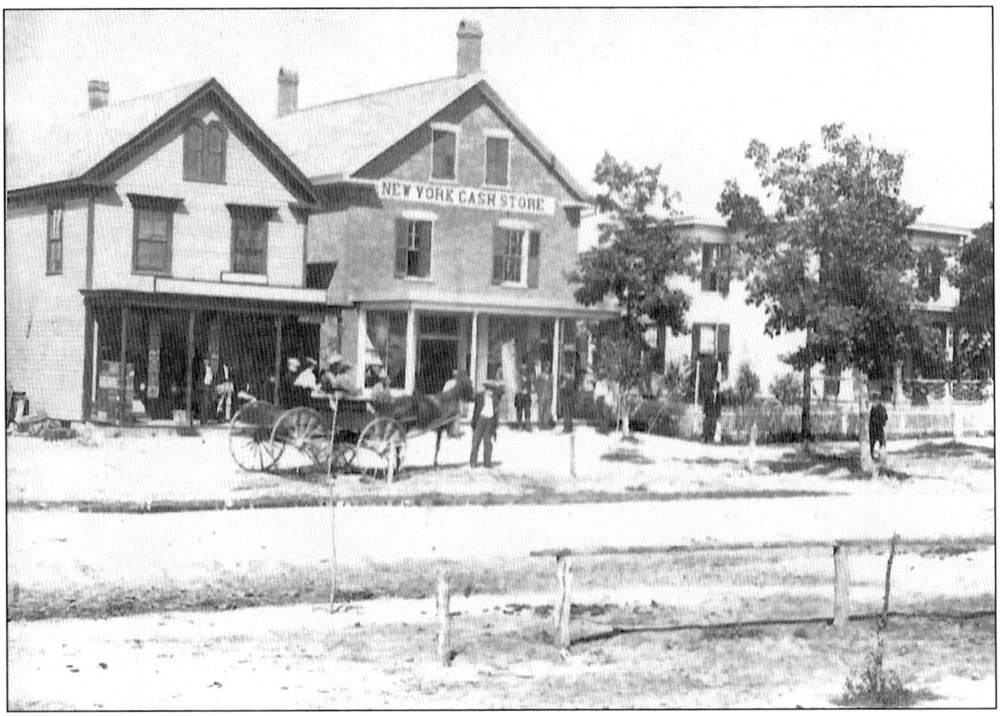

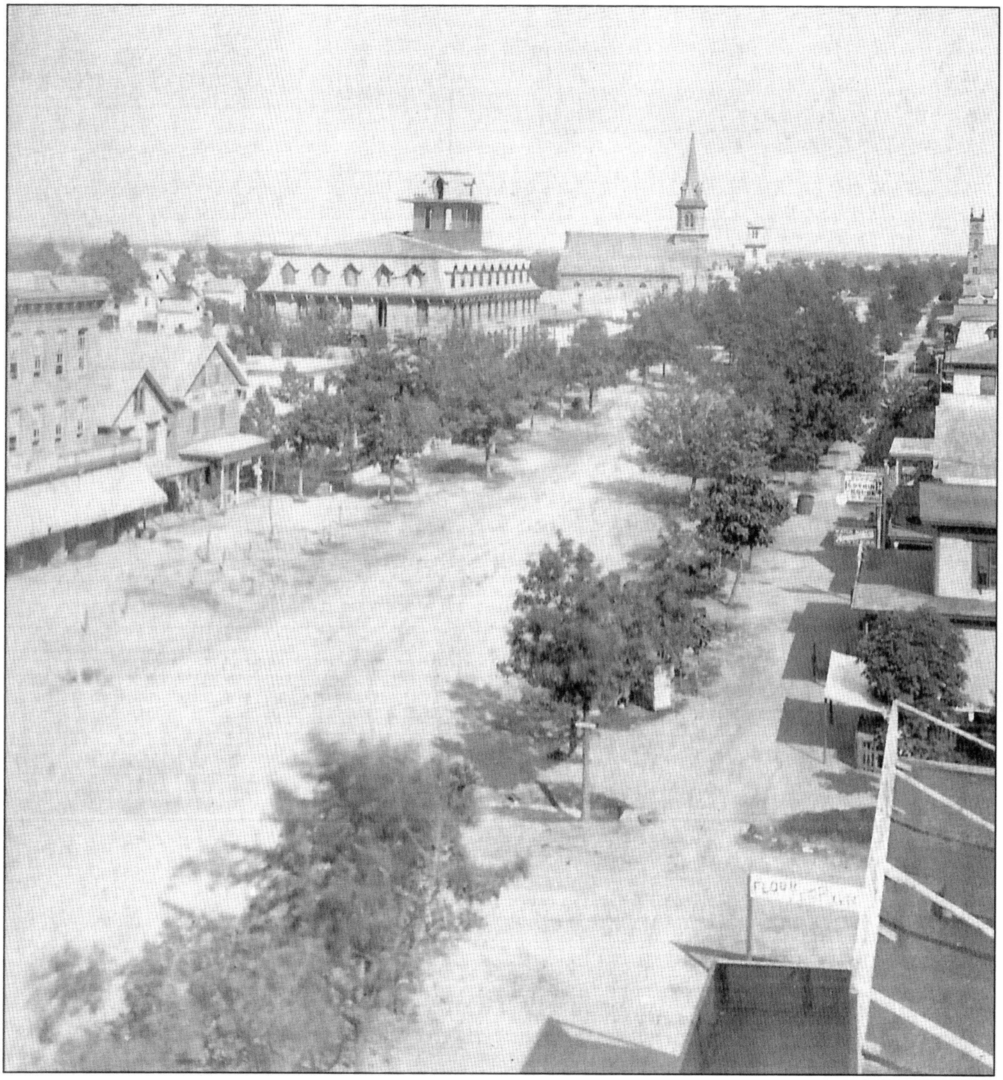

VIEW OF BAKER HOUSE. This 1876 view of Landis Avenue looking east from Sixth Street shows the prominent Baker House Hotel, advertised at the time as "being the largest and best between Philadelphia and Cape May." A four-story brick building surmounted by a large tower and observatory, the Baker House hosted important events and also important visitors to Vineland. Beyond the Baker House can be seen the steeples of the Methodist Episcopal church on the left, the Presbyterian church behind that, and the Baptist church on the right. (Photograph by L. D. Johnson of Vineland.)

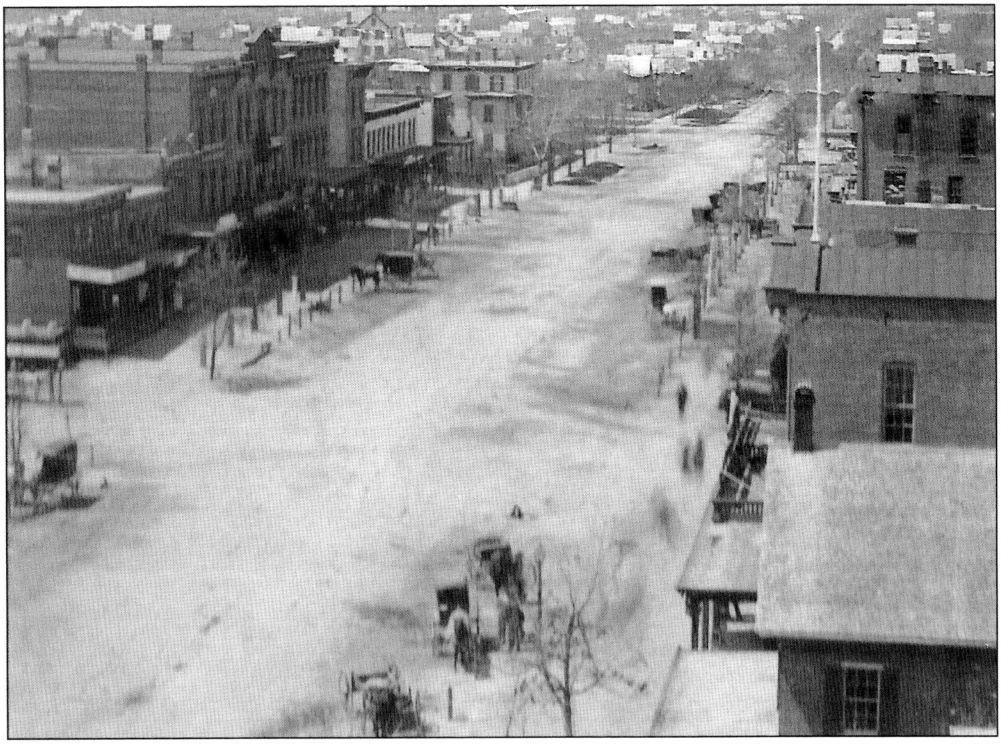

VIEWS FROM BAKER HOUSE, C. 1875. As a landscape and portrait specialist, photographer L. D. Johnson's stereoviews show Landis Avenue from the observatory of the Baker House Hotel with interesting scope and detail. Above, Johnson photographed southeast down Landis Avenue. The extensive development based on Charles K. Landis's precise layout for the borough can be appreciated in its early but developing stage. Below, Johnson turned his camera to Landis Avenue looking west. In each photograph, the views beyond the foreground offer the viewer the clear evidence of the impressive scope of construction true to Landis's initial plans for the use, design, and growth of the borough where housing and business would be located. The outlying land beyond the structures was the farmland—cleared, parceled, planted, and ready for new buyers.

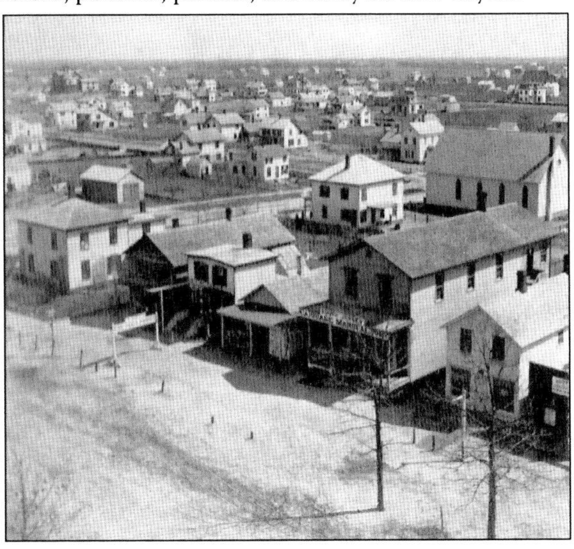

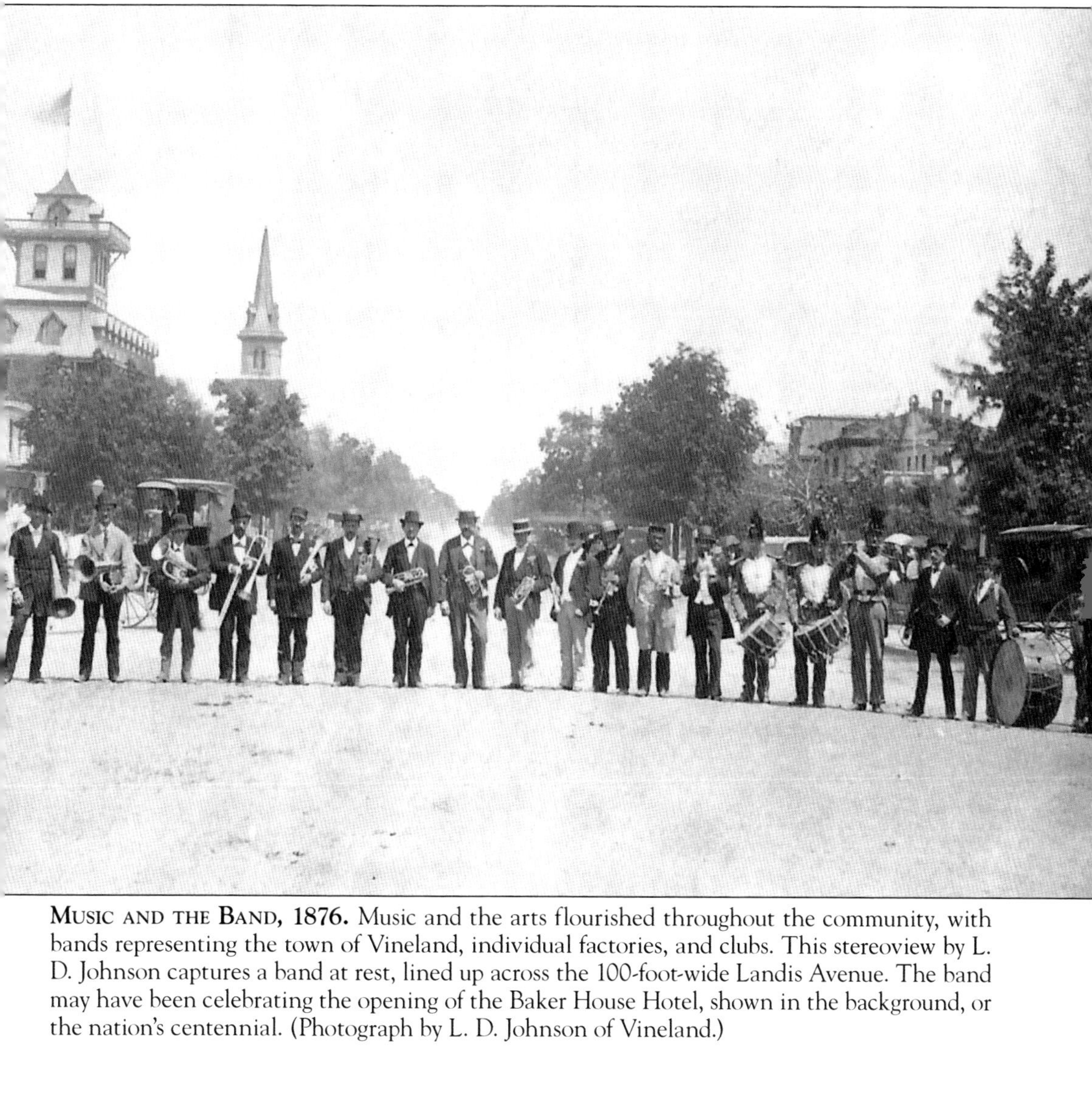

MUSIC AND THE BAND, 1876. Music and the arts flourished throughout the community, with bands representing the town of Vineland, individual factories, and clubs. This stereoview by L. D. Johnson captures a band at rest, lined up across the 100-foot-wide Landis Avenue. The band may have been celebrating the opening of the Baker House Hotel, shown in the background, or the nation's centennial. (Photograph by L. D. Johnson of Vineland.)

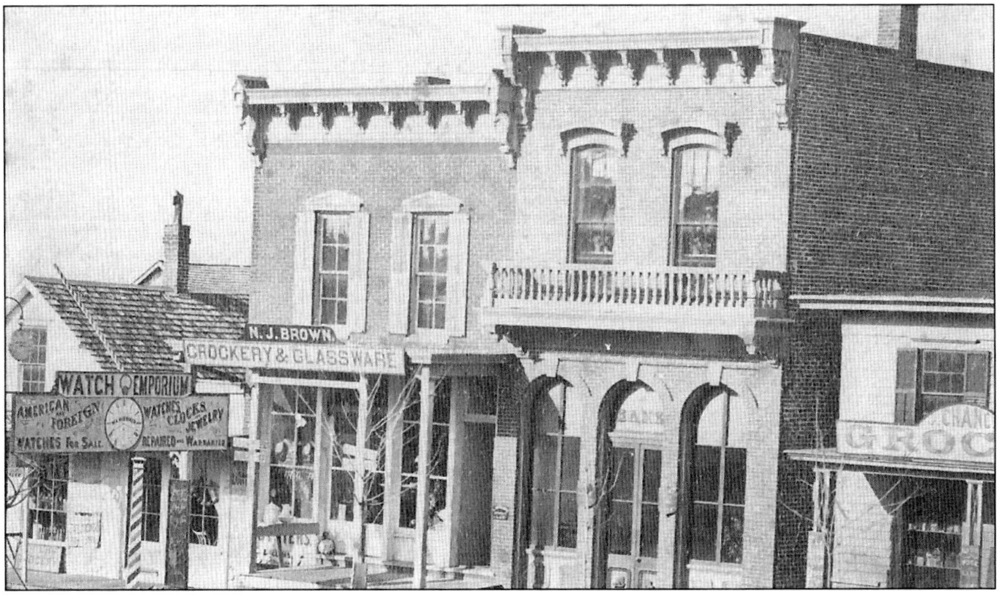

FIRE ON LANDIS AVENUE, 1872. The picture above shows the buildings on the north side of Landis Avenue before the fire. On July 6, 1872, a fire broke out, and the picture below shows its aftermath. The fire began in the small wooden building on the far left and quickly spread to the other buildings, demolishing the two wooden buildings and one brick building. The wooden building on the far right, Chance's Grocery, was torn down and dragged into the street to prevent the fire from reaching the neighboring brick building. Large brick buildings were soon after rebuilt on the sites of the destroyed buildings. The Vineland Hook and Ladder Company, Vineland's first fire company, was established almost immediately after this fire.

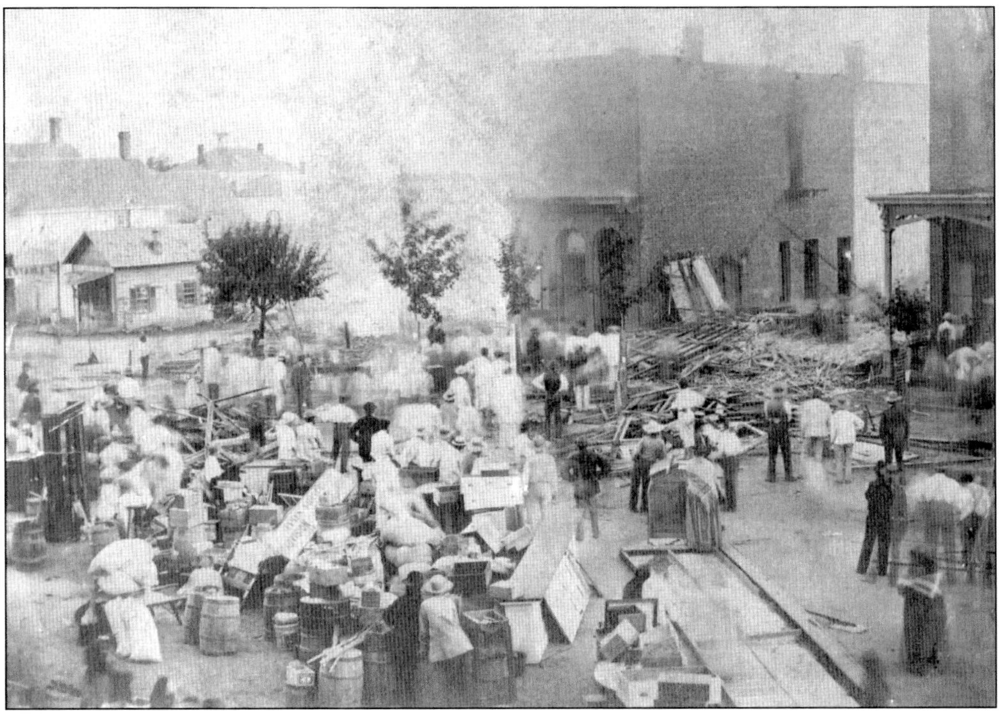

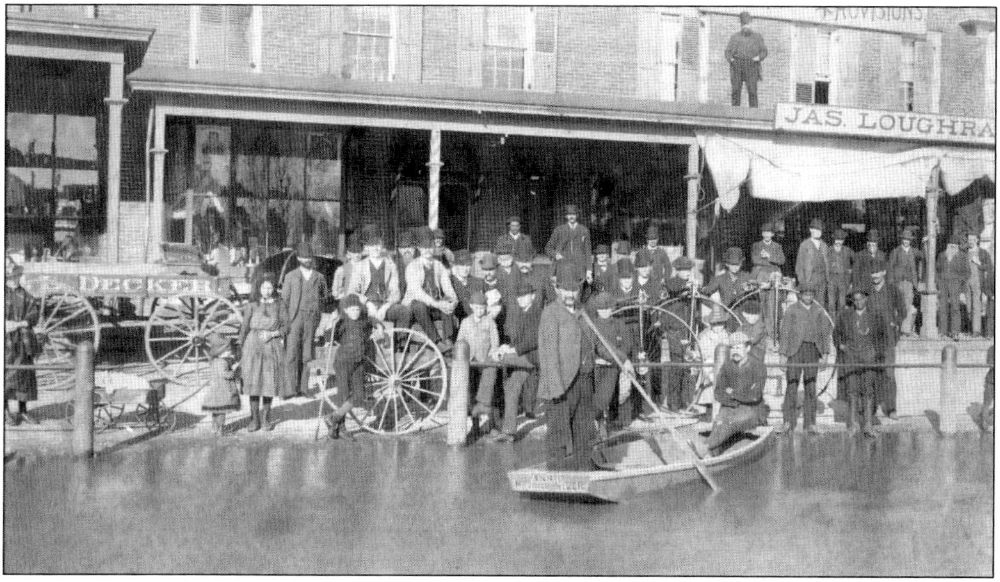

FLOOD ON LANDIS AVENUE, c. 1885. As citizens gather and wait for the photographer's shot, two do so aboard the Maurice River boat *Annie,* as if to make a statement. In the background is the office of James Loughran, who sold insurance for fire and tornados, but not for floods.

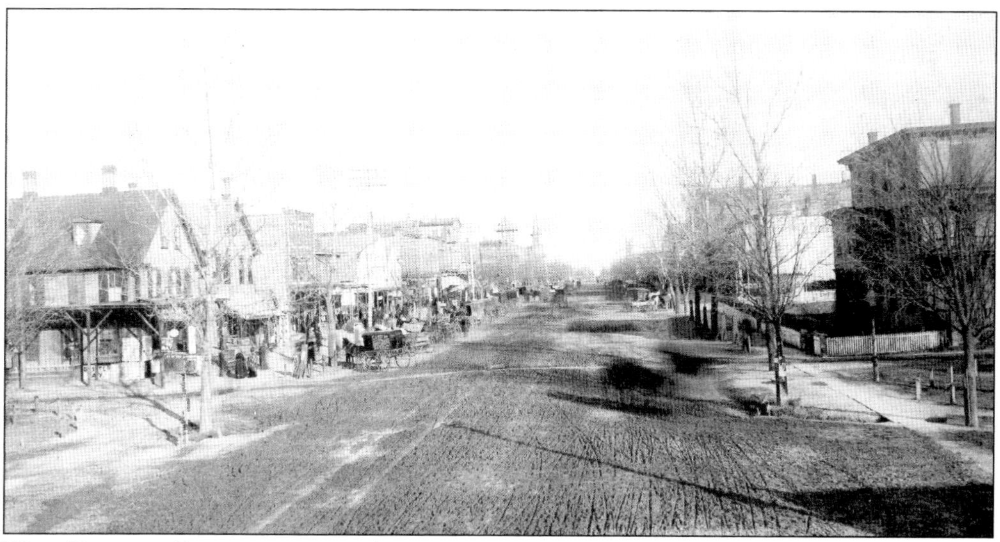

WELL-TRODDEN ROAD, c. 1885. This picture shows Landis Avenue looking east towards the Baker House Hotel. Deep ruts from traveling wheels can be seen in the road, showing its wear. A black buggy is seen parked in the left front of the picture with a sign on it that reads, "Cash for rags, metals and bones."

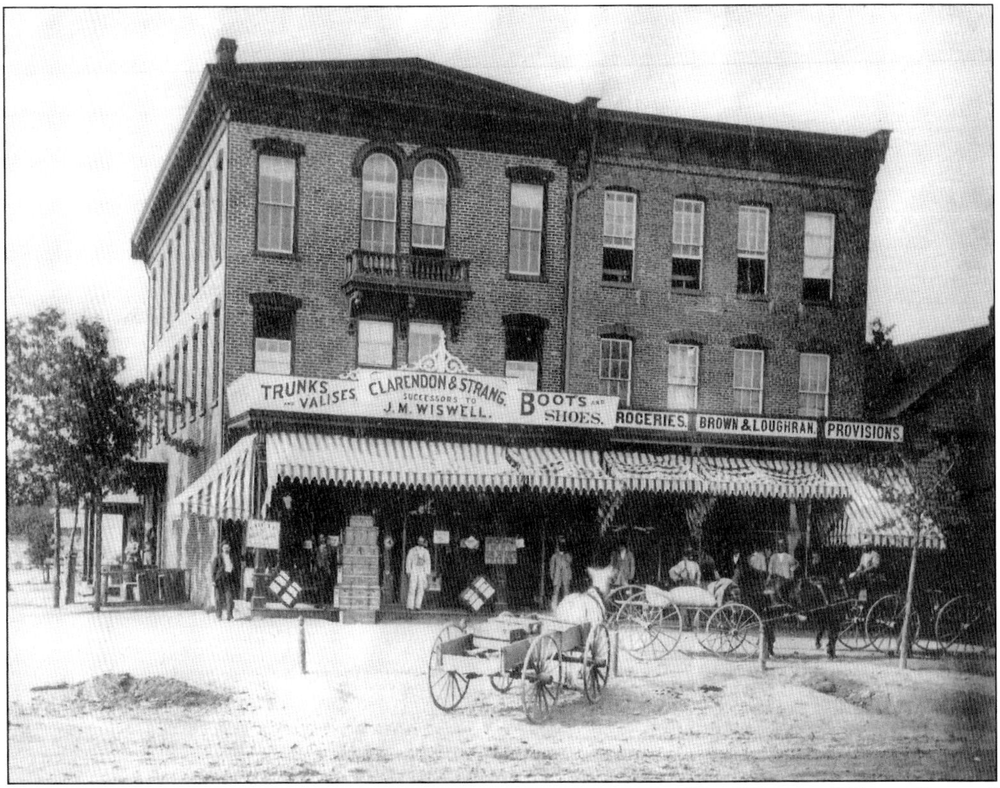

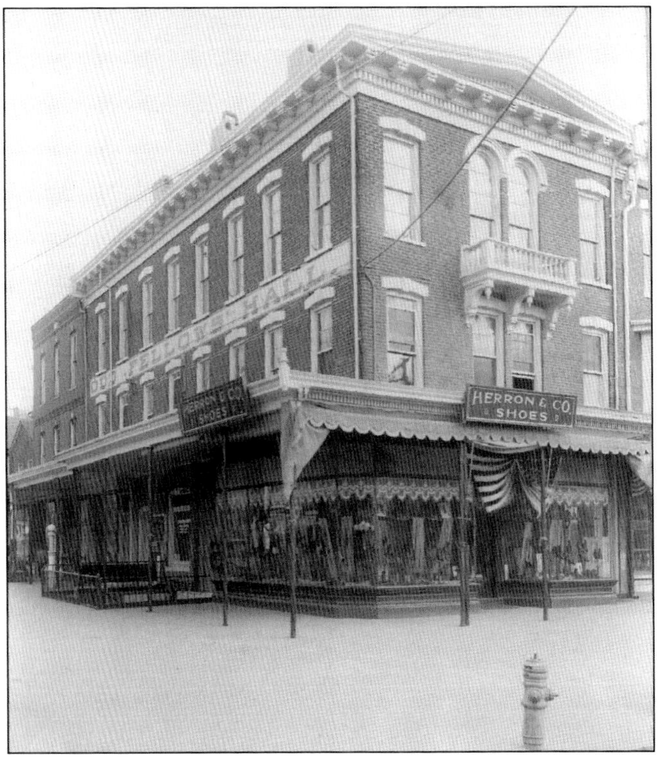

ODD FELLOWS' HALL. Erected in 1866 on the northeast corner of Sixth Street and Landis Avenue, the Odd Fellows' building (above) stood as an impressive center for trade, commerce, and the collegiality of its members. Prior to the social reforms necessitated by the industrial revolution, the Odd Fellows served its members with a focus on the social and financial needs of its members and their families. The picture at left shows the building around 1920. The fraternal order met on the second floor of the building while the first floor was used for retail stores. It continues to stand today as the oldest building on Landis Avenue.

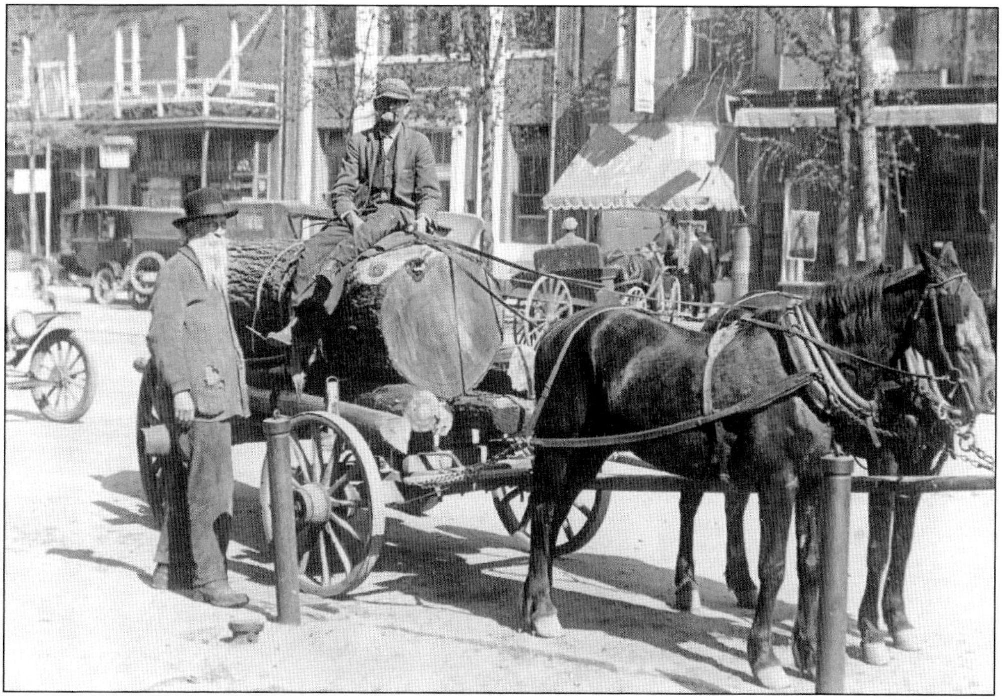

New Jersey Naturals, c. 1920. Both the men and the mode of transport shown above embody the unchanged means of business for some woodcutters and haulers of hay around 1920. The striking contrast of the horse and wagon with the automobiles in the background reflect the ease with which the old and the new existed side by side. New Jersey wood would be hauled this way to as far away as New York.

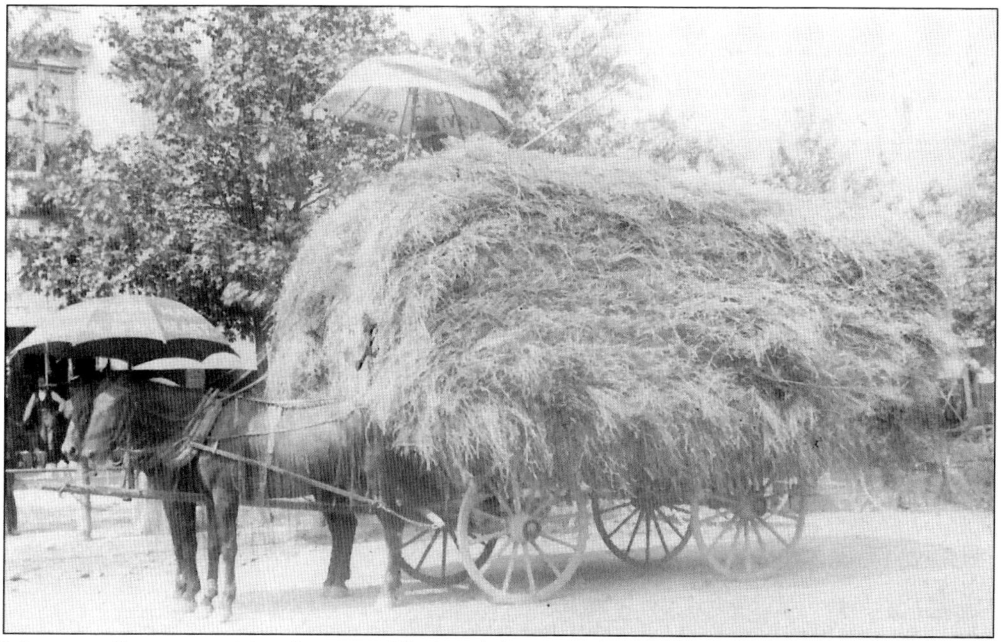

Man and Beast, c. 1890. A wagon filled with hay travels down Landis Avenue with umbrellas offering shade to both man and beast.

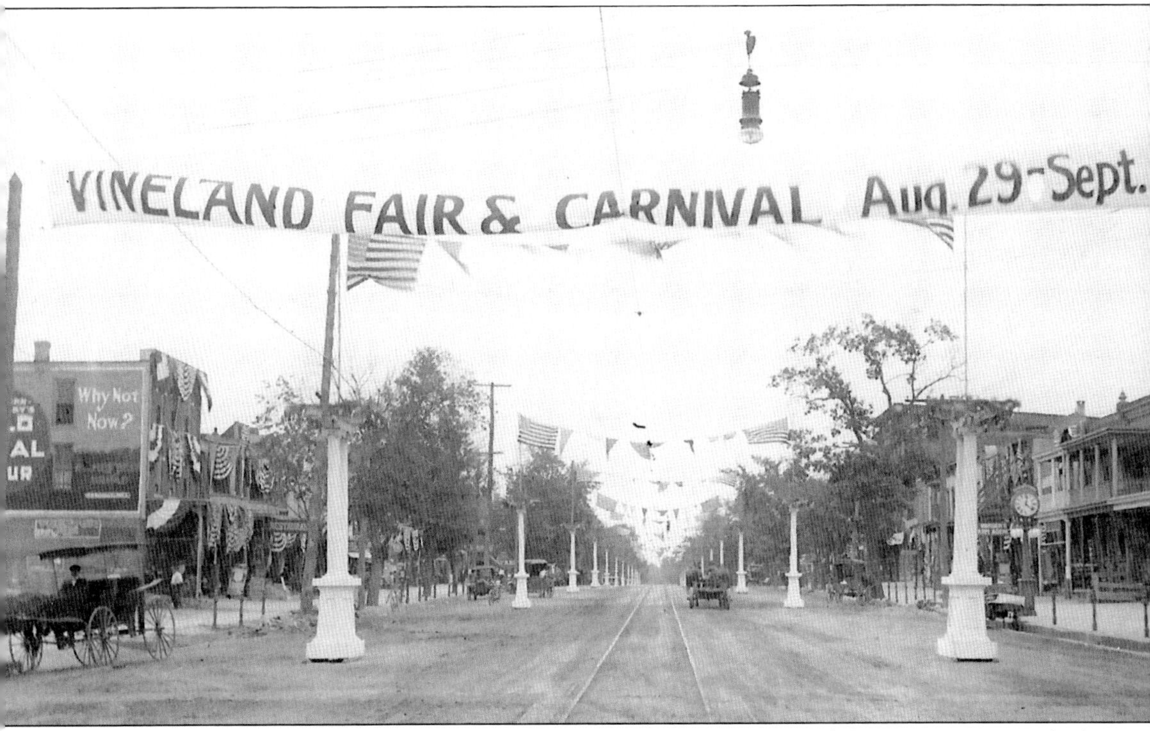

TOWARD THE FUTURE, C. 1910. With electric lines, automobiles, and the iconic avenue clock, seen far right, this photograph of Landis Avenue presents the beautiful Old World style that was so much an inspiration to Charles K. Landis's original vision. The 100-foot-wide boulevard, lined with trees and gas lights, invited the gathering of its citizens for festive occasions. The Vineland Fair and Carnival was only one of the regularly planned festivities honoring the city, its citizens, and the spirit of the community.

Three

Firsts in Vineland

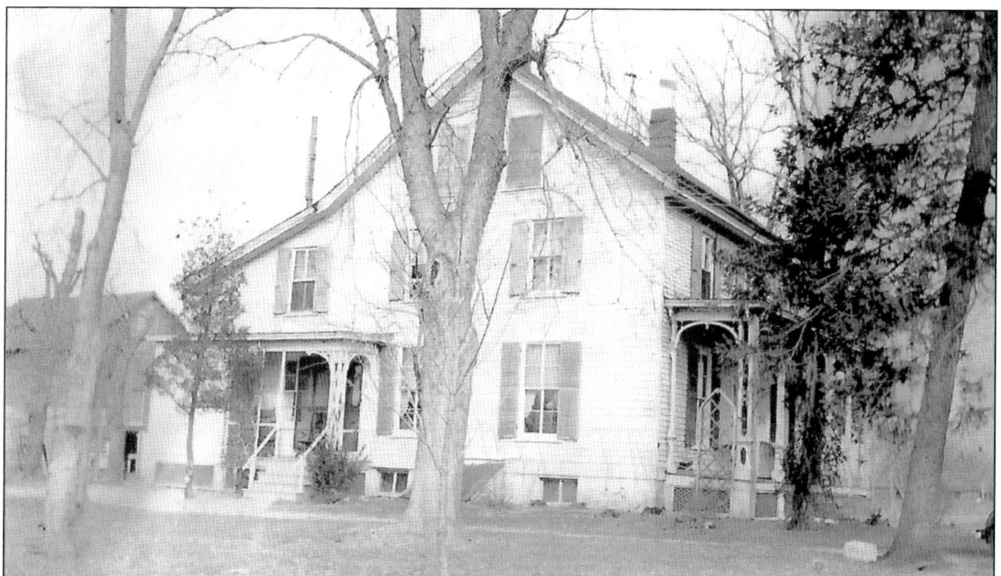

First Post Office. In 1860, Andrew Sharp built this home on land that later became the corner of Main Road and Park Avenue. In 1861, after some initial opposition, Charles K. Landis was granted the right to establish a post office in Vineland and was appointed its first postmaster. He rented rooms in this home to use as his headquarters and as Vineland's first post office. The first post box is displayed in the Vineland Historical and Antiquarian Society Museum.

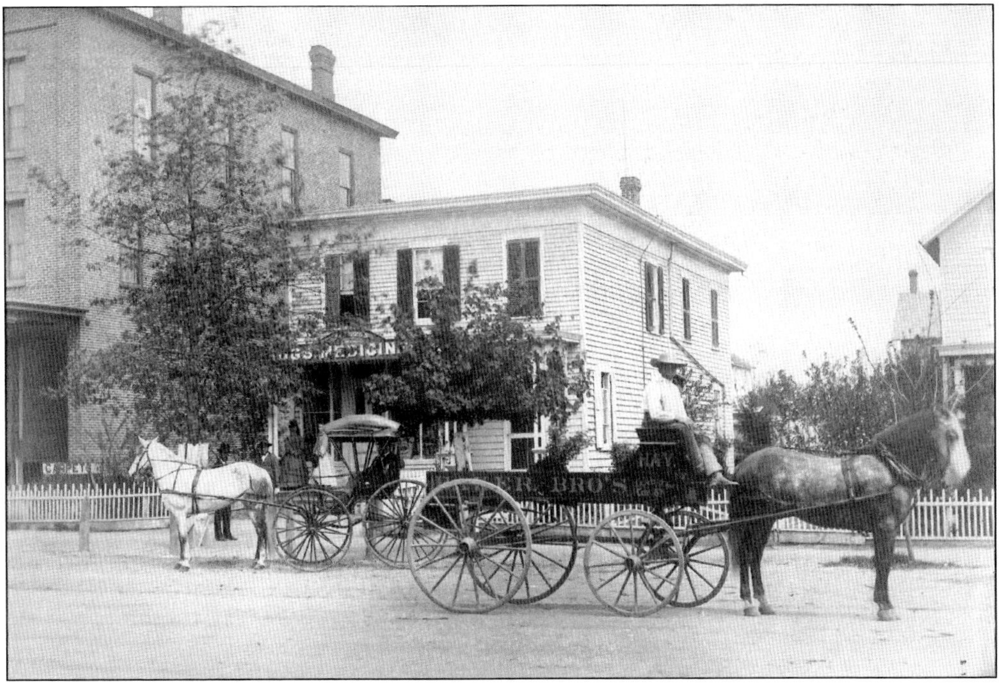

Vineland's First Pharmacy. In 1865, Dr. John R. Elton moved to Vineland and established the Pioneer Drug Store on Landis Avenue near Sixth Street. It was there that Vineland's first physicians came to have their prescriptions compounded. Elton continued the business until 1881, when he sold it to Dr. Joseph A. Conwell, who later became the ninth mayor of Vineland.

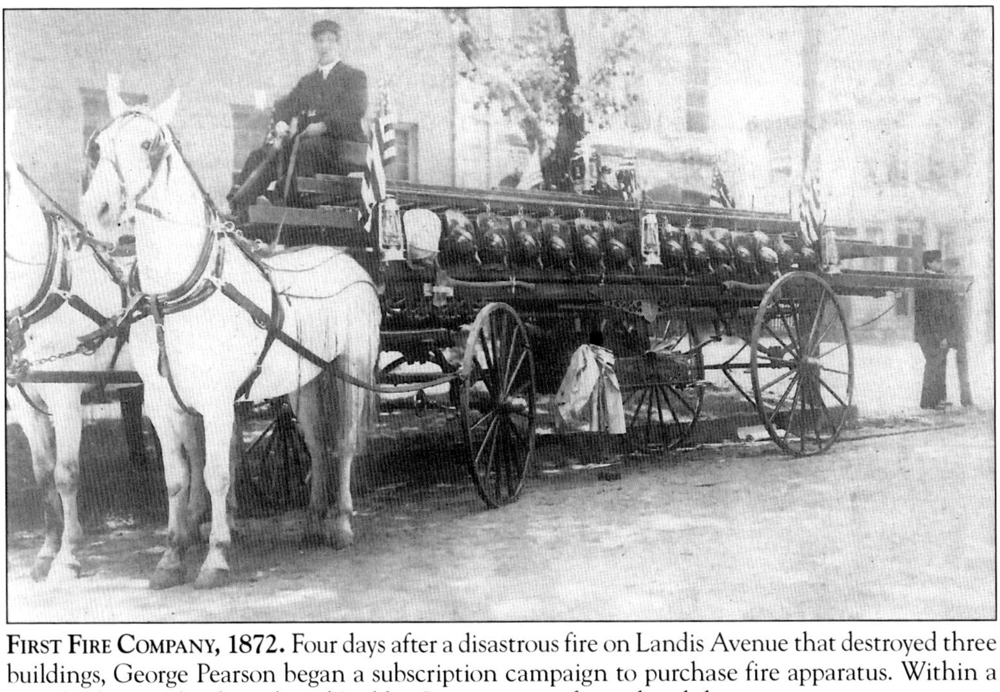

First Fire Company, 1872. Four days after a disastrous fire on Landis Avenue that destroyed three buildings, George Pearson began a subscription campaign to purchase fire apparatus. Within a month, the Vineland Hook and Ladder Company was formed and the necessary equipment was acquired. The company's horse-drawn vehicle is shown being driven by Charles Sharp.

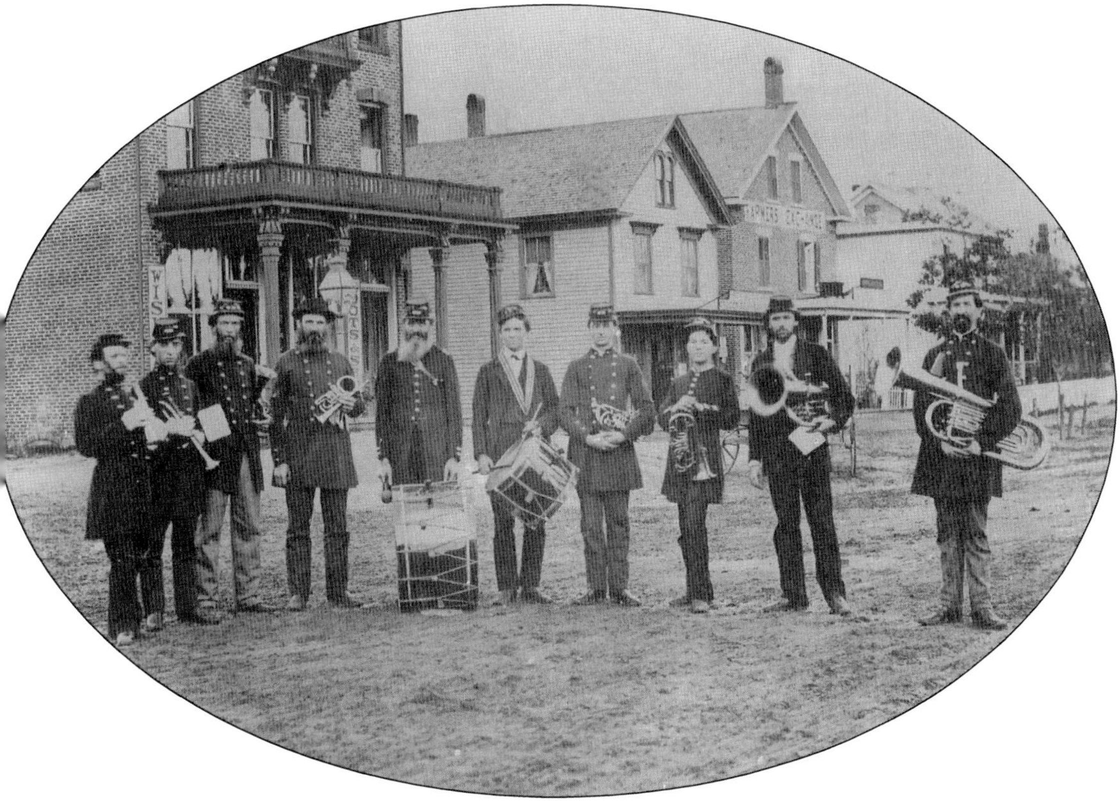

VINELAND'S FIRST BAND. About 1866, the first band to form in the town posed for this picture on Landis Avenue, in front of the newly finished Odd Fellows' Hall. The band members are, from left to right, J. C. Barrett, Frank Hopkins, Mr. Beech, R. Lang, Ira Thompson, Mert Crowell, Lewis Gould, Andrew Cross, Walter Cansdell, and George A. Cheever. The band members represented a distinct variety of townspeople: Barrett, the band leader, was a shoemaker; Crowell was a butcher; Cheever owned the paper box manufactory; and Hopkins owned a pocketbook manufactory. The band played regularly in Plum Street Hall.

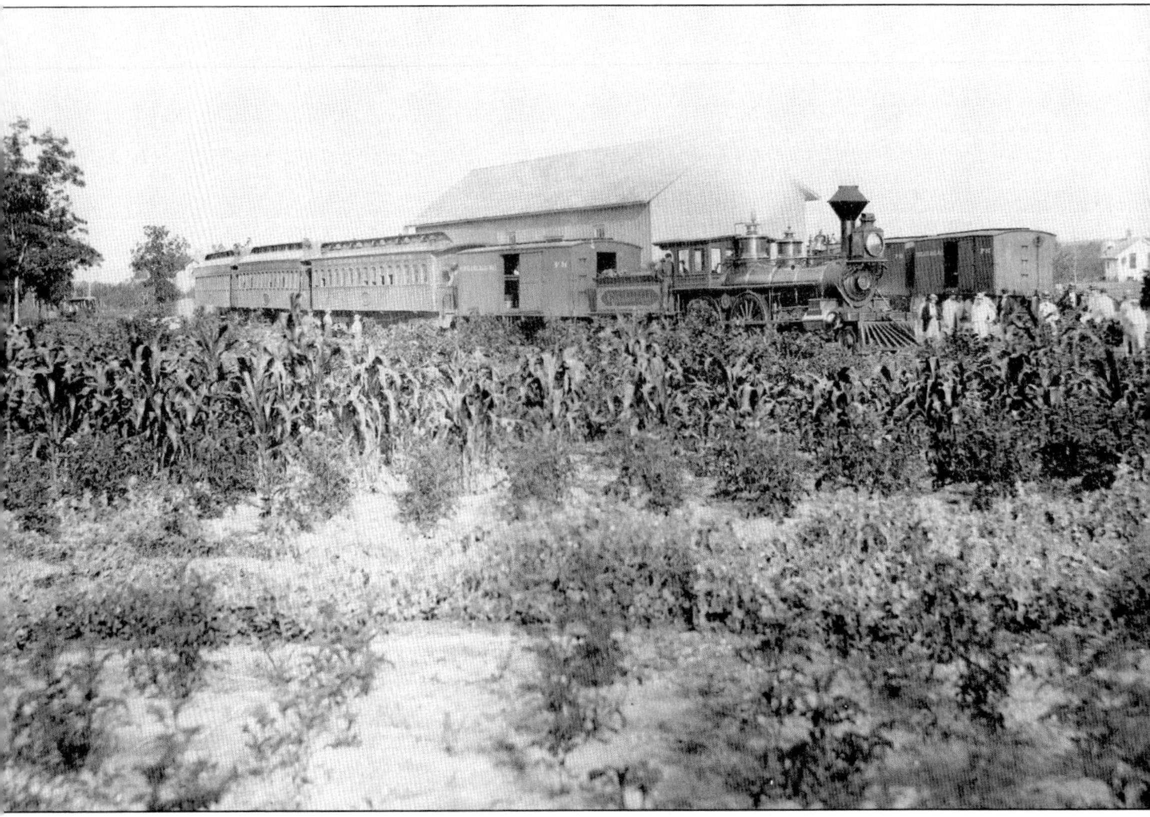

FIRST TRAIN ON VINELAND RAILWAY, 1872. In order to ship produce to the markets of New York, Boston, Newark, and Philadelphia, citizens of Vineland organized the Vineland Railway to run from Vineland to Atsion, New Jersey. Charles K. Landis was its first director and president. The first passenger train to run on the completed road left Vineland on August 9, 1872. In 1873, the road was sold to pay its debts and consolidated with the New Jersey Southern Railroad.

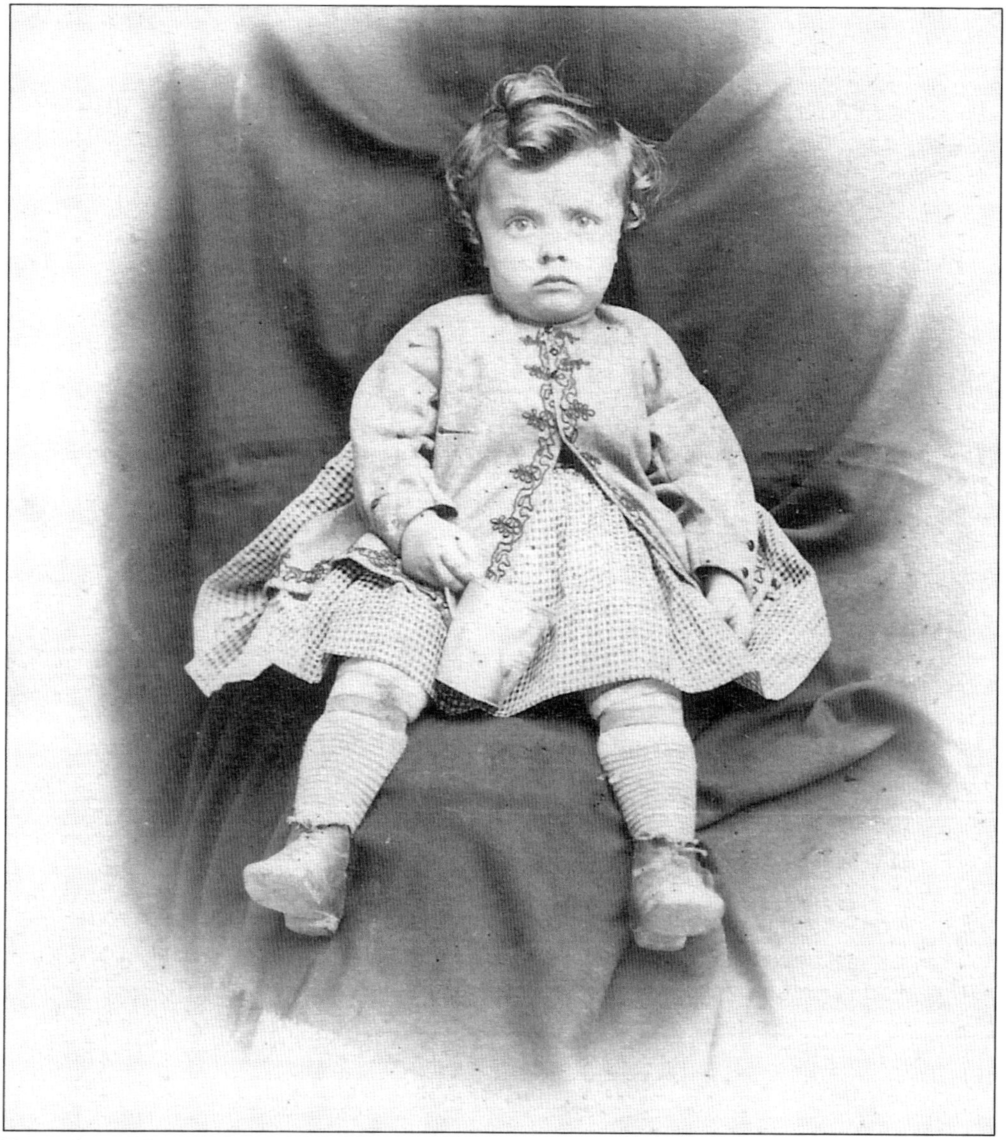

First Child Born in Vineland. On January 16, 1862, Willie Channing Richardson was born to Chester and Hattie Richardson, who had moved to Vineland a few months earlier from Vermont. Richardson received a commemorative cup from Charles K. Landis on which was inscribed, "Willie Channing Richardson, the first born in Vineland. Presented by the Founder." By 1890, Richardson had moved to Massachusetts and never again lived in the town of his birth. (Photograph by David Astle of Vineland.)

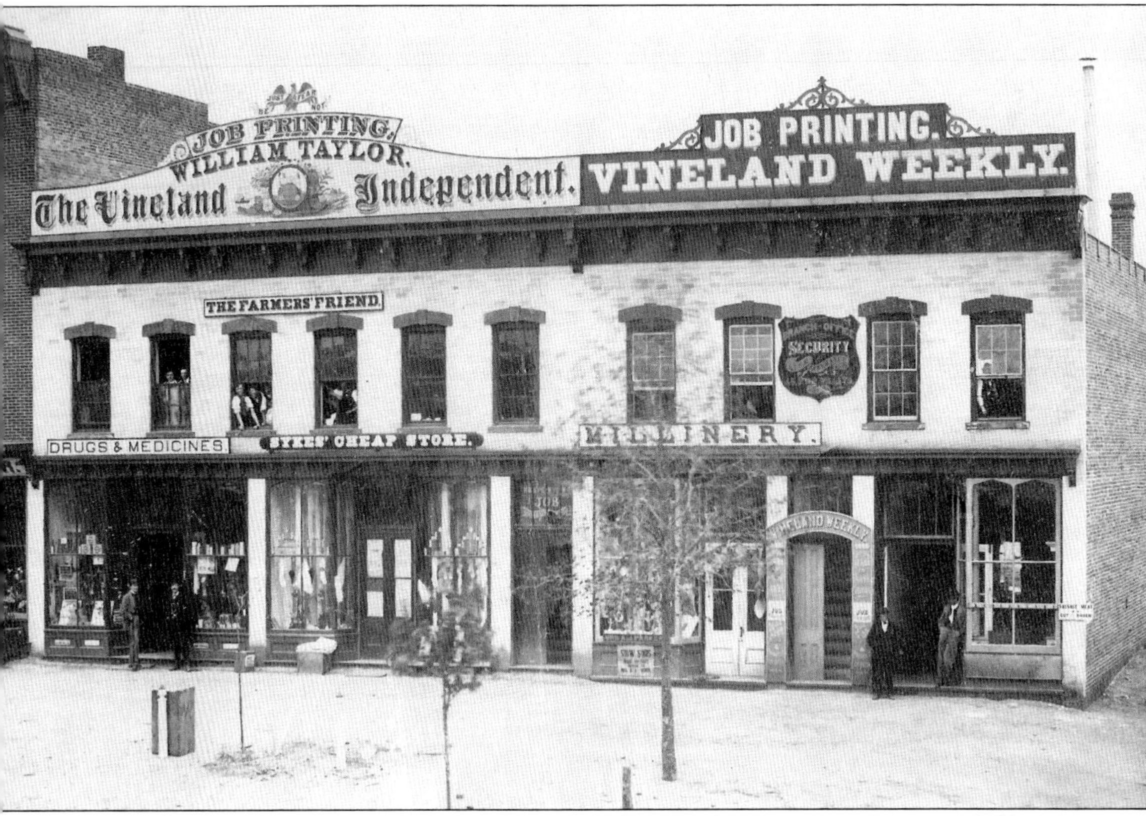

NEIGHBORS AND BITTER RIVALS. This late-1860s photograph captures a rather remarkable scene, that of the offices of Vineland's two newspapers, the *Vineland Independent*, and the *Vineland Weekly*, both being within the confines of a single building with just a common wall between them. The *Vineland Weekly*, Vineland's first newspaper, was established in 1865 by Francis P. Crocker. Its inaugural edition of September 9, 1865, notes "it will be our main object to make our paper an acceptable local sheet, dedicated especially to the interests of the place of our adoption . . . matters which will serve to promote the prosperity of Vineland, will ever be considered of paramount importance. All that pertains to its moral, intellectual, educational, financial and agricultural prosperity, will we trust, be discussed with freedom." It was largely under the influence of Charles K. Landis. Within several years, a number of early settlers, dissatisfied with the progress of the community, furnished the financial backing to start a competing, independent newspaper, the *Vineland Independent*, which commenced publication on March 2, 1867.

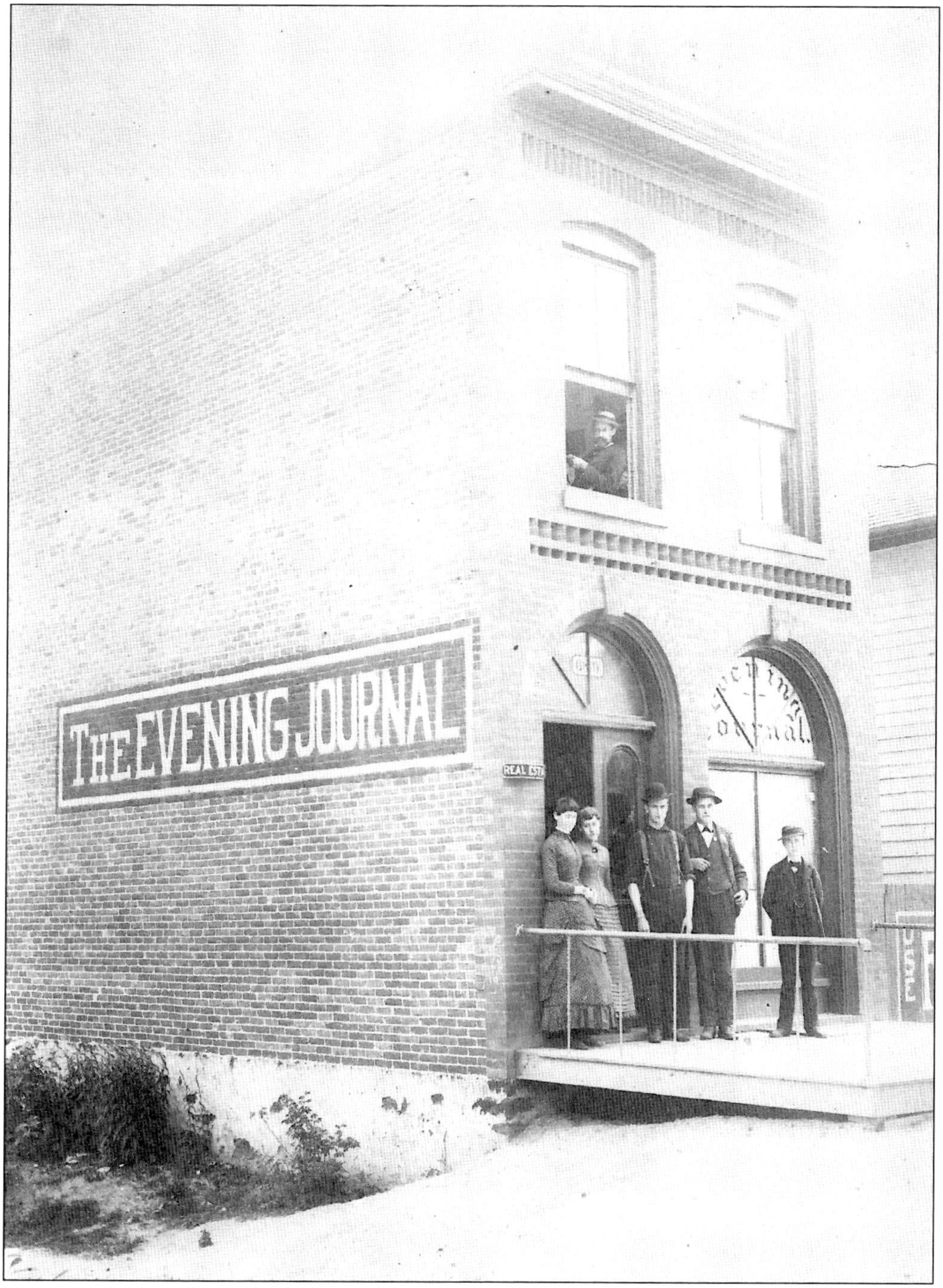

VINELAND'S FIRST DAILY NEWSPAPER, C. 1881. In 1875, Walter E. Cansdell established the *Daily Journal*, the first daily newspaper published in Vineland. A year later, he sold the business to Benjamin F. Ladd, who, in 1880, changed the paper's name to the *Evening Journal*. Ladd remained owner and editor of the paper until his death in 1913. In 1942, the *Journal* merged with the *Daily Times* and became the *Times Journal*. It continues today as the *Daily Journal*. (Photograph by Keystone Instantaneous View Company of Philadelphia.)

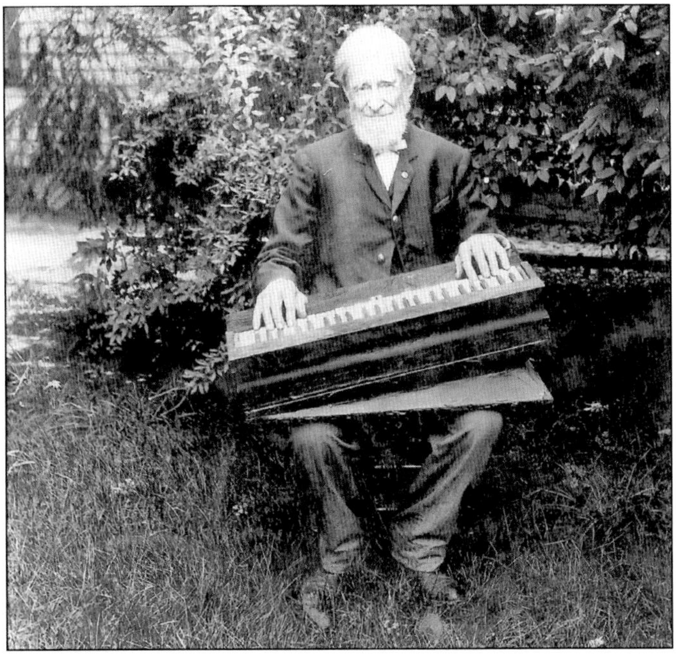

First Instrument in Vineland. In 1864, John A. Washburne claimed title to operating the first musical instrument with piano keys used in the town. Hundreds of people would go to hear him play it. In 1911, Washburne, a Civil War veteran and music teacher, posed with the lap organ at the age of 78. The organ, built in 1847, is on display in the Vineland Historical and Antiquarian Society Museum.

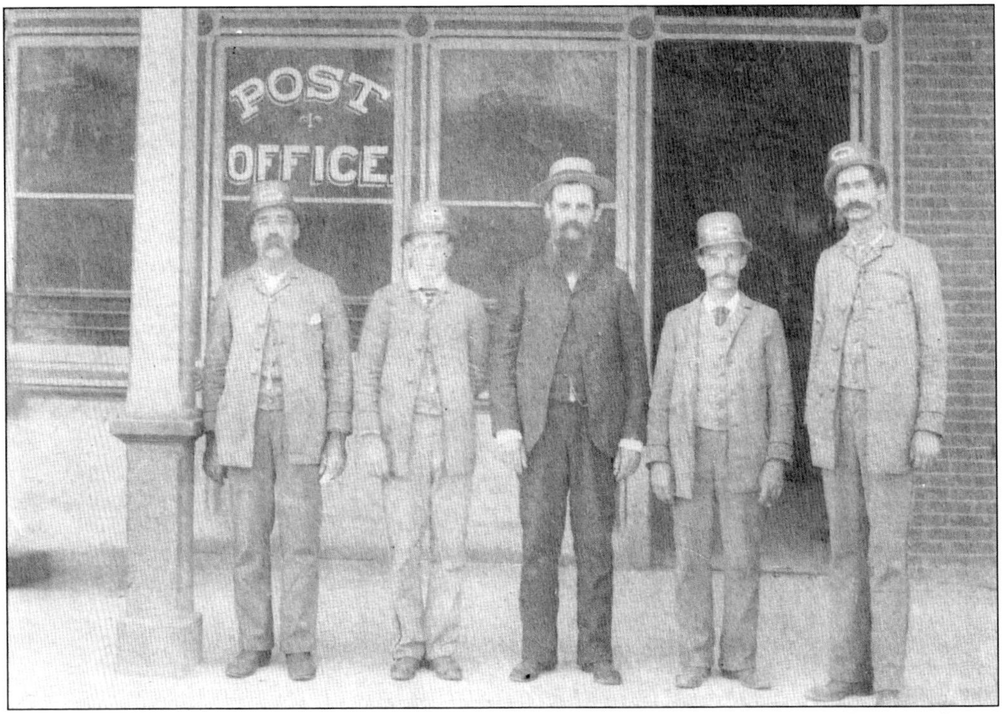

First Mail Carriers, 1892. In 1890, the Vineland Post Office established a Rural Free Delivery system, whereby town residents no longer had to pay a fee for their mail to be delivered to their homes. During that year, there were 26 mailboxes set up around Vineland, attached to lamp posts where possible. The first mail carriers are shown in this picture. From left to right are Albert Keyser, George Boynton, postmaster Arthur T. Parsons, Jesse C. Schoonmaker, and Thomas P. Bowman.

First Telephone Company. In 1894, Elwood C. Potter established Vineland's first telephone company with eight subscribers at $1 per month. Potter, seated in the middle in the picture below, was an electrician, photographer, and entrepreneur who worked for many years to build up his telephone company. Al Zehnder, the first operator of the company, is shown at right at work in 1896. When the demand became too much to handle himself, Potter sold the business to a company that in turn sold it to Bell Telephone Company. With his profits, he became the second person in Vineland to purchase an automobile.

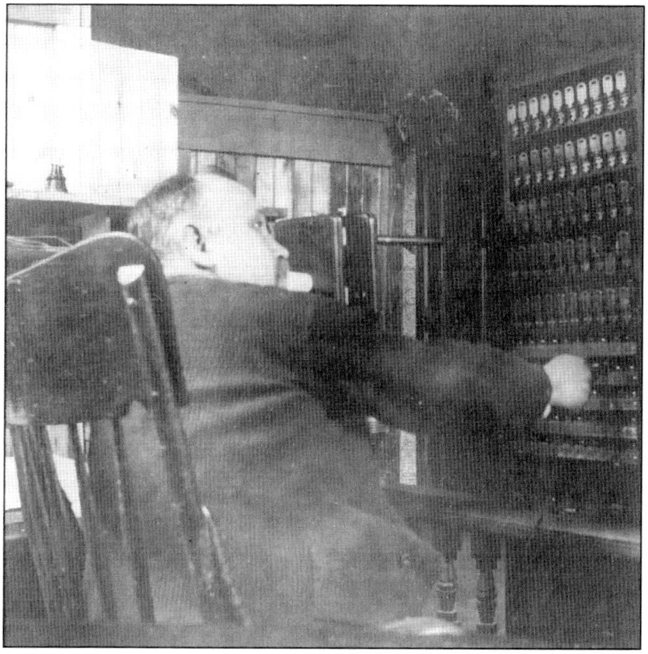

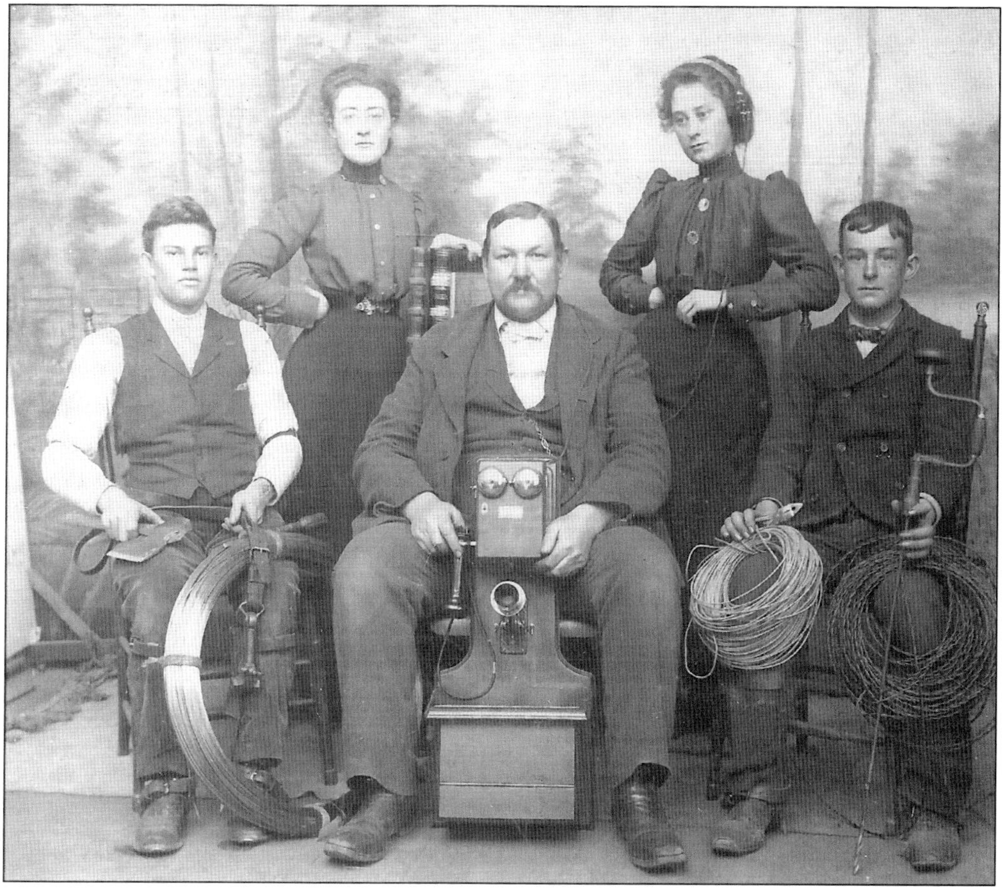

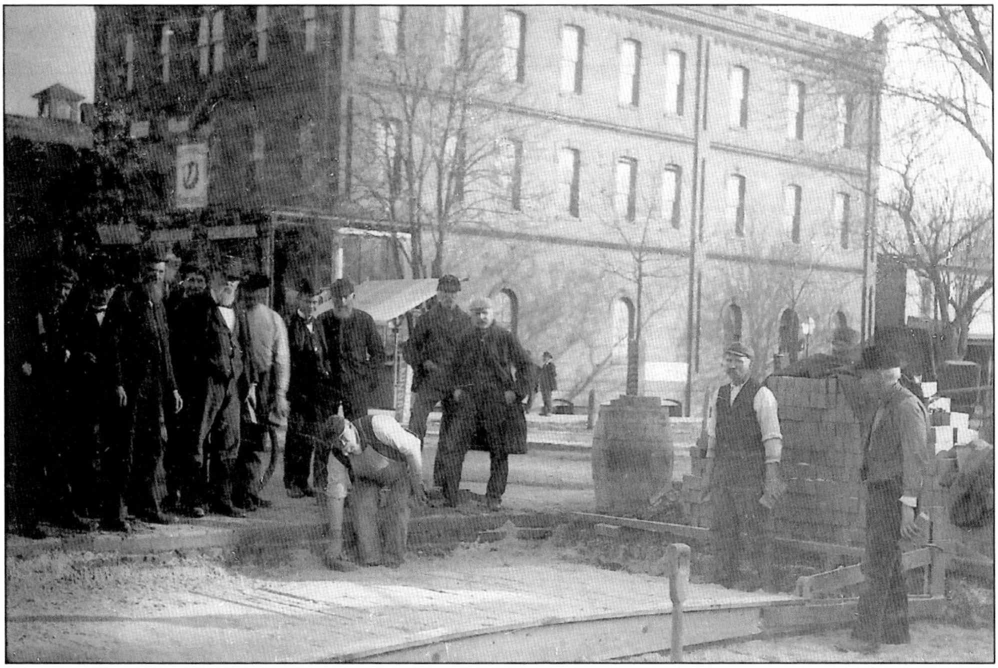

LAYING THE FIRST BRICK ON LANDIS AVENUE, 1900. In 1900, when Landis Avenue was first being paved with bricks, the mayor of Vineland gathered with the workmen on the 500 block in front of the Diamond Social Club. The picture above shows one of the workmen, Pat Downey, laying the first brick. The picture below shows Mayor Charles P. Lord laying a brick adjacent to the brick already laid by Downey. However, both pictures are labeled as the laying of the first brick on Landis Avenue.

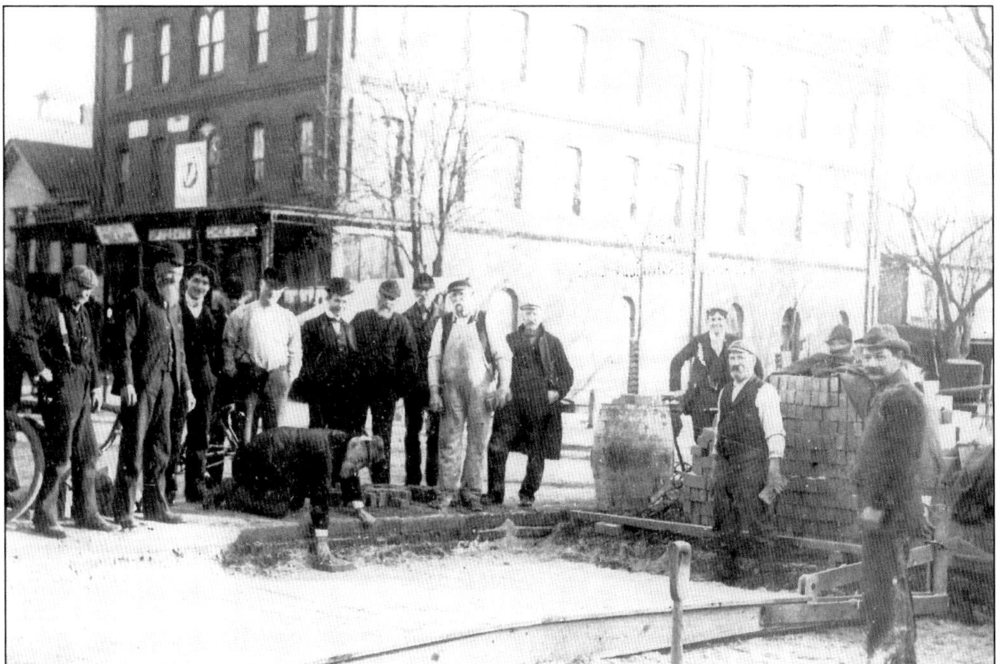

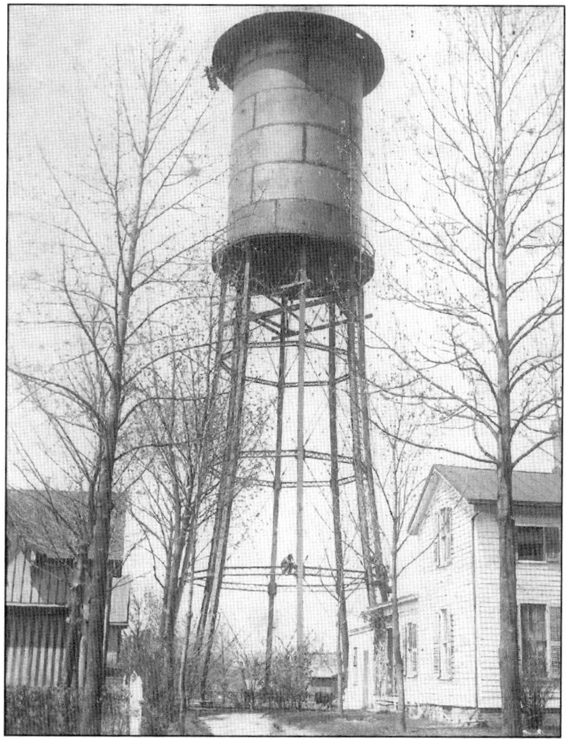

First Water Tank, c. 1900. The first water storage tank to be built in Vineland was located between Wood and Plum Streets. It held approximately 175,000 gallons. The six men who built it are shown below.

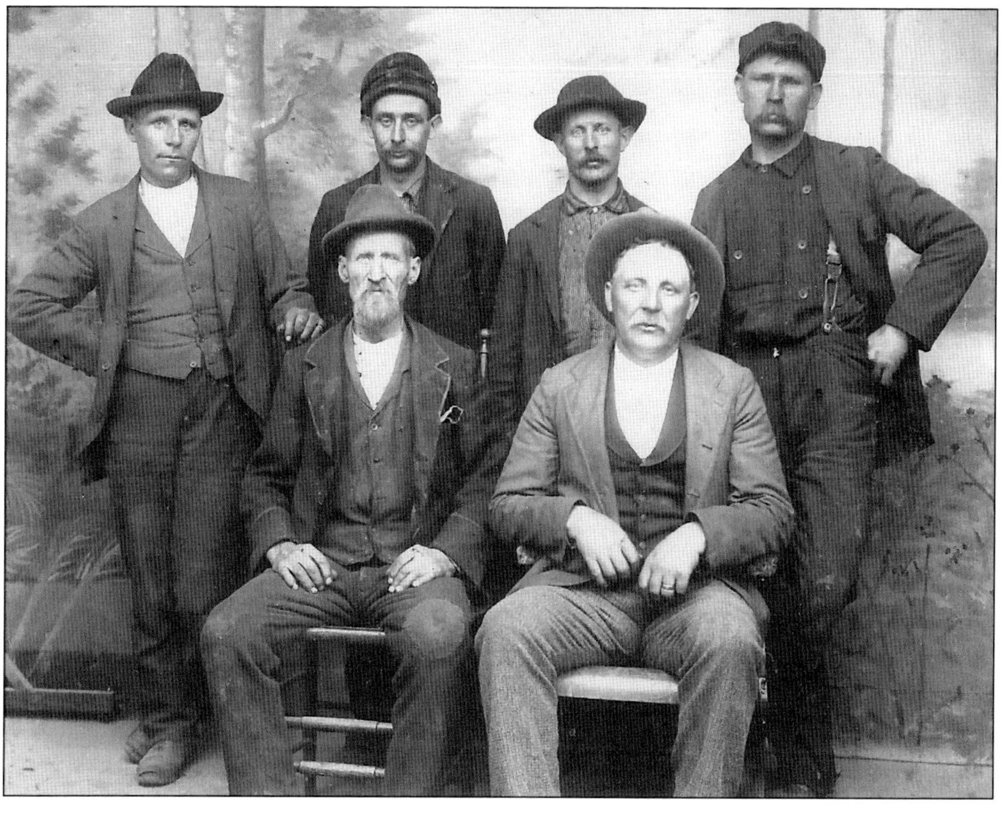

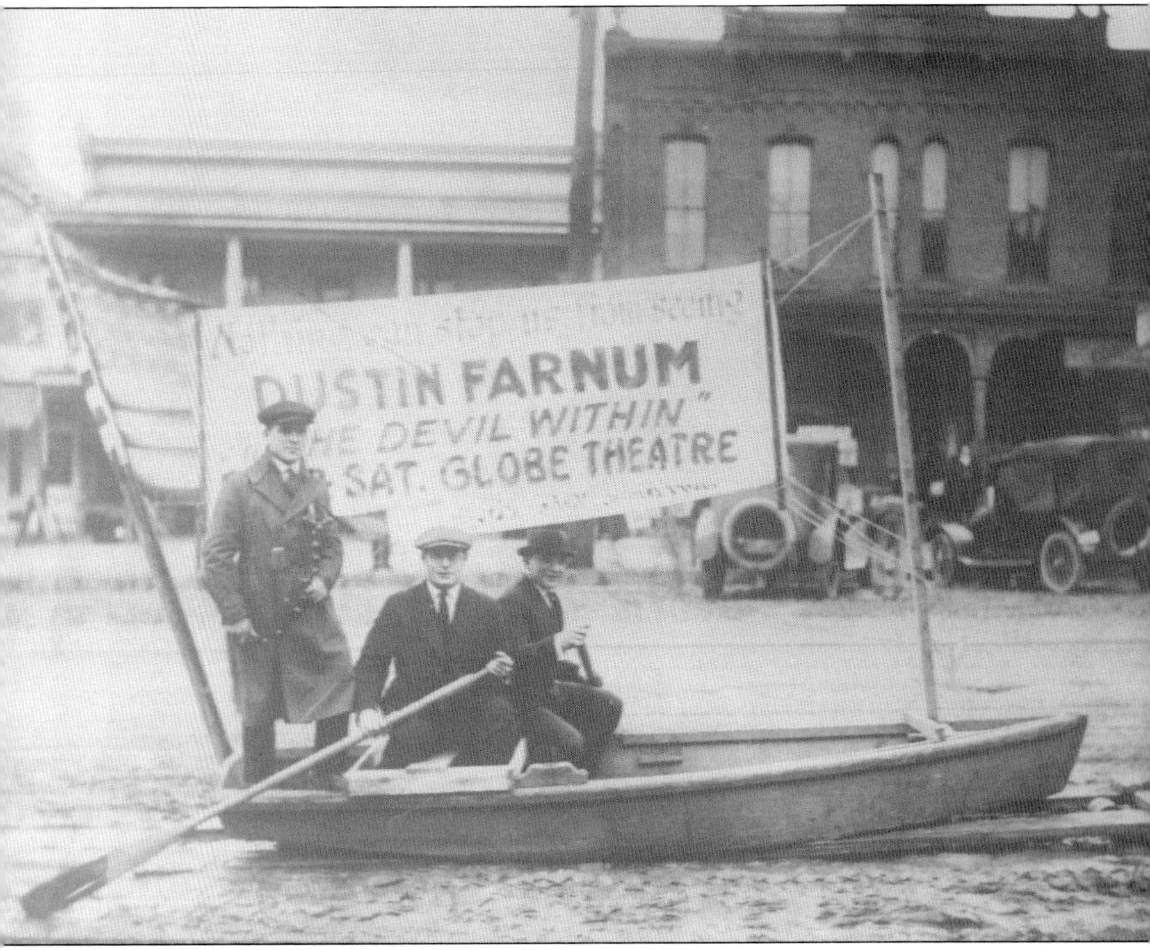

Avenue of Mud. In 1921, Vineland residents amplified their protests against the poor condition of Landis Avenue, which they referred to as the "River of Mud." Three businessmen rode down the avenue in a row boat, attached by a rope to an automobile that pulled them. In the picture above are, from left to right, Julius Lelli, Herbert Lubin, and Eugene Mori. During the ride, Lelli rang a cord of sleigh bells while Lubin and Mori manned the oars.

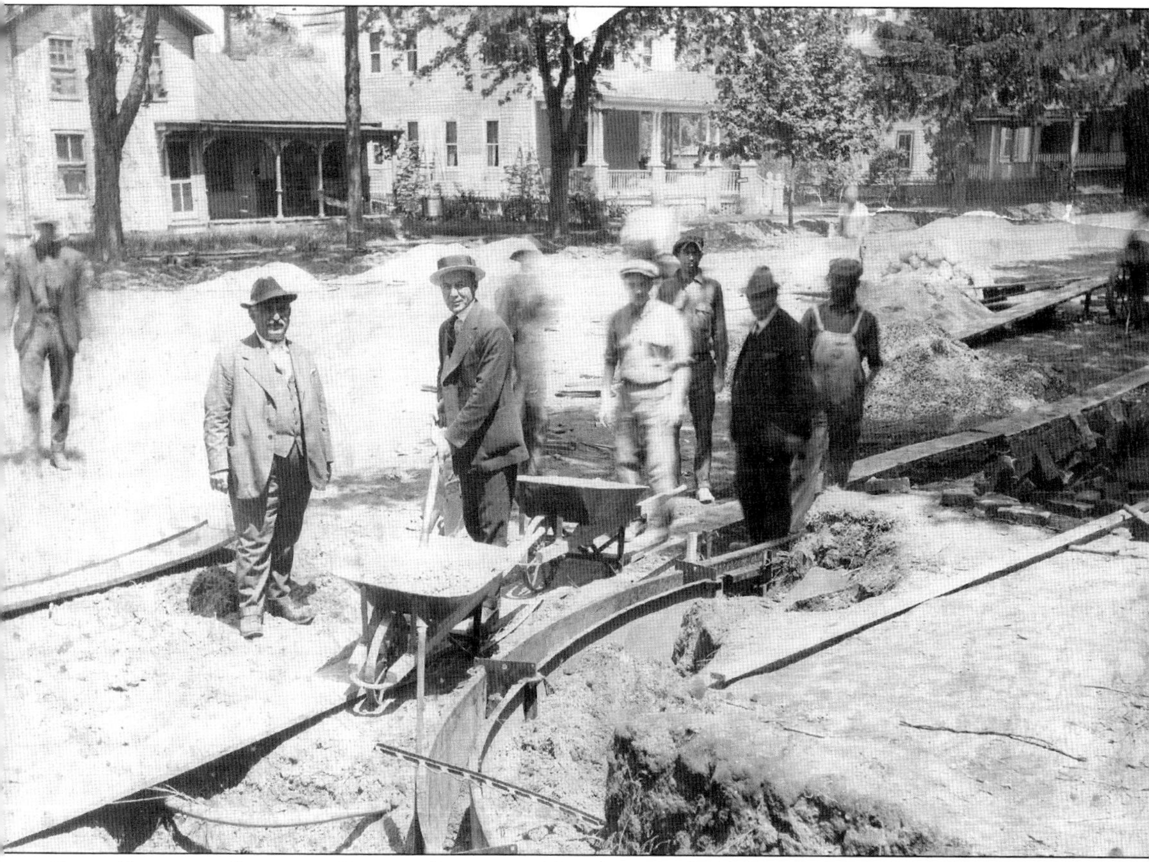

First Concrete Paving of Landis Avenue, 1921. A week after Julius Lelli, Herbert Lubin, and Eugene Mori led the protest against the River of Mud, borough commissioners approved several paving ordinances, including one calling for the avenue to be paved. In 1922, Mayor Ferdinand Koetz posed for the camera as he mixed the cement that laid the first curbing on Landis Avenue. (Photograph by Roland G. Robbins of Vineland.)

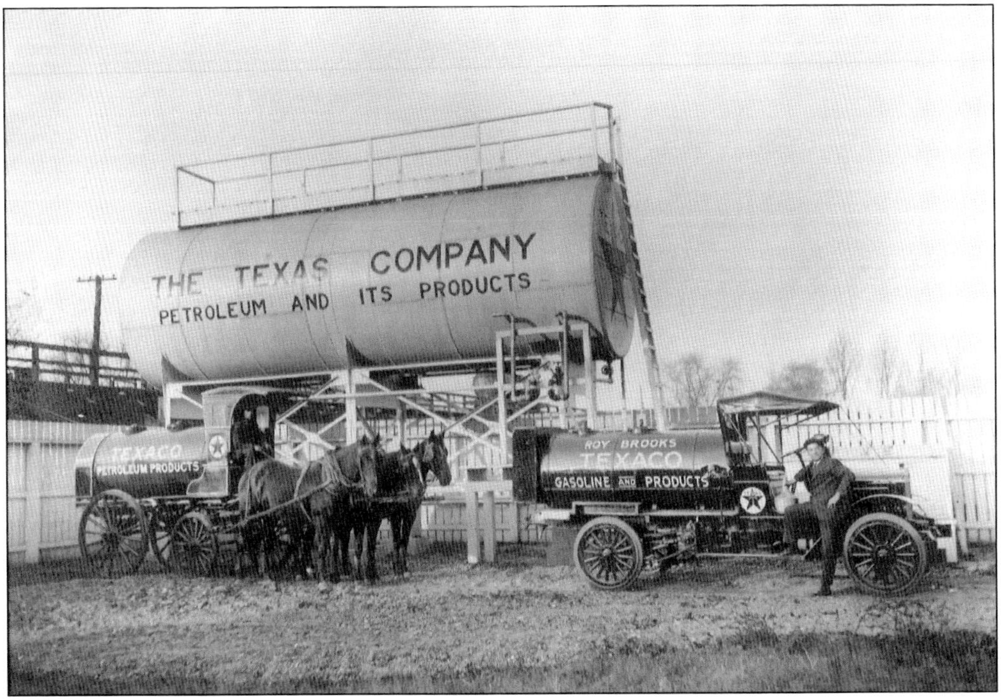

FIRST TANK TRUCK IN VINELAND, 1917. This picture shows the first motorized tank truck to be used in Vineland, together with the horse-drawn vehicle it replaced. Both were used by Roy Brooks of East Avenue at his gasoline station.

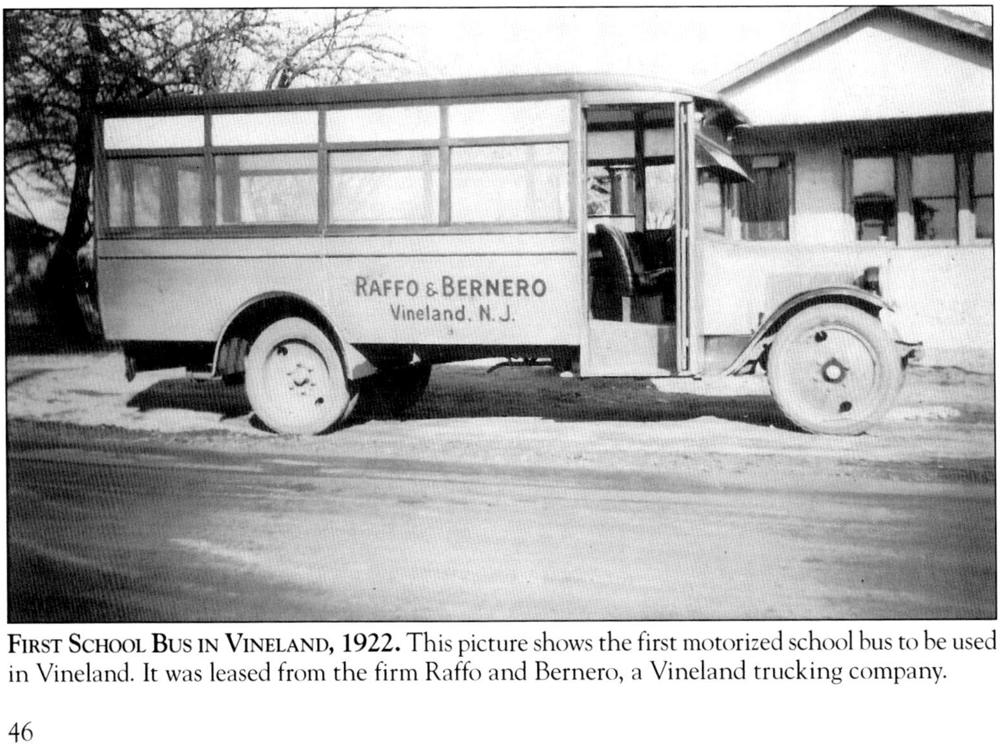

FIRST SCHOOL BUS IN VINELAND, 1922. This picture shows the first motorized school bus to be used in Vineland. It was leased from the firm Raffo and Bernero, a Vineland trucking company.

Four

INDUSTRY IN VINELAND

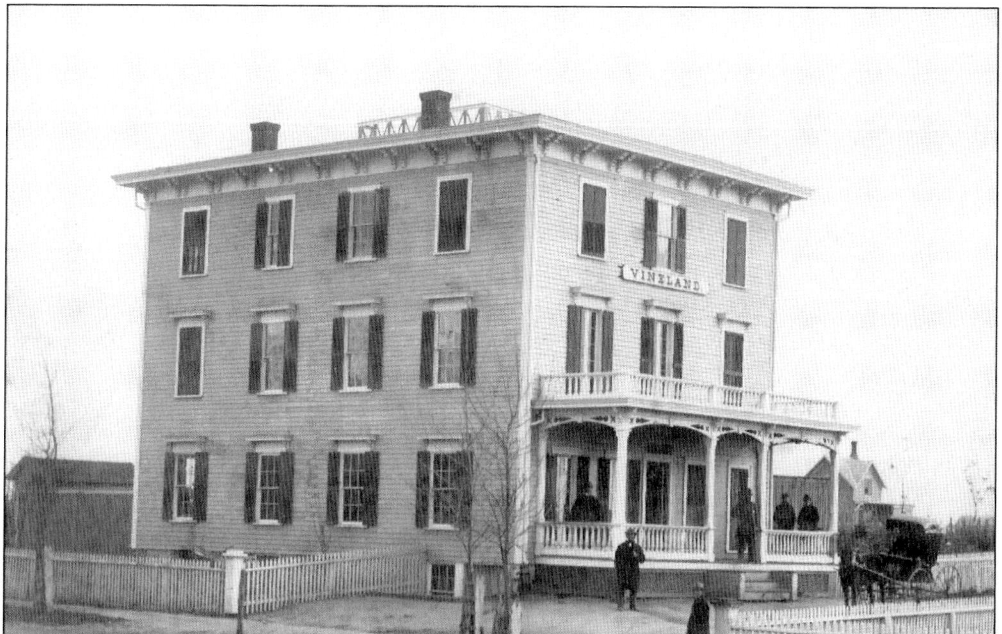

HOTEL VINELAND, 1865. To accommodate regular visitors to Vineland, especially those seeking to purchase real estate, a hotel was erected at the Boulevard and Landis Avenue, which was the center of activity after the addition of the new railway station. The hotel boasted modern accommodations and housed many well-known figures of the time and region. Charles K. Landis constructed an office attached to the hotel in order to quickly and efficiently attend to the needs and curiosities of visitors to the new town. (Photograph by Union Gallery of Vineland.)

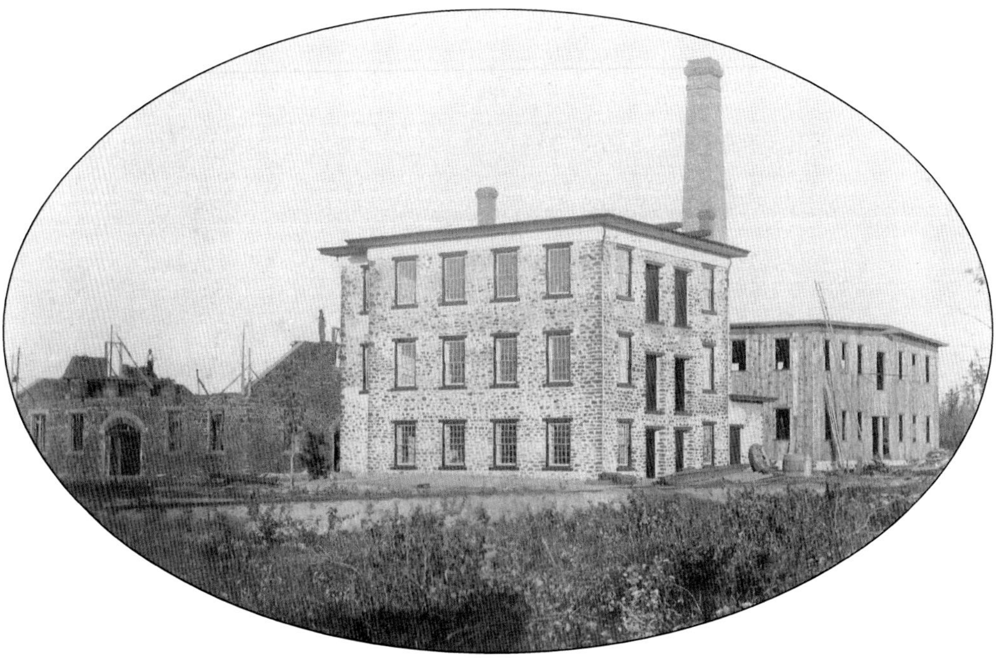

STEAM AND FLOUR MILL, 1865. Charles K. Landis built a steam and flour mill on the south side of Vineland in 1865. Landis built several factories during Vineland's early development to give employment to those who settled in the town and to help provide the town with necessary products or services. (Photograph by Union Gallery of Vineland.)

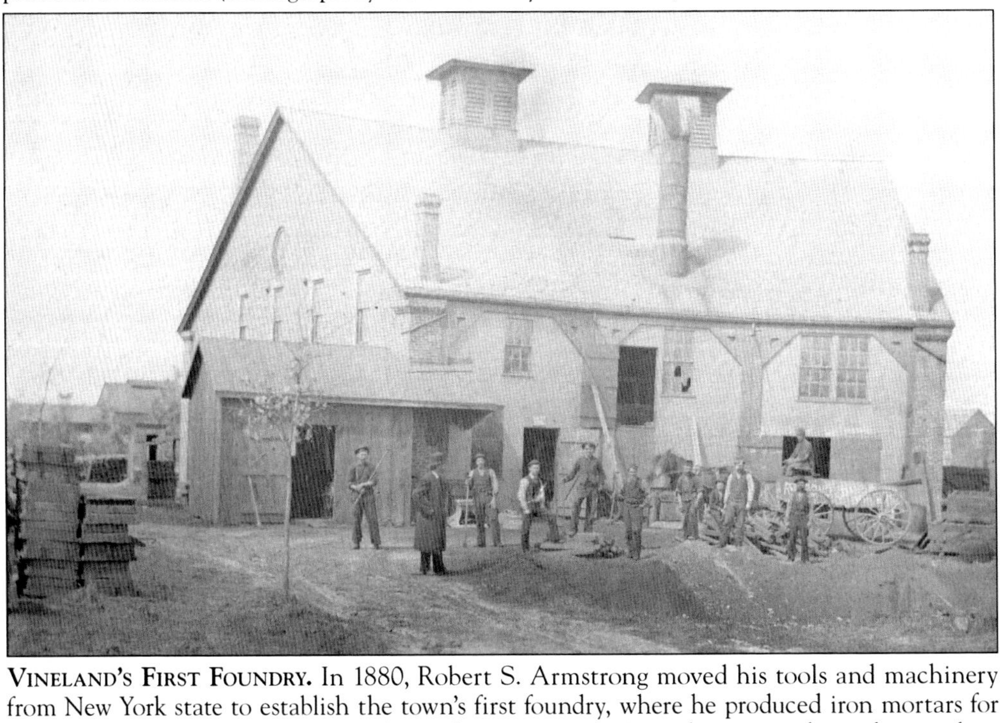

VINELAND'S FIRST FOUNDRY. In 1880, Robert S. Armstrong moved his tools and machinery from New York state to establish the town's first foundry, where he produced iron mortars for pharmacists and iron standards for shoemakers. Armstrong's products were shipped to markets across the nation, from New York City to San Francisco.

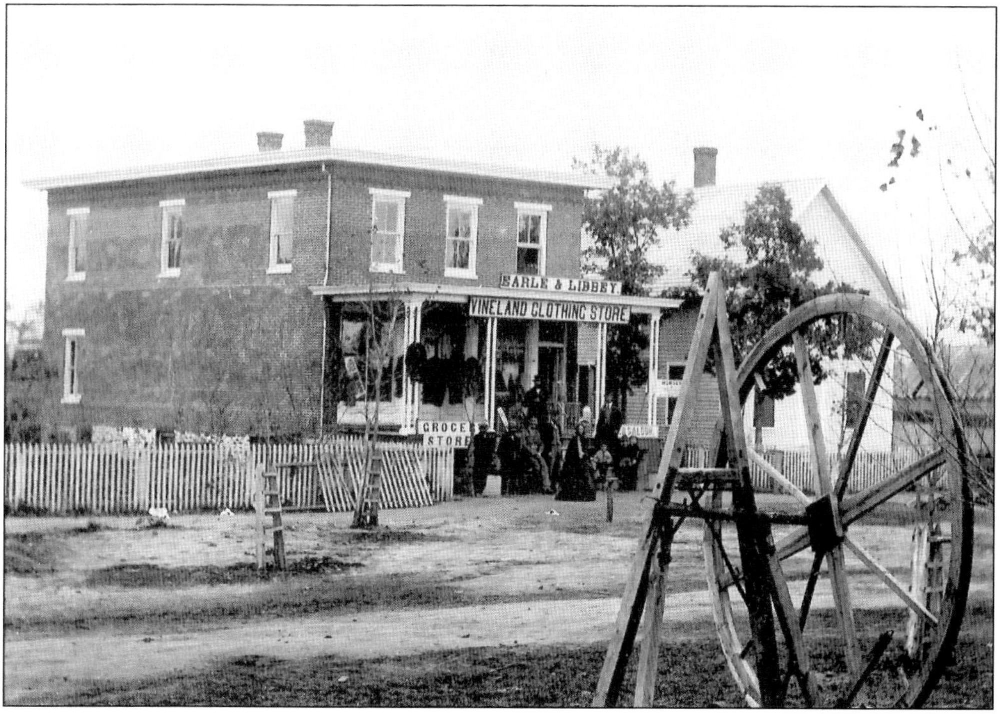

A Vineland Clothing Store, 1865. This picture shows the Earle and Libbey Clothing Store, with some of its wares prominently displayed on the porch. As the signage reflects, the building also contained a grocery store and a saloon. (Photograph by Union Gallery of Vineland.)

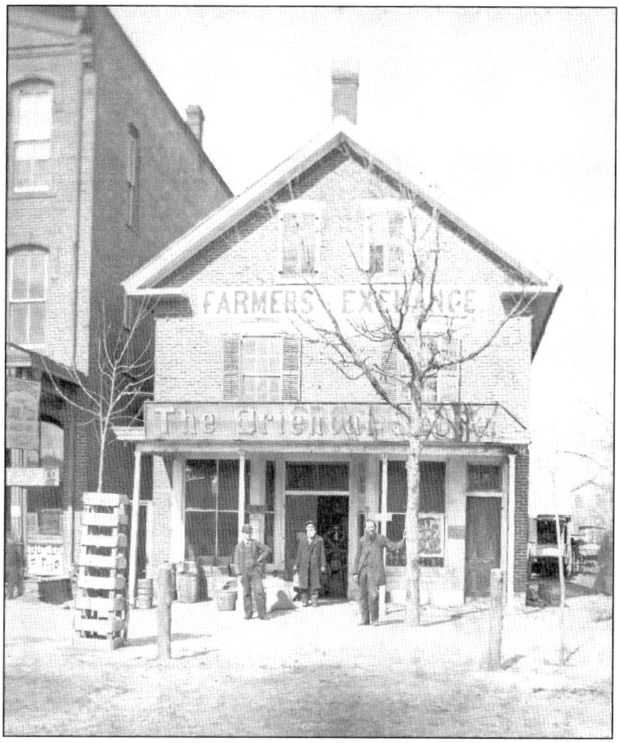

Farmers' Exchange Bank, c. 1880. This picture shows an early banking institution on Landis Avenue, called the Farmers Exchange, that catered to the banking needs of farmers who settled in Vineland. In 1889, it became the Tradesmens Bank and Trust Company, which operated independently until 1939.

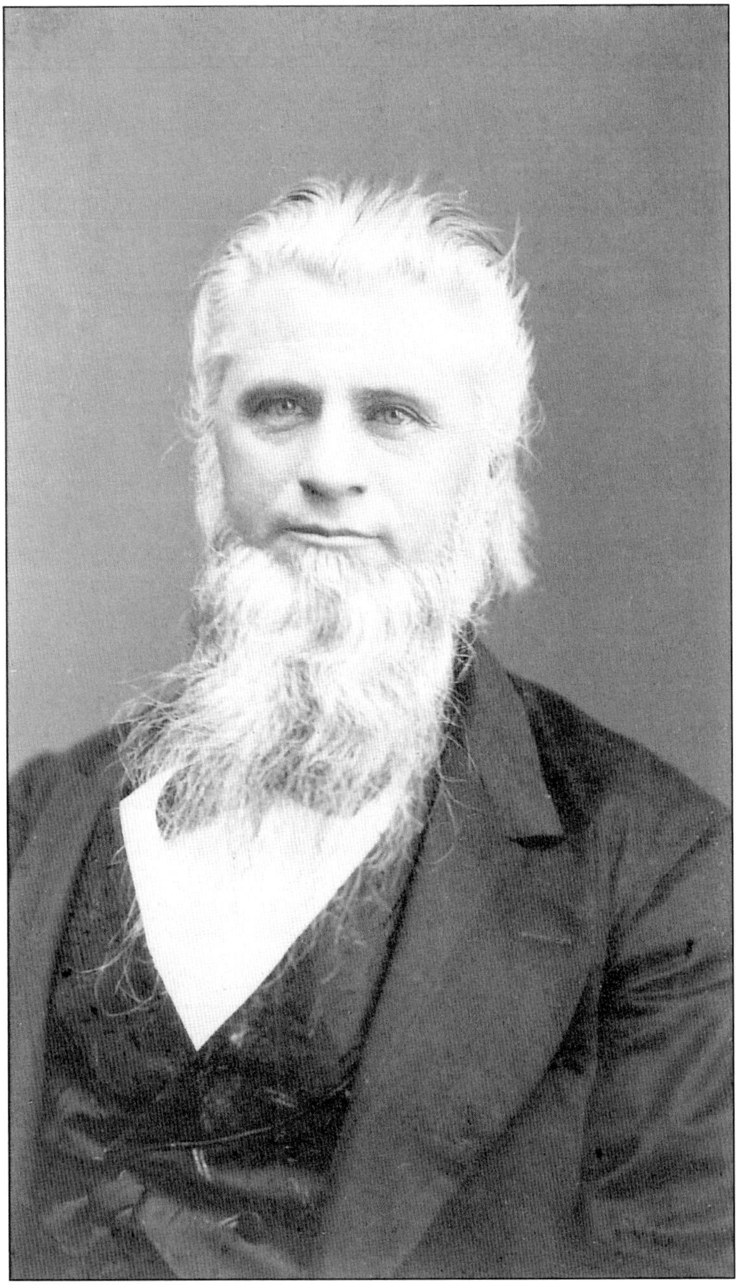

Dr. Thomas B. Welch. In 1865, Welch moved to Vineland with his family to begin a dental practice, a profession in which he continued until 1880. In 1881, he established a dental depot in Philadelphia that became one of the largest stores of its kind in the nation, and published a magazine known as *Welch's Monthly*, which soon became the nation's most popular dental journal. However, Dr. Welch is best known for having developed a method of preserving wine in an unfermented state. In 1869, having been elected recording steward of the Vineland Methodist Episcopal Church, he protested against wine for communion. When he was told he could provide whatever he wished, he created his "unfermented wine." The concoction was sold under that name for 20 years before its name was changed to grape juice. (Photograph by L. D. Johnson of Vineland.)

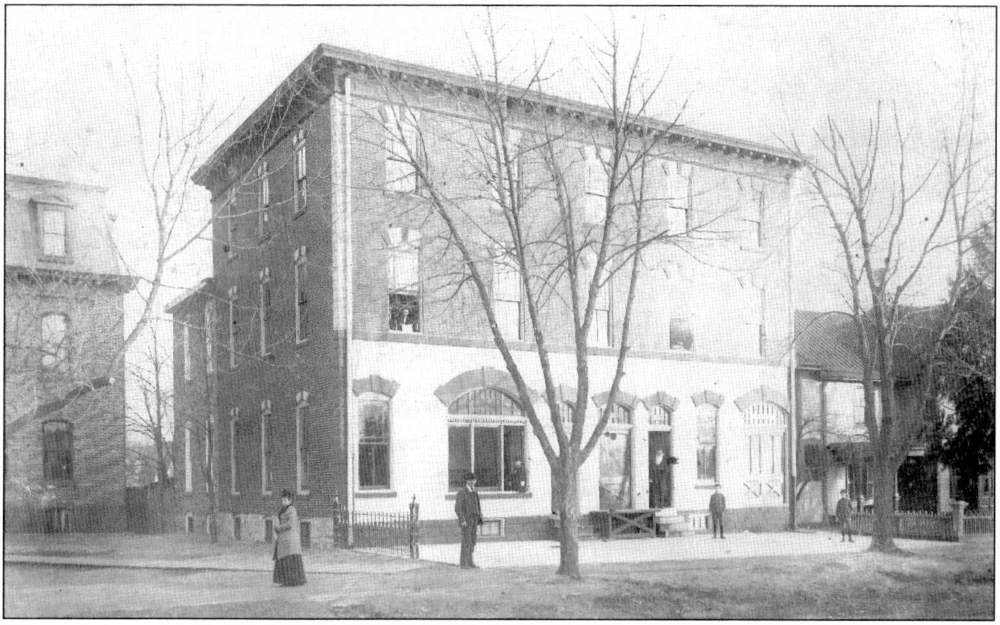

Welch's Grape Juice. By 1890, the Welch Grape Juice Company had become a household name. In 1892, Welch erected a three-story warehouse on Wood Street, shown above. The interior of the company's office in that building is shown below. For years, most of the world's supply of Welch's Grape Juice was produced in Vineland. In the early 1900s, when the company began moving its operations to New York state, several other grape juice manufactories opened in Vineland, including the Vineland Grape Juice Company, Breck's Grape Juice, and Duffy's Grape Juice. (Photograph by Elwood C. Potter of Vineland.)

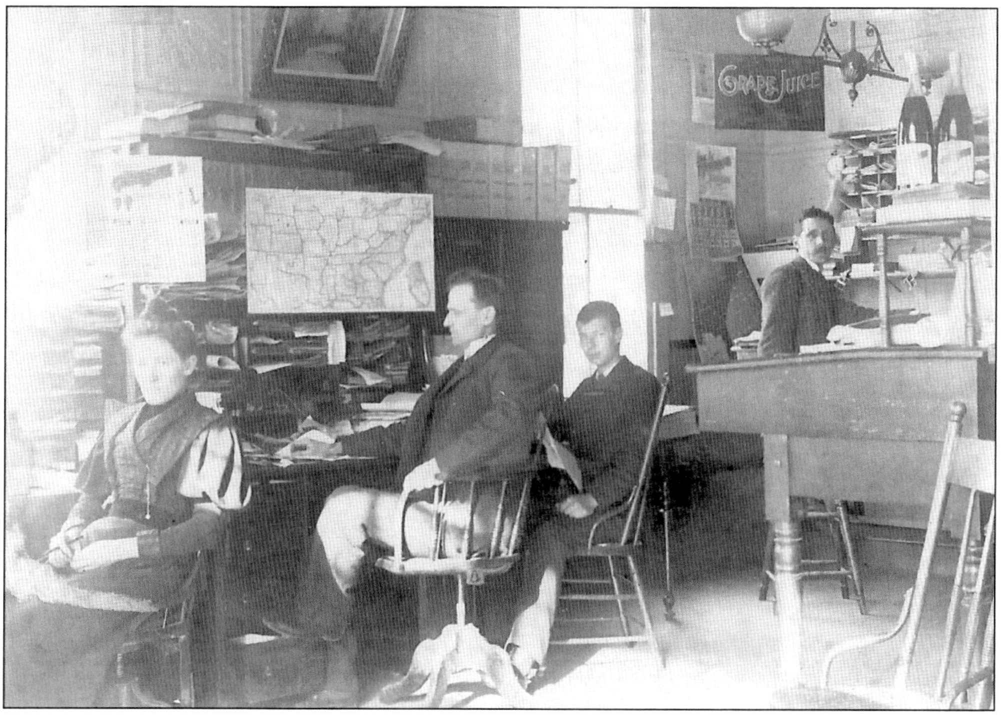

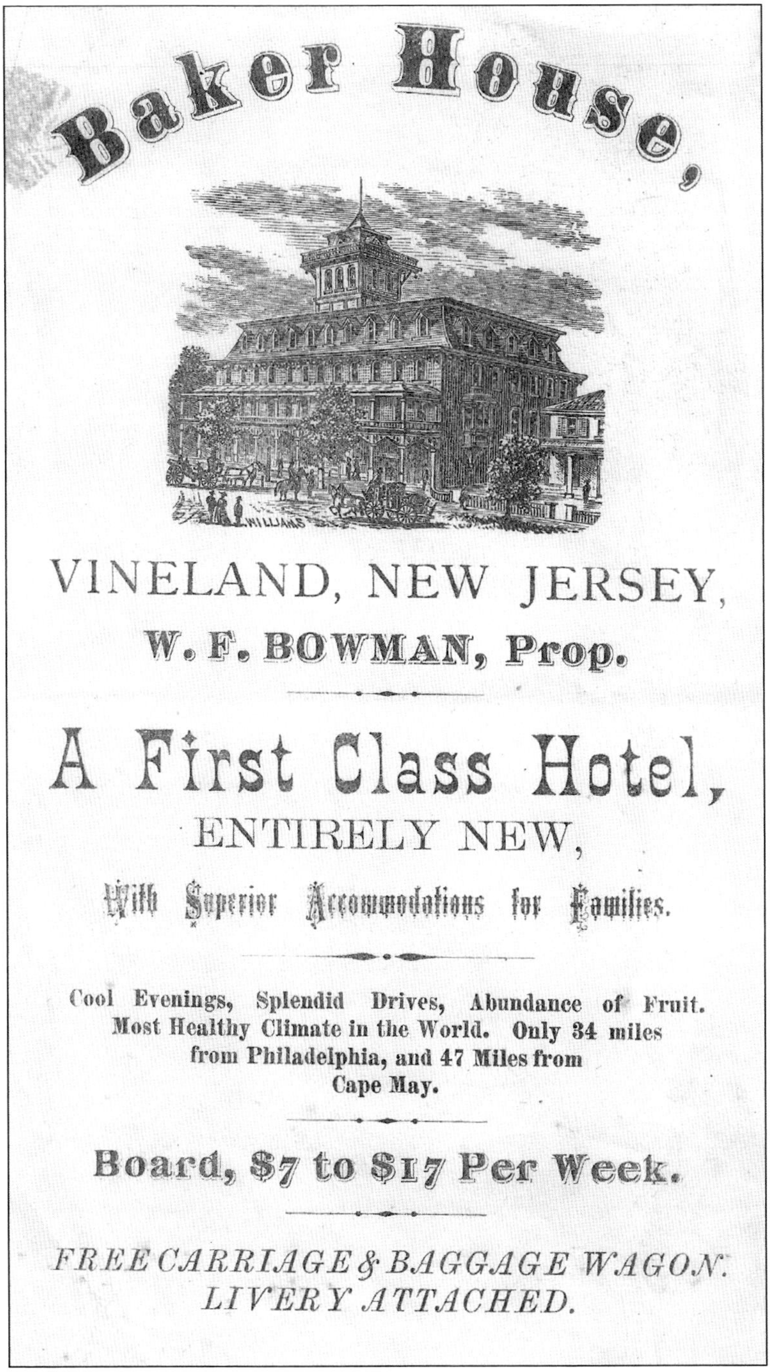

BAKER HOUSE. In 1876, brothers Philip and Latimer Baker constructed a large building on Landis Avenue called the Baker House, which consisted of a hotel and general stores. At the hotel's largest capacity, it had 100 rooms. Philip Baker was a New Jersey state senator and president of the Vineland Tradesman's Bank. The Baker brothers founded the town of Wildwood and eventually gave up their interests in the Baker House. Pictured above is an advertisement for the hotel from its early years, with a wood-engraved illustration by Richard A. Williams, a Vineland pioneer.

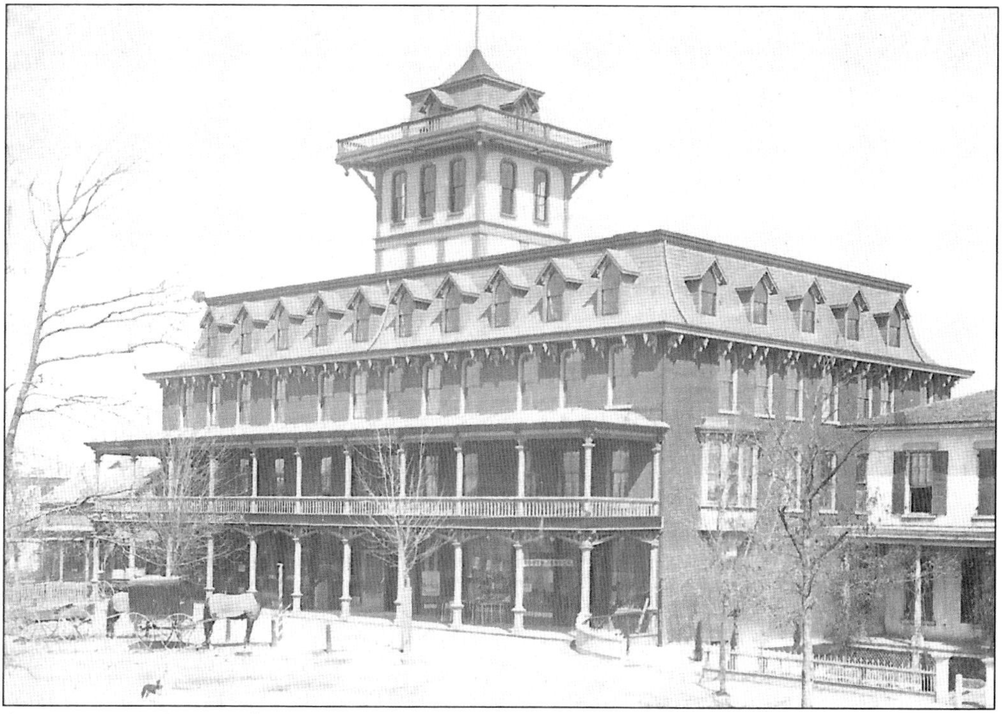

A First-class Hotel. The picture above shows the 65-foot-high hotel shortly after its construction. In 1876, when the Baker House first opened to the public, it was decorated with $9,000 worth of furniture. The picture below shows the interior of the hotel, with guests seated in the parlor room. The hotel was heated by steam and lighted by gas. Sand was placed between the floors in an effort to make it fireproof. Notwithstanding, the Baker House was destroyed by fire in 1940. (Photographs by L. D. Johnson of Vineland.)

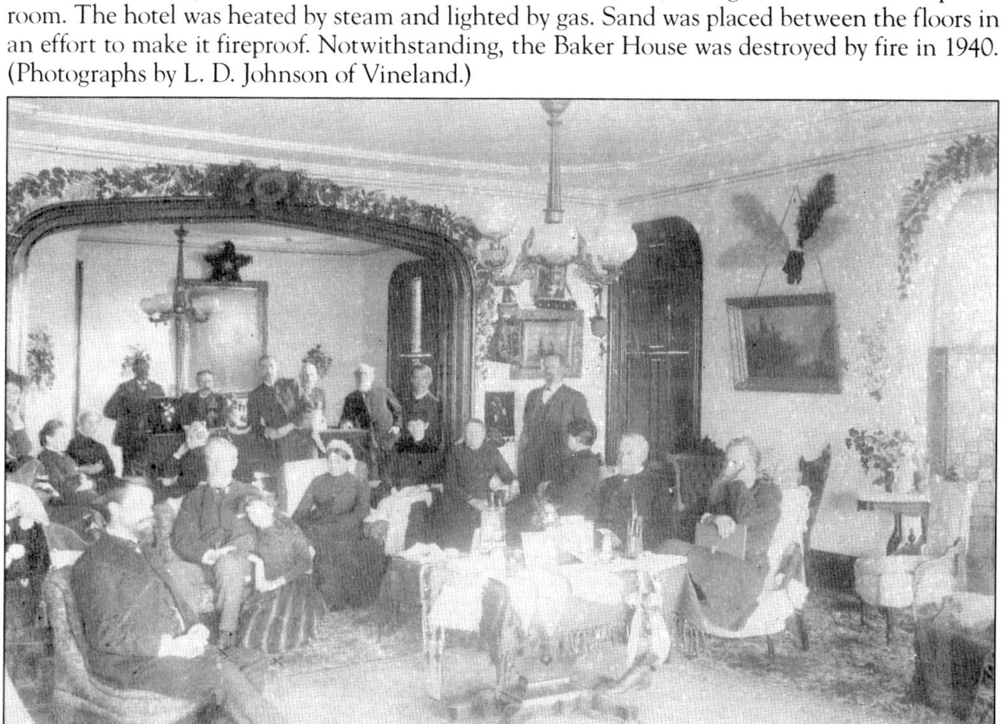

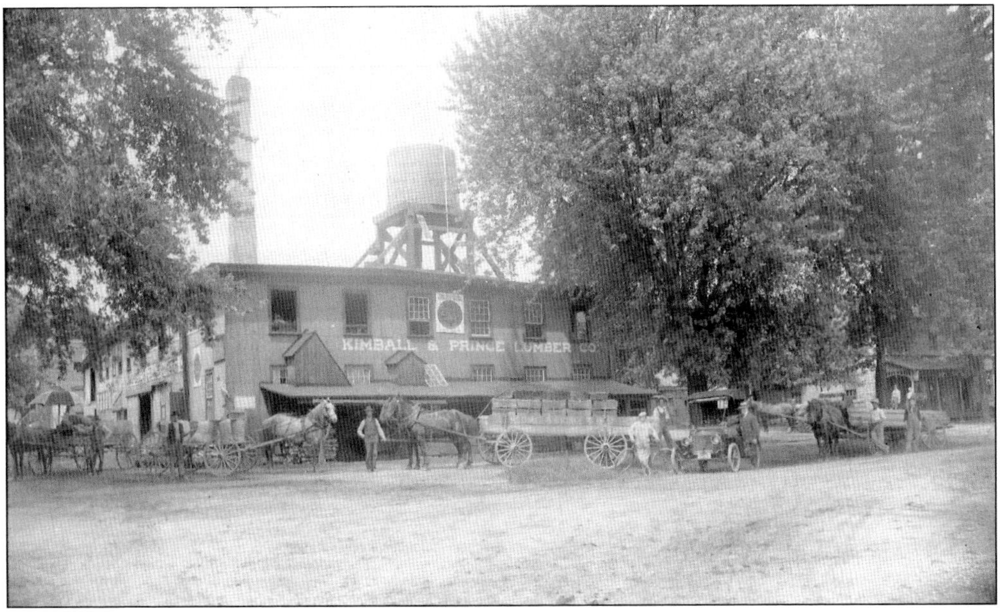

Kimball and Prince Lumber Company. In 1866, Myron J. Kimball moved to Vineland and, two years later, married Clara A. Prince, daughter of William V. Prince. In 1871, Messrs. Kimball and Prince purchased a lumber company on the corner of the Boulevard and Almond Street. Kimball, who was also president of the Vineland National Bank, served as president and manager of the company until his death in 1915.

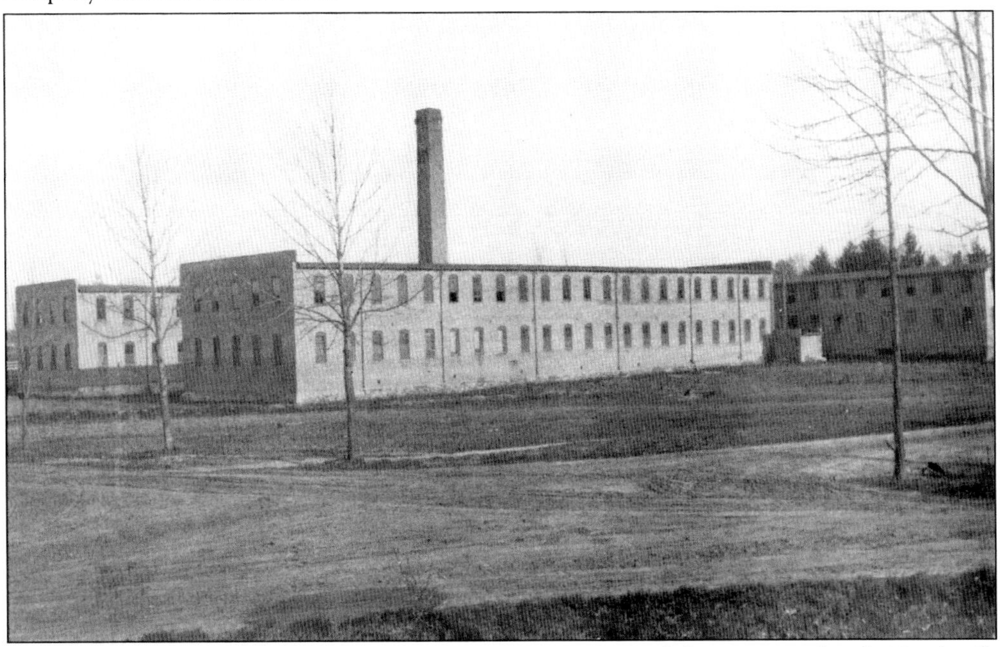

Thomas Hirst Rug Factory. In 1888, Thomas Hirst successfully negotiated with Vineland's Board of Trade to acquire 5 acres of land on which he would build a factory to manufacture rugs. The factory employed several hundred people and shipped its products across the nation, but after having been charged with polluting the Maurice River with liquid waste, the factory was closed in 1910.

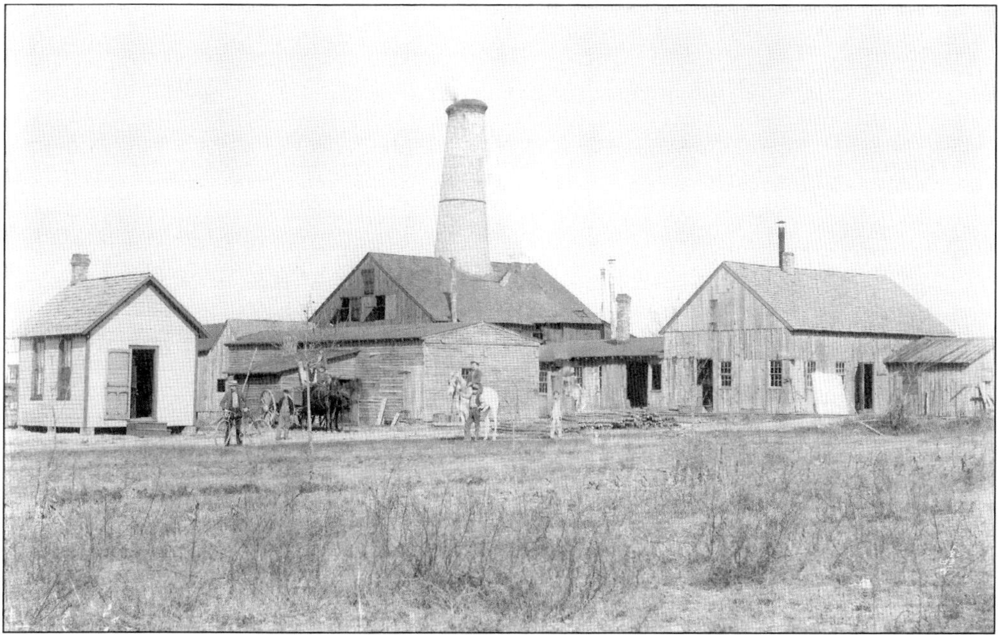

Durand Glass Factory. In 1897, Victor Durand Sr. established the Vineland Flint Glass Company, which soon after was run by his son Victor Durand Jr. The company manufactured scientific and clinical glassware. In 1904, the company's first factory, shown above, burned down and was replaced with a brick building. The picture below shows several of the factory workers. By the 1920s, Durand had shifted the factory's focus to art glass, and what he produced made him famous in the glass industry. In 1931, he was in an automobile accident and was killed by the glass from his car's windshield.

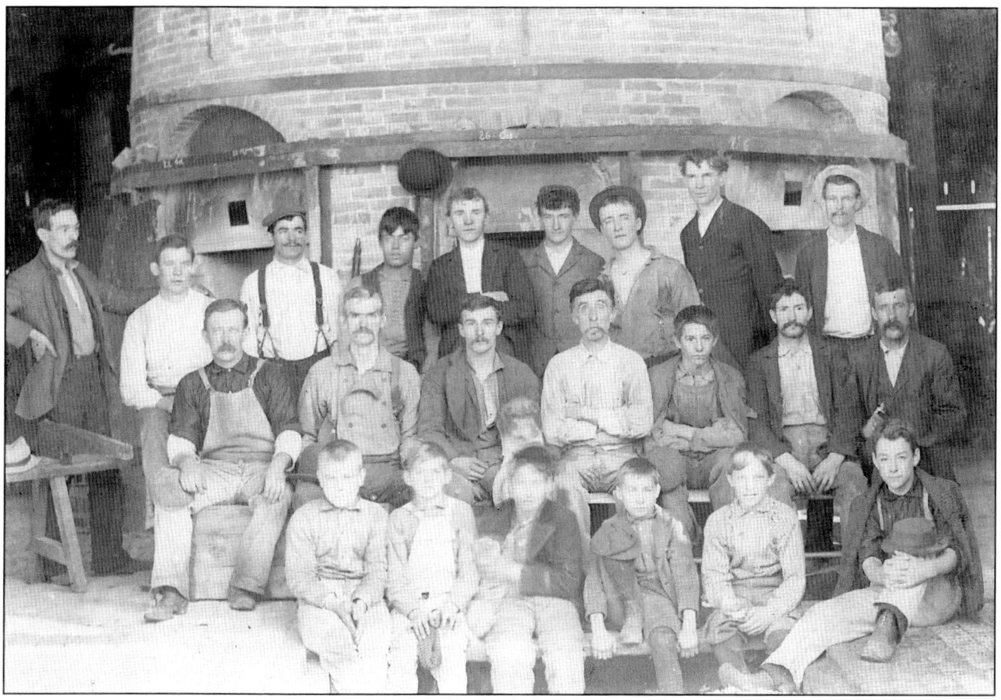

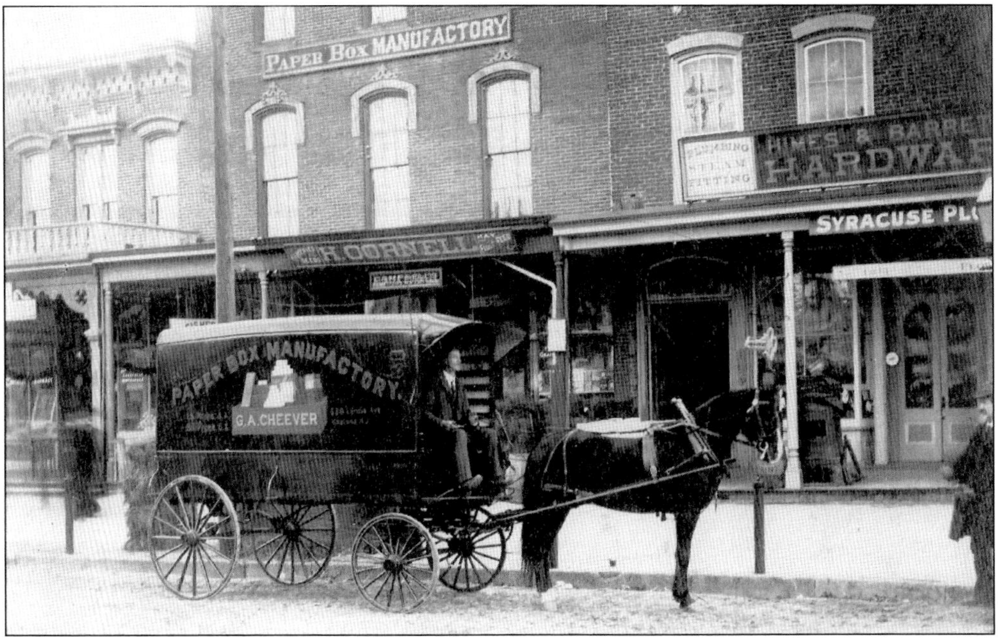

ONE-OF-A-KIND BUSINESS IN SOUTH JERSEY. In 1867, David A. Cheever moved to Vineland and established a paper box manufactory. Upon his death in 1882, his son George A. Cheever purchased and expanded the company, the first of its kind in South Jersey. Its specialty was grape boxes, but it also made thousands of boxes annually for various glass firms in the area. Because of the demand for business, it employed a large force of men and women to keep the factory running constantly. By 1905, as shown in the picture above, the factory was located on the 500 block of Landis Avenue. In the picture below, from left to right, the following women are shown at work: Joanna Buck, Emma Ewan, Lula Eilenberg, Mary Jost, Ada Ayers, Bertha Cronk, Mary Austin, and Ella Fiske. After Cheever's death in 1907, the company passed through several owners before dissolving in the late 1920s.

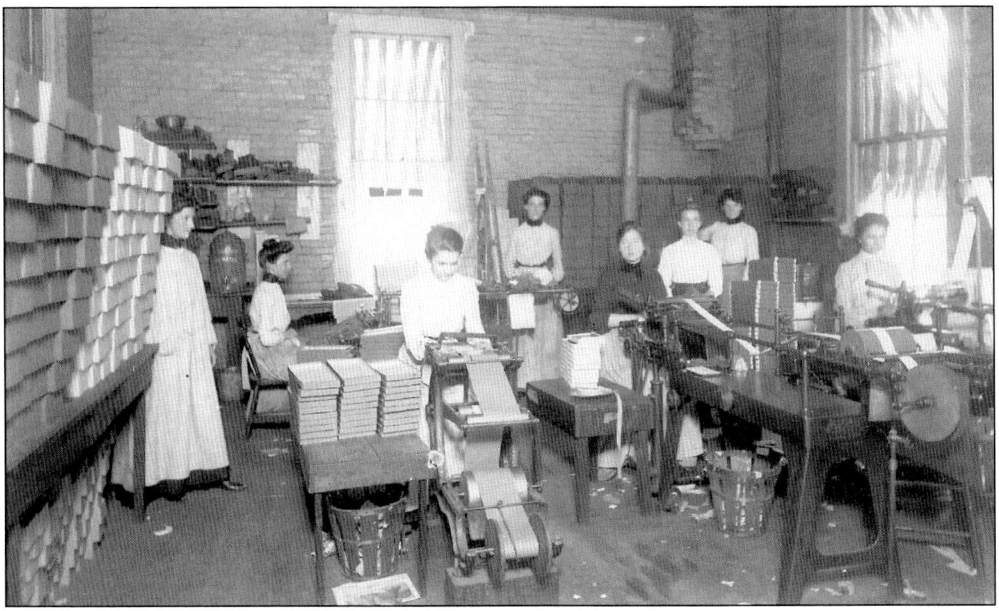

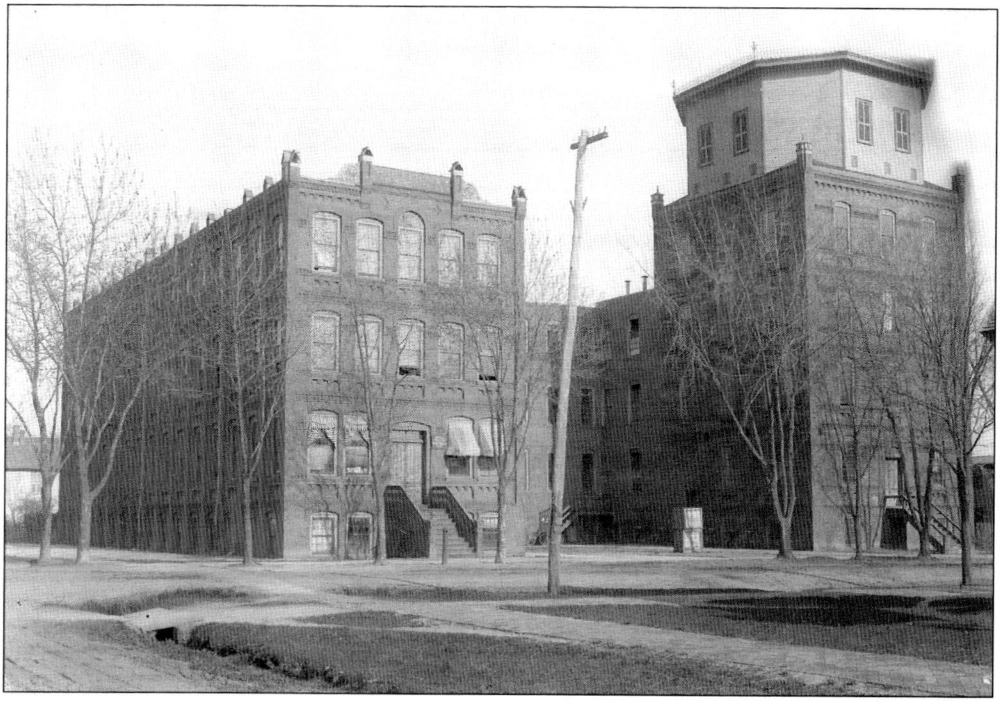

VINELAND'S LARGEST SHOE FACTORY, C. 1900. In 1875, Charles P. Keighley opened a small shoe factory in a rented room with about 10 employees. In 1884, after moving his business space several times, he built a four-story brick factory on the corner of Sixth and Montrose Streets. Less than 10 years later, he more than doubled the size of the factory, shown above. By 1897, the factory employed 450 people and made 1,500 pairs of shoes a day. The picture below is a group of its workers, which includes several young boys. Keighley dominated the industry in South Jersey through his innovations in shoe machinery, for which he held several patents.

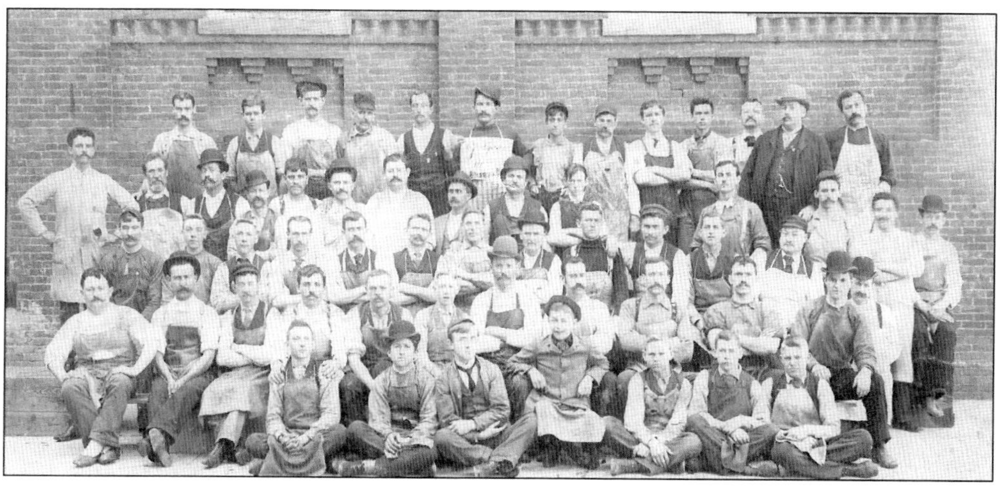

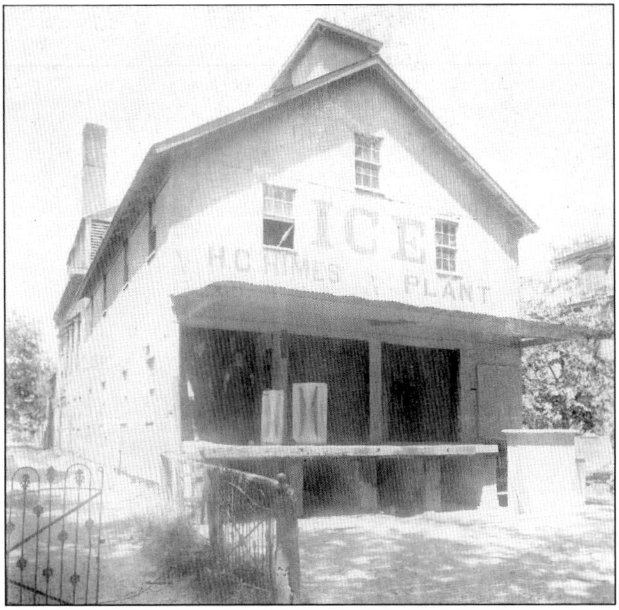

H. C. HIMES ICE PLANT. In 1898, H. C. Himes moved to Vineland and purchased a refrigerating plant on Elmer Street. He continued to operate the business until 1920, when he sold his interests in the company, but maintained an active role in the plant until it was yet again sold to a larger company in the 1930s.

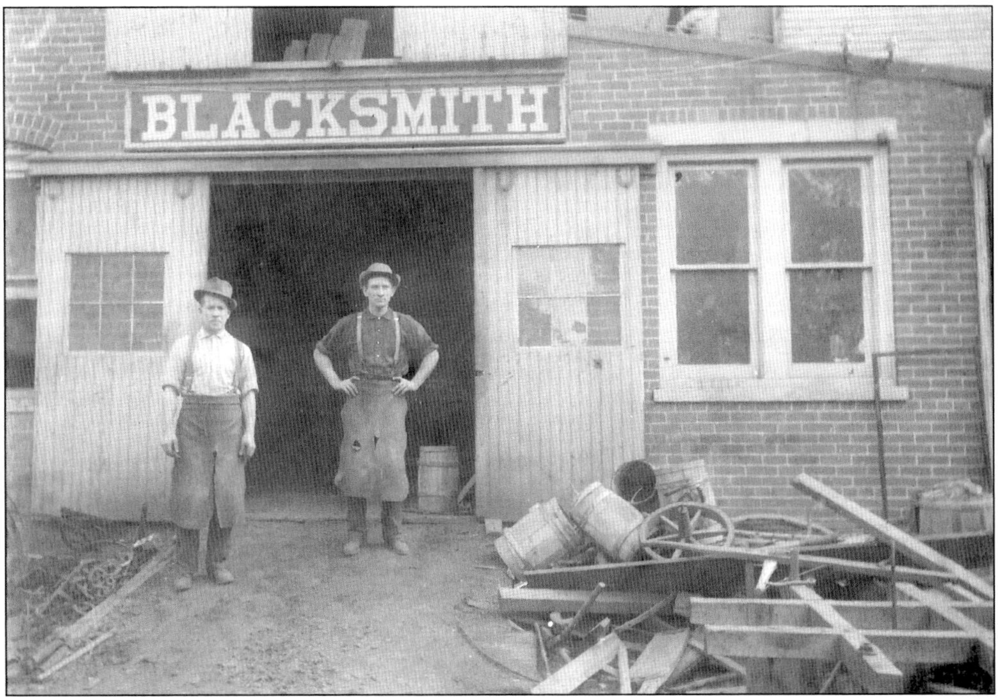

BLACKSMITH'S SHOP, C. 1912. This picture shows a blacksmith's shop on Landis Avenue. The men pictured are William Z. Little (left) and William Darnstadter. Charles K. Landis stated that when he first established Vineland, the town was in great need of a blacksmith. He engaged a man from Philadelphia who immediately changed his mind. Landis then convinced a blacksmith from Vermont to set up shop in Vineland. However, when he opened his business, some New Jersey natives convinced him that no one would need blacksmith work in such a forsaken place, which discouraged him so much he left the next morning. However, 50 years later, there were several blacksmiths in Vineland.

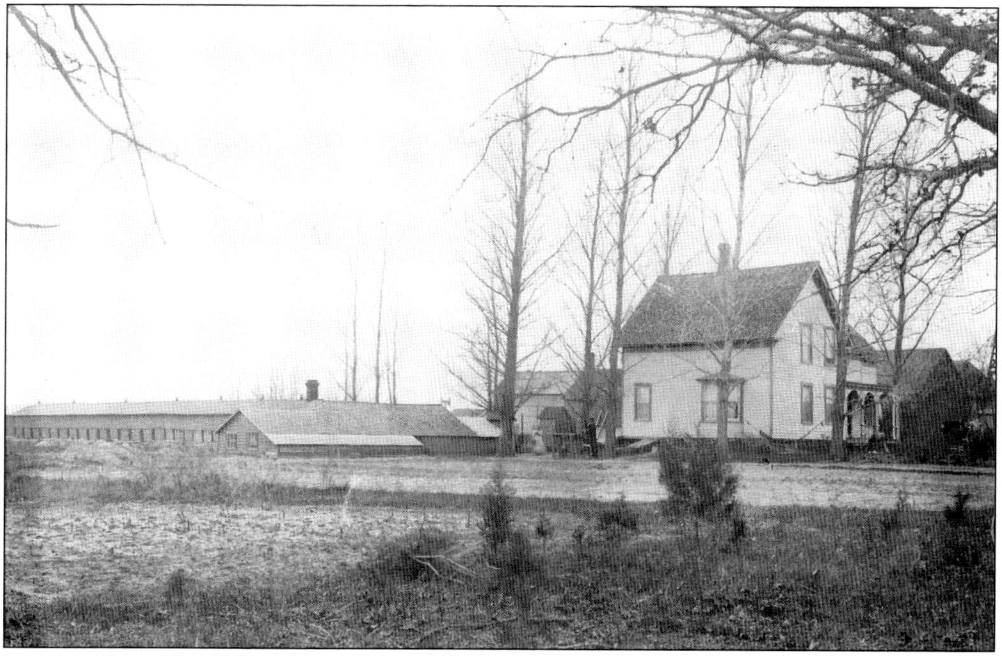

Arnold Farm. In 1868, Albert P. Arnold moved to Vineland and established a 5-acre farm on Malaga Road. In 1887, he began to raise chickens to sell and, after 10 years, was averaging 63,000 broilers a year. In 1908, he changed the focus of his farm to the production of eggs and became the most successful poultry farmer in Vineland on a farm spanning over 80 acres. Arnold contributed to the rise of the town's poultry industry, which led to Vineland being called the "Egg Capital of the World."

Little Robin Duck Farm. In 1906, Horace G. Huey established an 18-acre duck farm on West Landis Avenue, near Mill Road and the Little Robin Branch Stream. Within a year, the Little Robin Duck Farm could accommodate 7,000 ducklings. By 1920, the farm produced over 30,000 ducks per year, which were sold directly to hotels. The use of innovative technology and the large scale of the farm attracted many visitors and helped it achieve statewide fame.

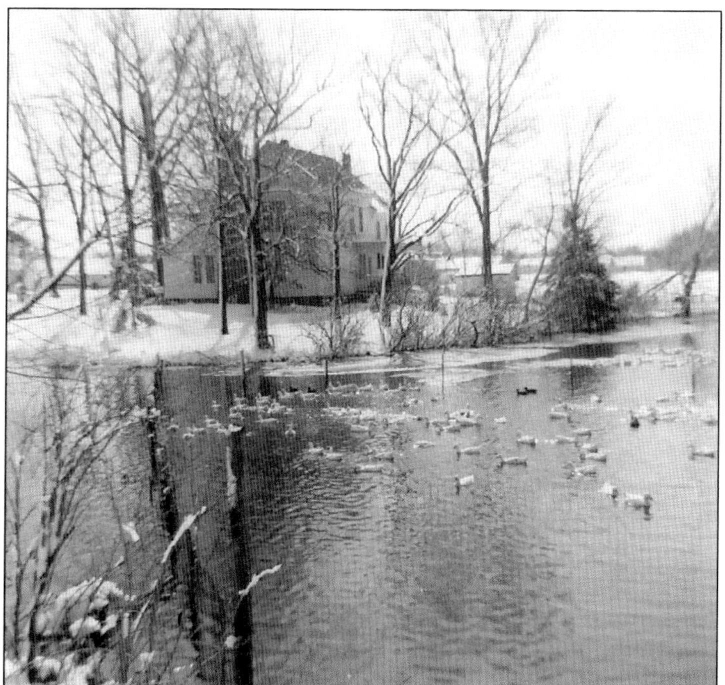

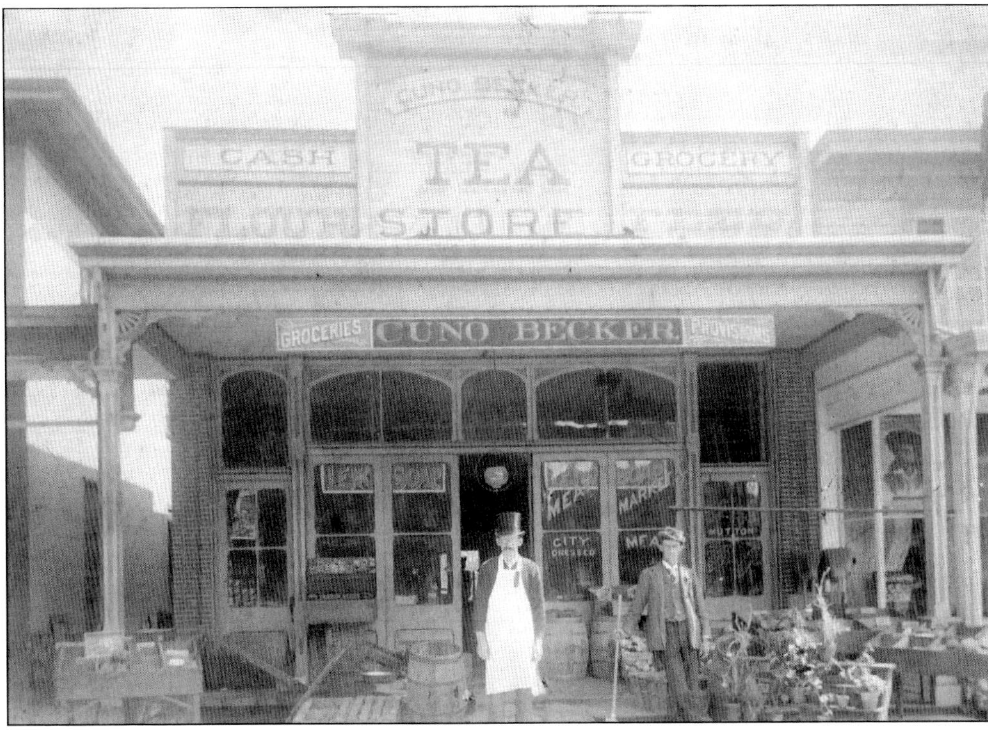

CUNO BECKER TEA STORE, C. 1890. The picture above shows the outside of Cuno Becker's Tea Store, with Becker in an apron standing directly under the store's sign. The store was located on East Avenue in a building once occupied by John W. Potts's grocery store. The picture below shows the inside of the Becker Tea Store with barrels of fruits and vegetables. The store was successful for many years and expanded to offer a wide variety of food products; at one time it even employed six butchers.

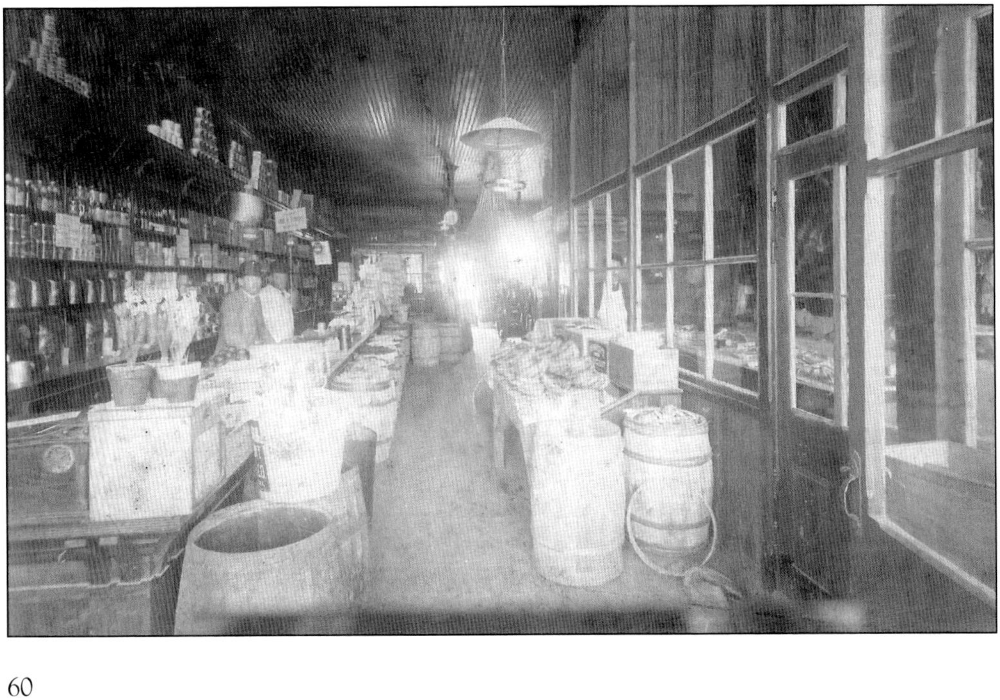

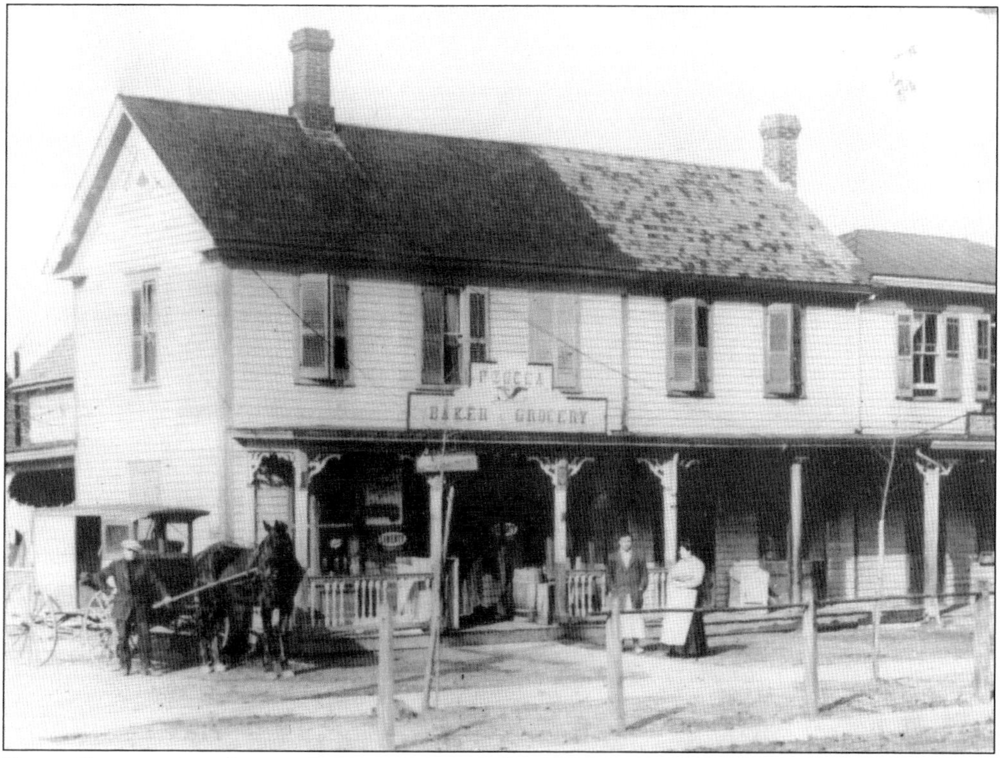

Zucca Bakery, 1910. In 1896, Peter Zucca, an Italian immigrant, established a bakery in Vineland. He began only making bread but, by 1910, was selling a complete line of baked goods. His son Ernest A. Zucca worked in the bakery from the age of nine and, in 1923, assumed ownership of the business. By the 1940s, Zucca operated four delivery routes in the area and sold his products, both wholesale and retail. The bakery continued to be popular throughout its duration in Vineland. In 1955, Zucca retired, giving the business to his children, who continued to operate it for several decades thereafter.

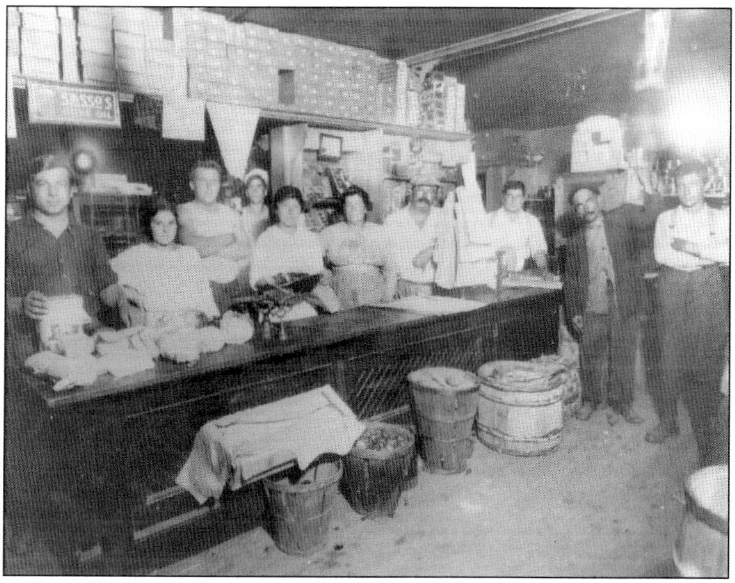

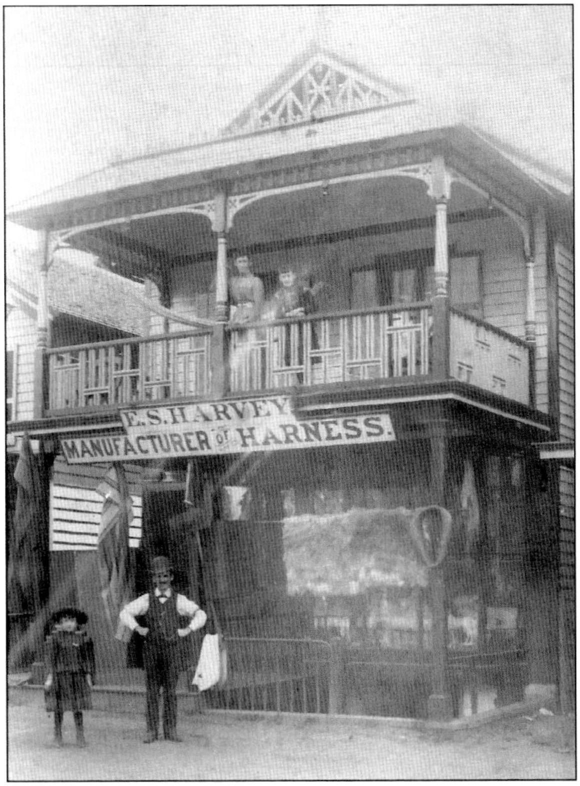

E. S. HARVEY HARNESS STORE, c. 1890. About 1870, Edwin S. Harvey moved to Vineland and established a harness business on the 600 block of Landis Avenue. Harvey is shown at left, in front of the store together with his wife and daughters. Harvey continued to operate the business until his death in 1912.

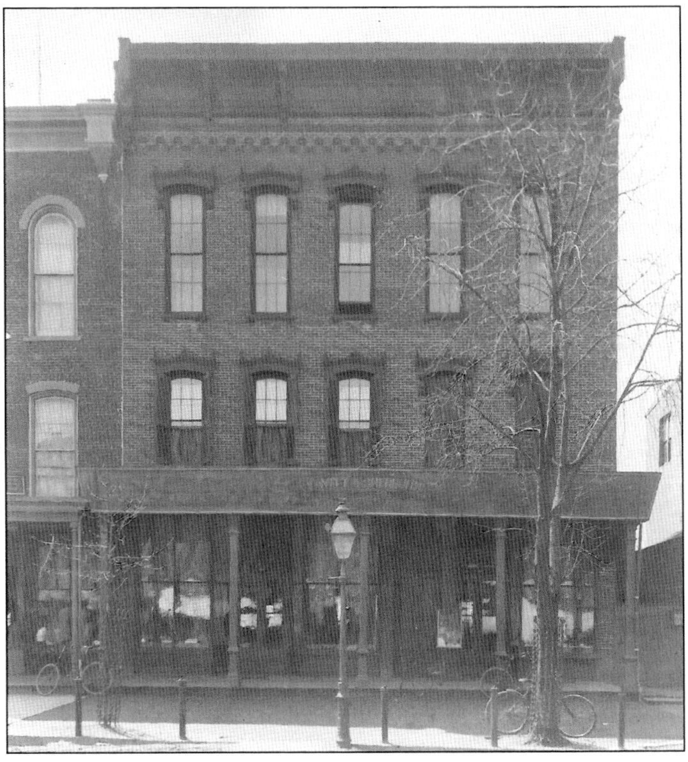

LEAVITT AND SHERBURNE DRY GOODS STORE. About 1868, Victoria Sherburne, along with Abby F. Leavitt, whom she met in Boston and with whom she shared an ambitious and progressive spirit, moved to Vineland to establish a dry goods store. From its beginning, their store was a success. In 1869, they constructed a large brick building on Landis Avenue, shown at right. For many years, the store was the leading dry goods and variety store in South Jersey. Eventually the partnership dissolved, and after a short career alone, Sherburne retired and became the second wife of Dr. Thomas B. Welch.

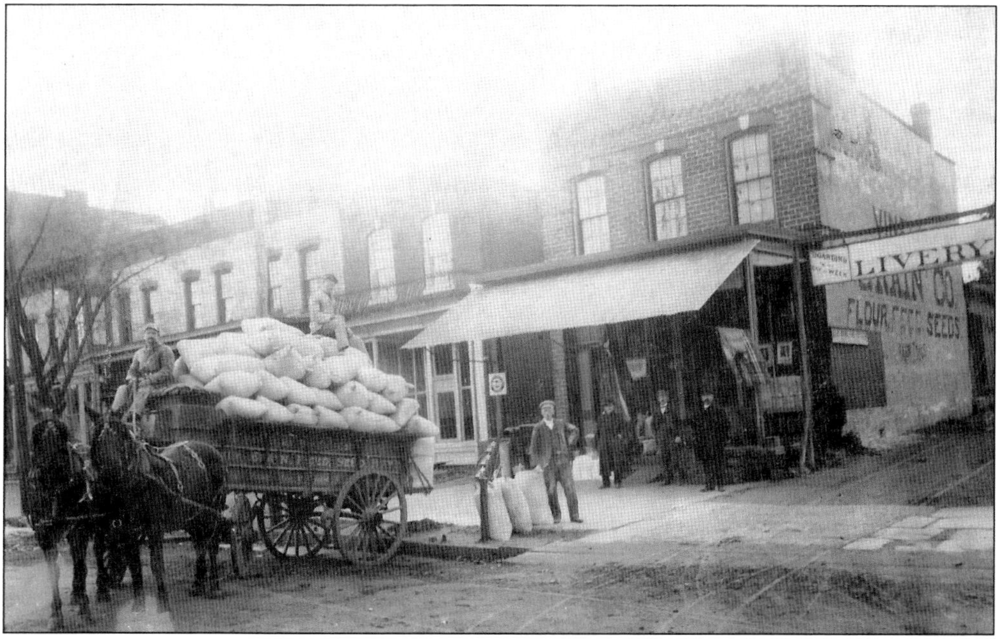

VINELAND GRAIN COMPANY, C. 1890. About 1889, the Taylor Brothers opened the Vineland Grain Company on the 500 block of Landis Avenue, managed by Stuart F. Morris. The company marketed grain, flour, feed, hay, and straw.

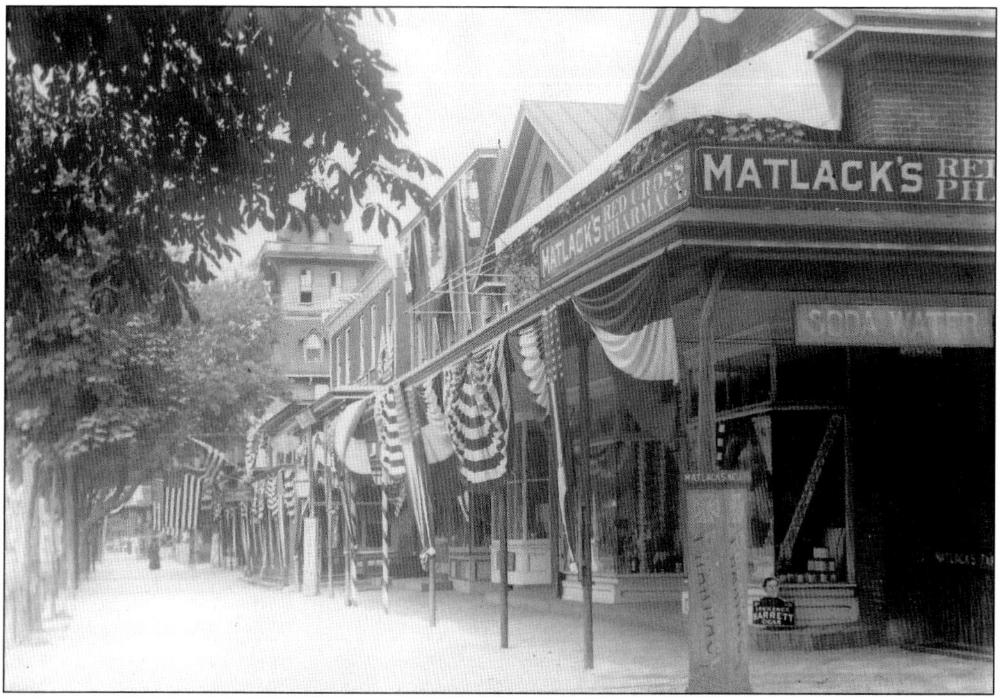

MATLACK'S RED CROSS PHARMACY, 1911. In 1902, Walter B. Matlack graduated from the Philadelphia College of Pharmacy and, in 1914, opened a pharmacy on the corner of Landis Avenue and Seventh Street. He continued to operate at that location until 1934, when he moved the business to Landisville.

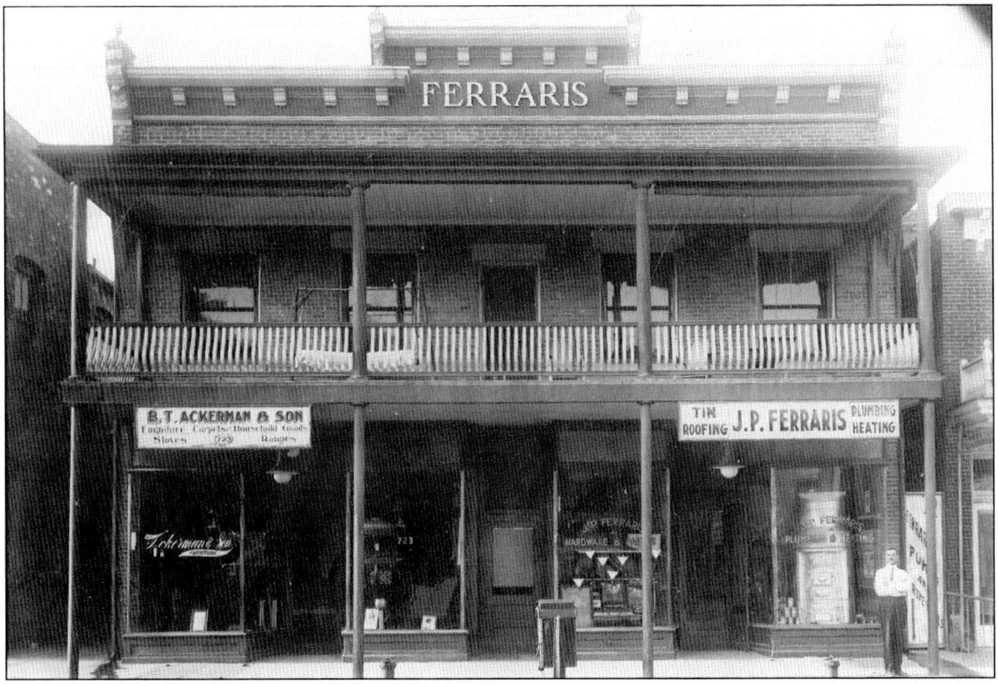

JOSEPH P. FERRARIS. In the 1870s, Ferraris moved to Vineland with his parents to establish a farm on Garden Road. In 1903, he opened a plumbing and heating business, which grew into a successful enterprise. In 1911, Ferraris erected the building shown above on the 700 block of Landis Avenue. Upon completion of the building, he opened a retail store in connection with his business, which he operated until his death in the 1940s. (Photograph by Roland G. Robbins.)

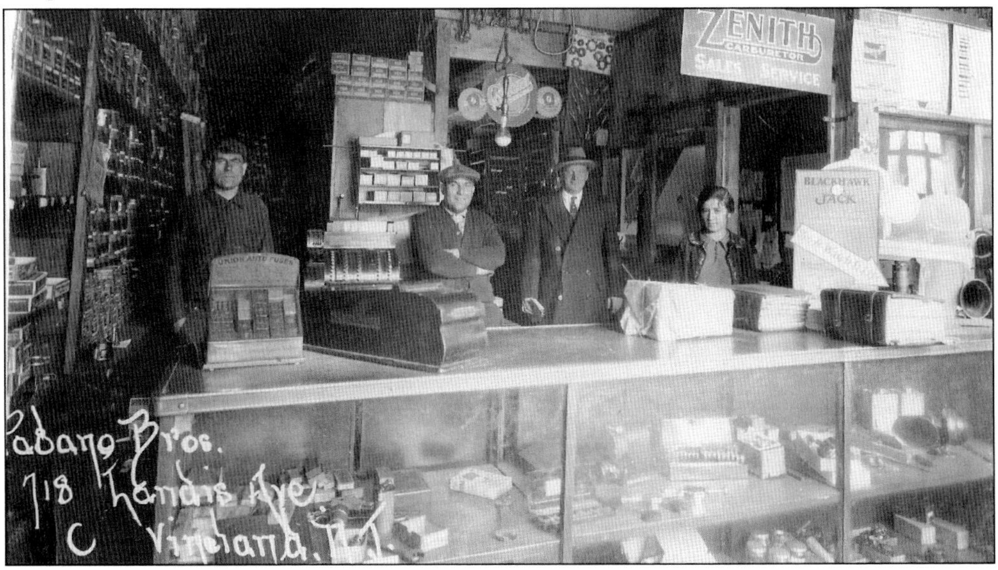

PAGANO BROTHERS. In 1918, at the close of World War I, Stephen F. Pagano and his brothers Thomas and John organized the firm of Pagano Brothers. They purchased an established automobile repair shop and continued that business while expanding with the retail store shown above. Their father, Angelo Pagano, born in Italy, was the first Italian youth to settle in Vineland. (Photograph by Eastern Photo Company of Wilmington.)

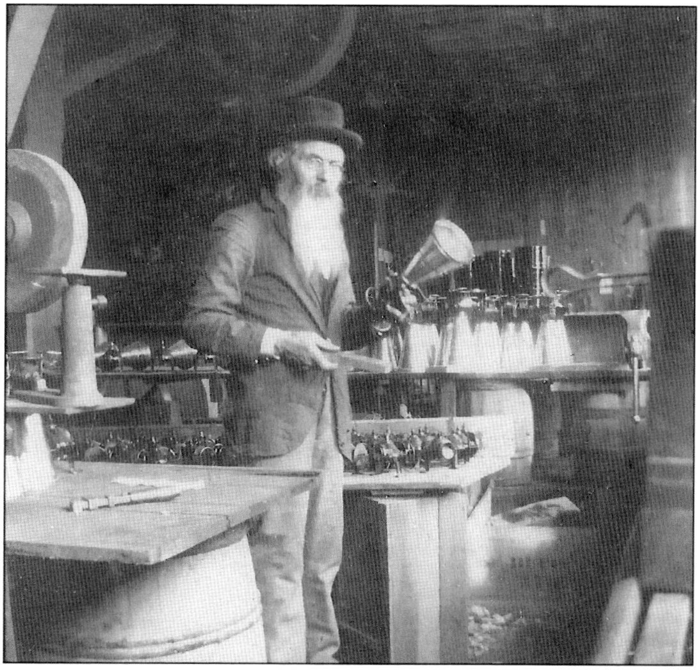

A Vineland Inventor. In 1864, William A. Daggett moved to Vineland and began inventing and improving household objects. His Daggett Clothes Horse, a frame on which clothes were hung to dry after washing them, was used all over the country. He built a factory on Wood Street and the Boulevard, when he manufactured another of his inventions, the Daggett Covered Roasting Pan. Daggett continued to operate a factory in Vineland until 1907, when, in his 85th year, he retired.

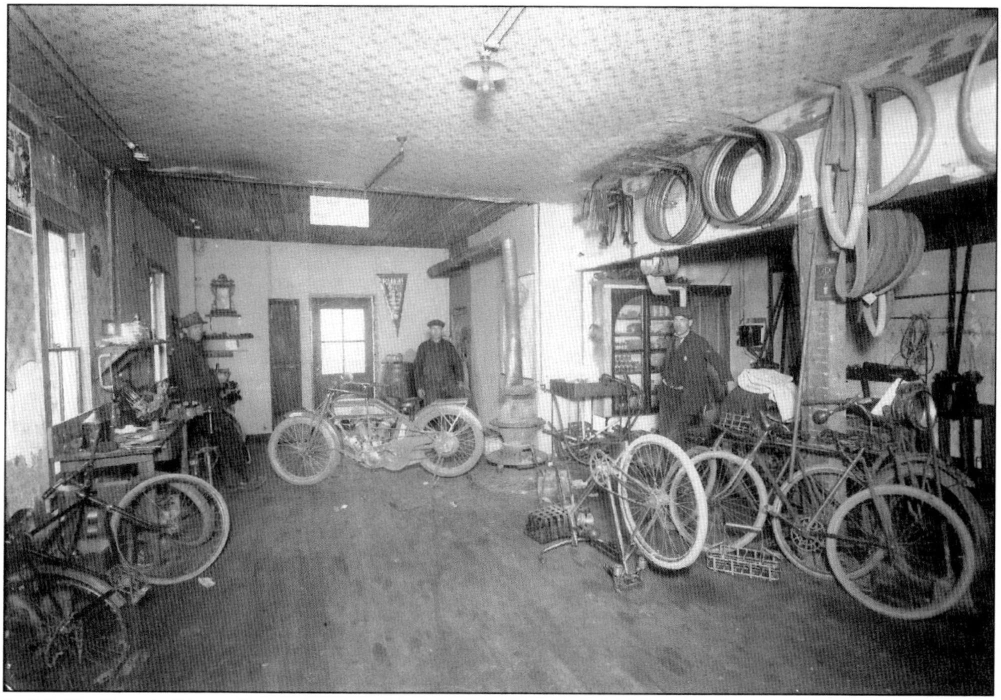

J. U. DuBois's Bike Shop. In 1913, DuBois, a native of Vineland, partnered with John W. Potts and established the Vineland Repair Shop on the 300 block of Landis Avenue. Four years later, DuBois bought out Potts's interest in the business and moved the store to the 700 block of Landis Avenue, where he continued to operate for many years. He became a distributor for Harley-Davidson motorcycles and carried one of the most complete lines of motorcycle and bicycle supplies in South Jersey.

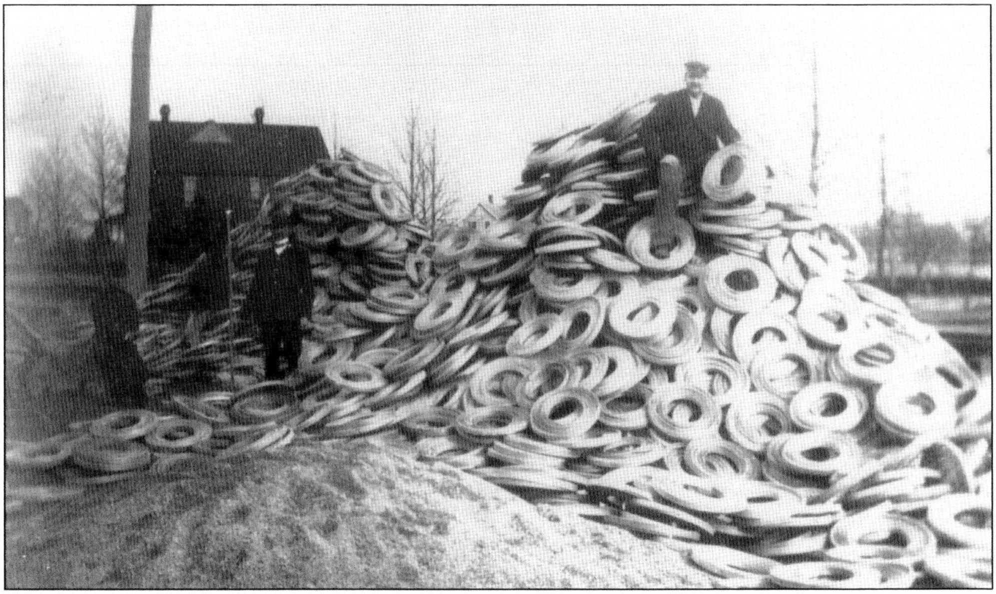

ELWOOD C. POTTER'S COOPERAGE. In the early 1900s, Potter engaged in the manufacture of wooden barrels. He is shown above, seated on a mound of metal hoops used to bind the barrels together. Shown below is the inside of his facility, where hundreds of finished barrels were stored. Potter was an eclectic businessman. His ventures included installing Vineland's first telephone system, making hammocks, and being an electrician, photographer, and weatherman. At one time, he devised a plan to harness the waterpower of the Maurice River to furnish electricity to the surrounding communities, but the project failed because there was not enough water during the summer.

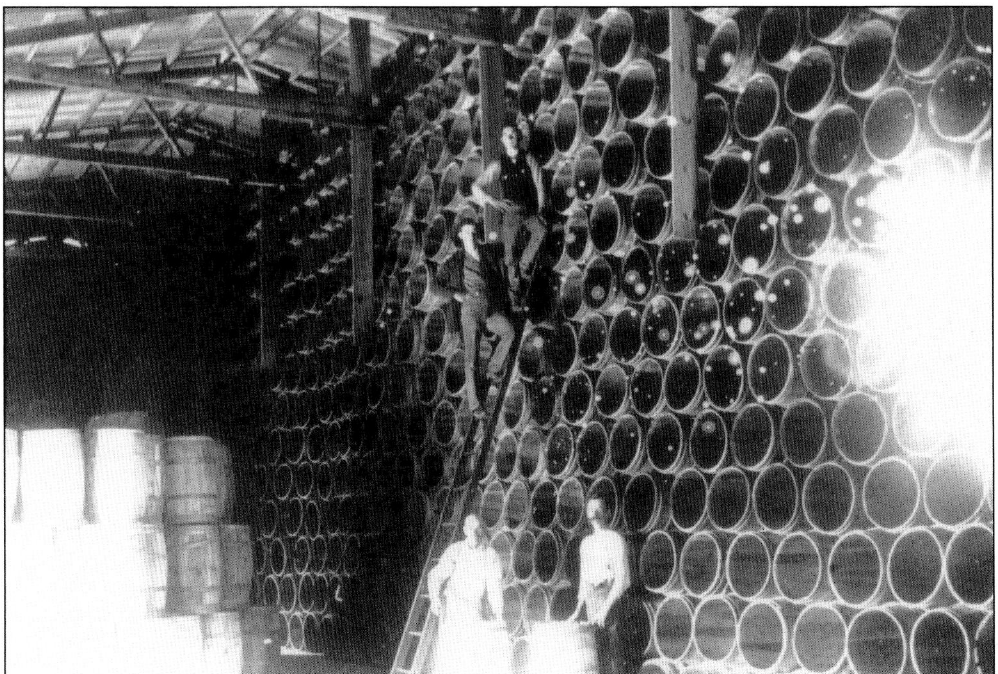

Five

Government in Vineland

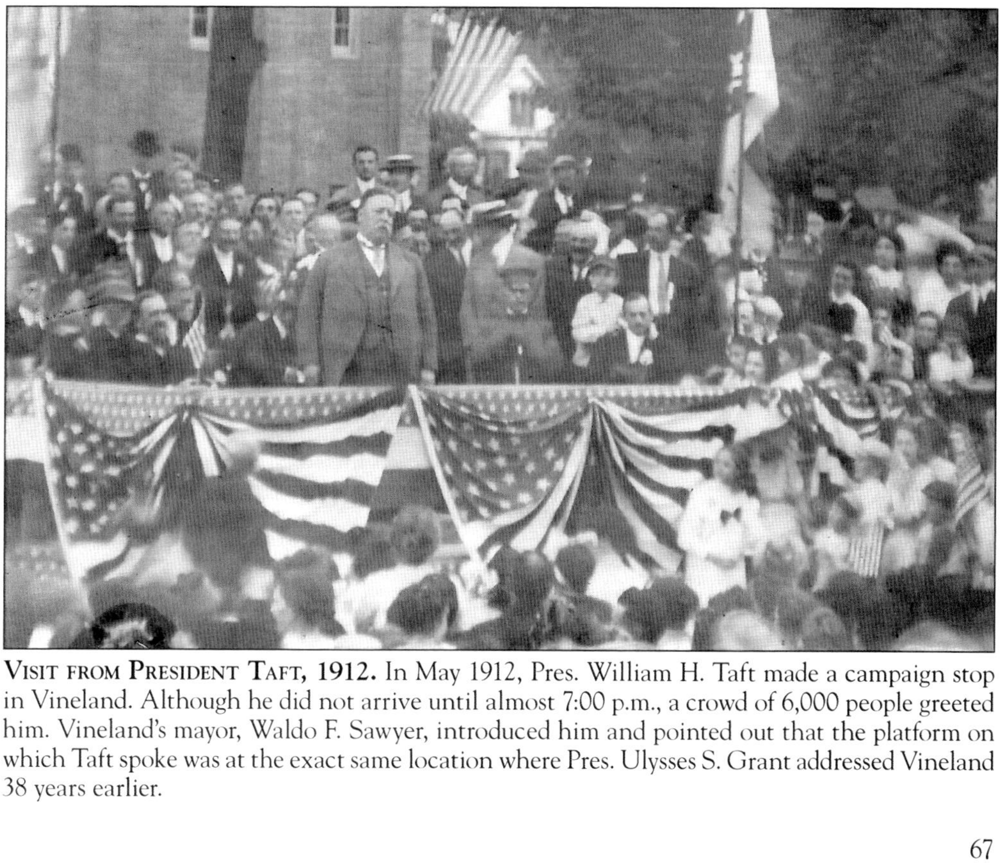

Visit from President Taft, 1912. In May 1912, Pres. William H. Taft made a campaign stop in Vineland. Although he did not arrive until almost 7:00 p.m., a crowd of 6,000 people greeted him. Vineland's mayor, Waldo F. Sawyer, introduced him and pointed out that the platform on which Taft spoke was at the exact same location where Pres. Ulysses S. Grant addressed Vineland 38 years earlier.

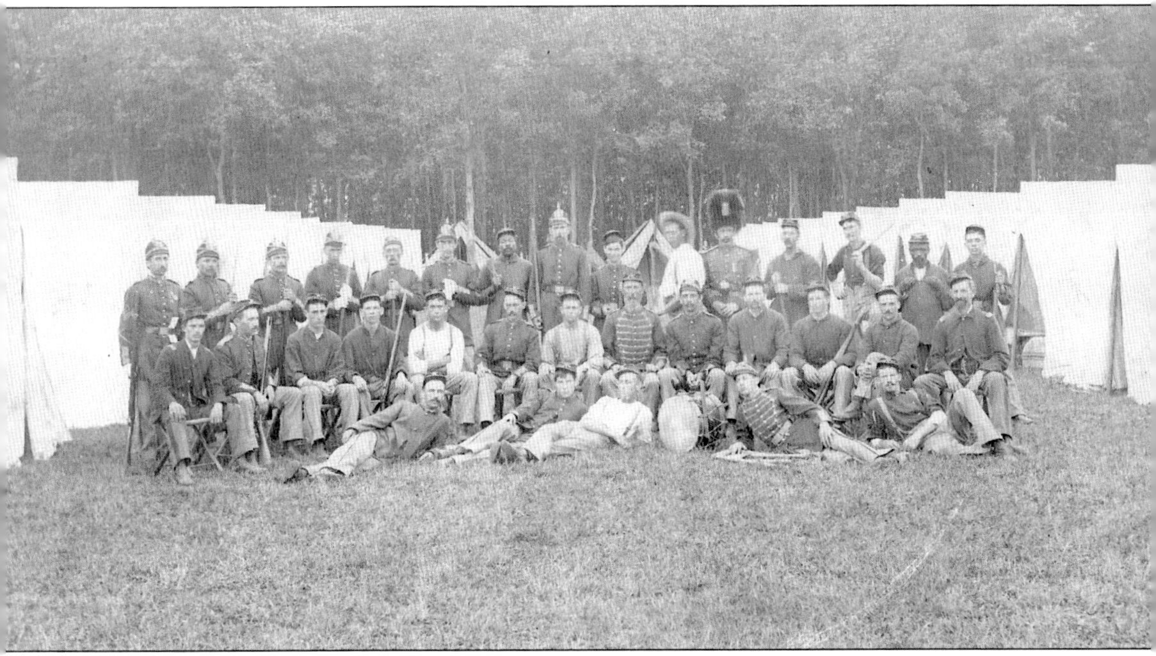

COMPANY K, C. 1875. The National Guard was represented in Vineland by Company K of the 6th State Regiment. It was first organized in 1873 as Company D of the 4th State Battalion, with George Souther as captain. Three of its subsequent commanders were Capts. George A. Cheever, O. W. Vernal, and L. W. Harris. Its armory was located in the Erickson Building on Landis Avenue. (Photograph by Walter M. Boyd of Red Bank.)

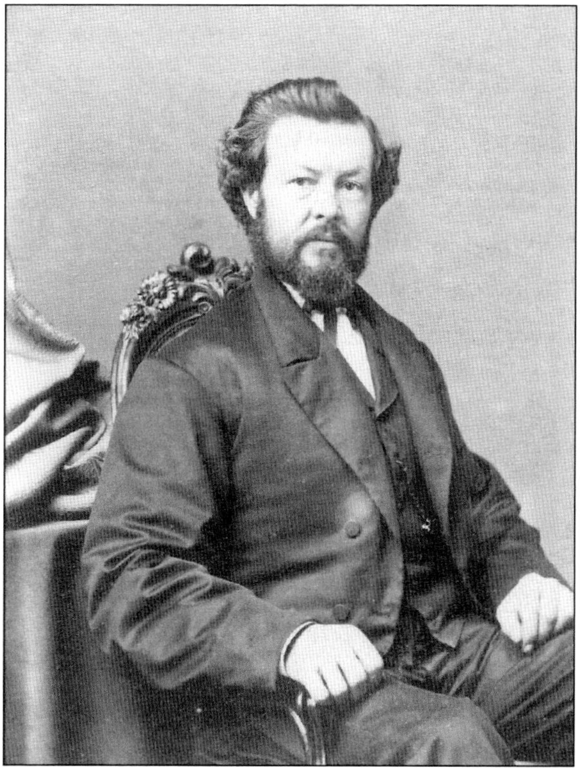

Joseph Mason. In 1872, Mason moved to Vineland to regain his health. Soon afterwards, he began publication of *Mason's Monthly*, a periodical devoted to horticulture. From 1881 to 1883, he served as the borough of Vineland's second mayor and was again elected to the office in 1900. During his second term, he explained to the city council his need for an additional source of income, whereupon council appointed him janitor of city hall. (Photograph by W. W. Wilson of Hartford.)

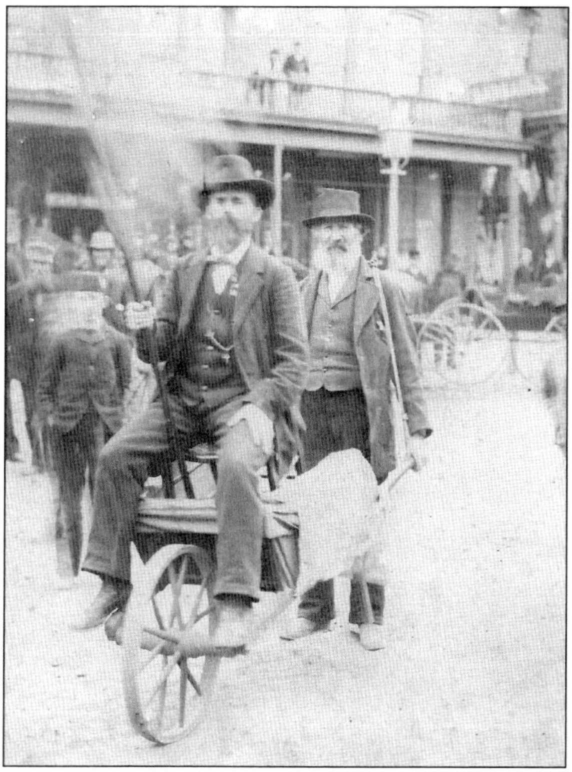

Wheelbarrow Campaign, c. 1885. Judge Eli B. Hendee, shown seated on a chair in a wheelbarrow and being pushed by Charles E. Greene, campaigned around Vineland in this manner for reappointment as county judge. In 1866, Hendee moved to Vineland as a farmer and continued in that profession while taking an active role in local politics until his death in 1914.

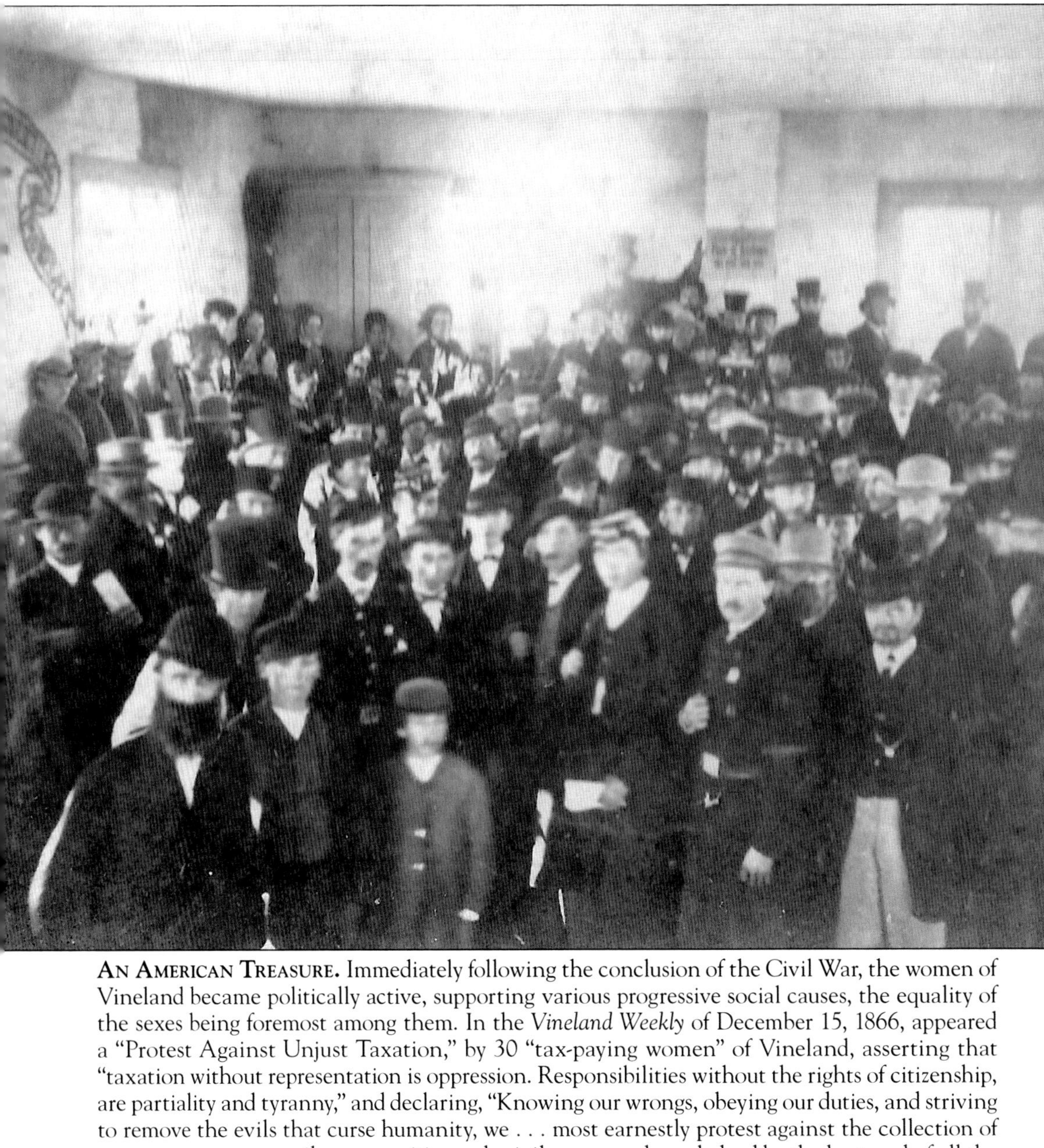

AN AMERICAN TREASURE. Immediately following the conclusion of the Civil War, the women of Vineland became politically active, supporting various progressive social causes, the equality of the sexes being foremost among them. In the *Vineland Weekly* of December 15, 1866, appeared a "Protest Against Unjust Taxation," by 30 "tax-paying women" of Vineland, asserting that "taxation without representation is oppression. Responsibilities without the rights of citizenship, are partiality and tyranny," and declaring, "Knowing our wrongs, obeying our duties, and striving to remove the evils that curse humanity, we . . . most earnestly protest against the collection of tax on our estates, until our capacities and privileges are acknowledged by the bestowal of all the rights of citizenship." In 1868, Vineland women cast symbolic ballots in the presidential election, an event captured in this photograph. Of the thousands of photographs in the collections of the Vineland Historical Society, this may well be the most historically significant; it is believed to be the earliest known photographic record of women voting anywhere in the United States. Also in the society's collections is the original cloth-covered ballot box into which the women cast their votes.

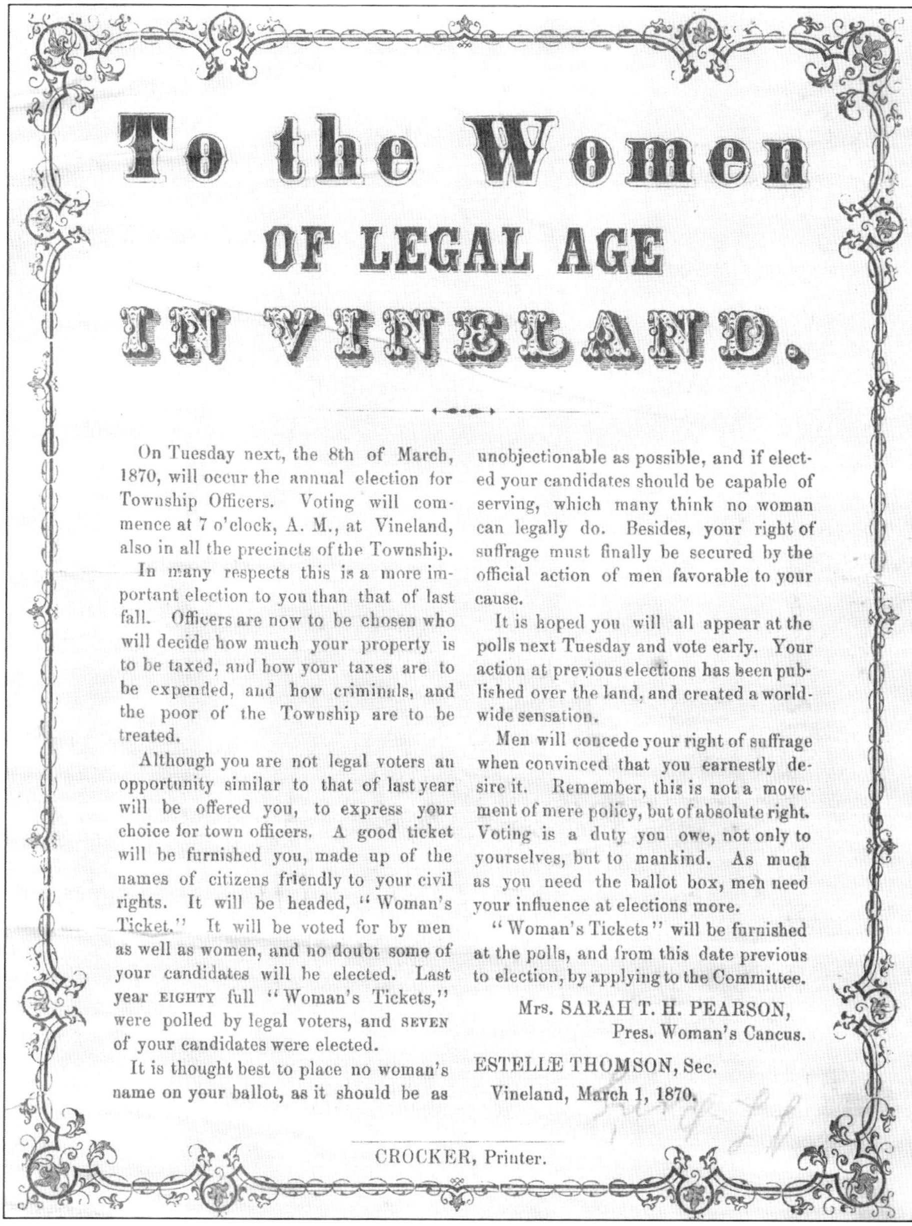

To the Women

OF LEGAL AGE

IN VINELAND.

On Tuesday next, the 8th of March, 1870, will occur the annual election for Township Officers. Voting will commence at 7 o'clock, A. M., at Vineland, also in all the precincts of the Township.

In many respects this is a more important election to you than that of last fall. Officers are now to be chosen who will decide how much your property is to be taxed, and how your taxes are to be expended, and how criminals, and the poor of the Township are to be treated.

Although you are not legal voters an opportunity similar to that of last year will be offered you, to express your choice for town officers. A good ticket will be furnished you, made up of the names of citizens friendly to your civil rights. It will be headed, "Woman's Ticket." It will be voted for by men as well as women, and no doubt some of your candidates will be elected. Last year EIGHTY full "Woman's Tickets," were polled by legal voters, and SEVEN of your candidates were elected.

It is thought best to place no woman's name on your ballot, as it should be as unobjectionable as possible, and if elected your candidates should be capable of serving, which many think no woman can legally do. Besides, your right of suffrage must finally be secured by the official action of men favorable to your cause.

It is hoped you will all appear at the polls next Tuesday and vote early. Your action at previous elections has been published over the land, and created a world-wide sensation.

Men will concede your right of suffrage when convinced that you earnestly desire it. Remember, this is not a movement of mere policy, but of absolute right. Voting is a duty you owe, not only to yourselves, but to mankind. As much as you need the ballot box, men need your influence at elections more.

"Woman's Tickets" will be furnished at the polls, and from this date previous to election, by applying to the Committee.

Mrs. SARAH T. H. PEARSON,
Pres. Woman's Caucus.

ESTELLE THOMSON, Sec.
Vineland, March 1, 1870.

CROCKER, Printer.

WOMEN'S TICKETS. In this rare handbill issued by the Woman's Caucus on March 1, 1870, Sarah T. H. Pearson calls upon the women of Vineland to participate in the upcoming election for township officers, women not having the legal right to vote notwithstanding. "Although you are not legal voters an opportunity similar to that of last year will be offered you, to express your choice for town officers. A good ticket will be furnished you, made up of the names of citizens friendly to your civil rights . . . It is hoped you will all appear at the polls next Tuesday and vote early. Your action at previous elections has been published over the land, and created a world-wide sensation. Men will concede your right of suffrage when convinced that you earnestly desire it. Remember, this is not a movement of mere policy, but of absolute right. Voting is a duty you owe, not only to yourselves, but to mankind. As much as you need the ballot box, men need your influence at elections more."

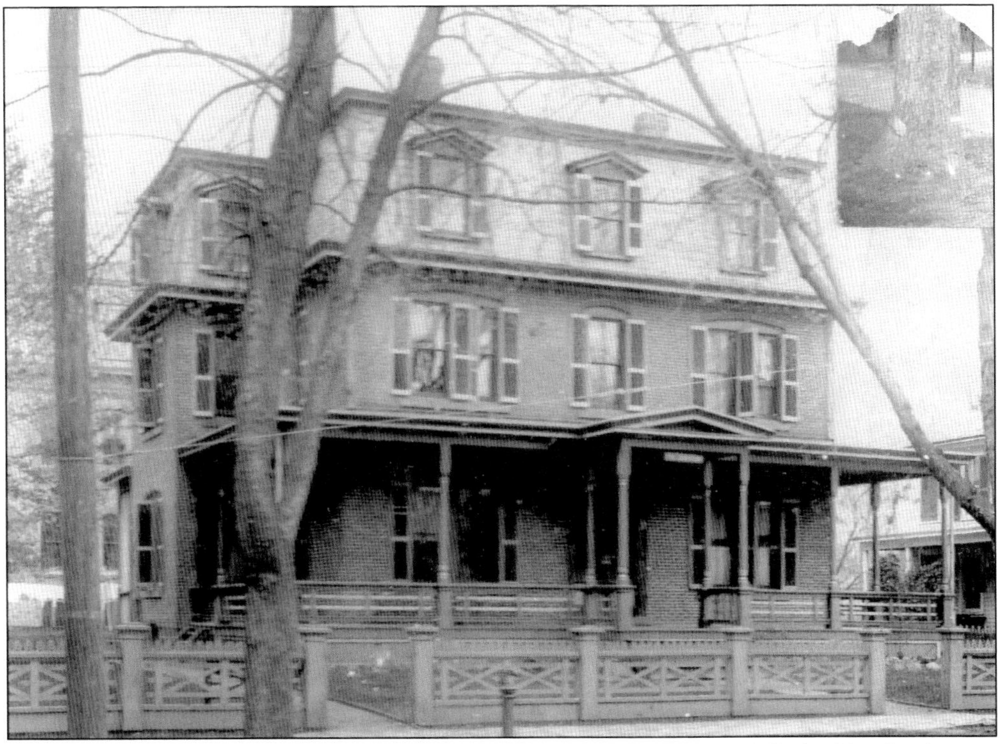

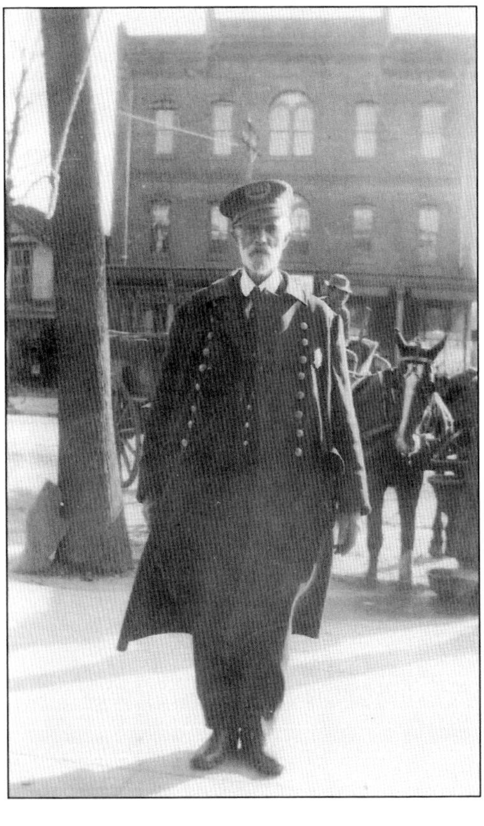

Boynton House. In 1917, the Vineland Police Department officially formed under the Borough of Vineland and Mayor Benjamin Stevens. The initial force was comprised of six men. For several years, the Boynton House, located on Wood Street, was used as the police department headquarters and an annex to city hall. The department's current building is located on this same site.

Chief Nick. Willard H. Nickerson moved to Vineland in the 1870s and began a long career of public service. The numerous offices he held in Vineland included fire chief of the Pioneer Fire Company, overseer of the poor, board of health inspector, truant officer, and deputy sheriff. When he died in 1920, he was the chief of police, having been a police officer for nearly 30 years. Weeks before his death, he wrote his autobiography and presented it to the Vineland Historical and Antiquarian Society.

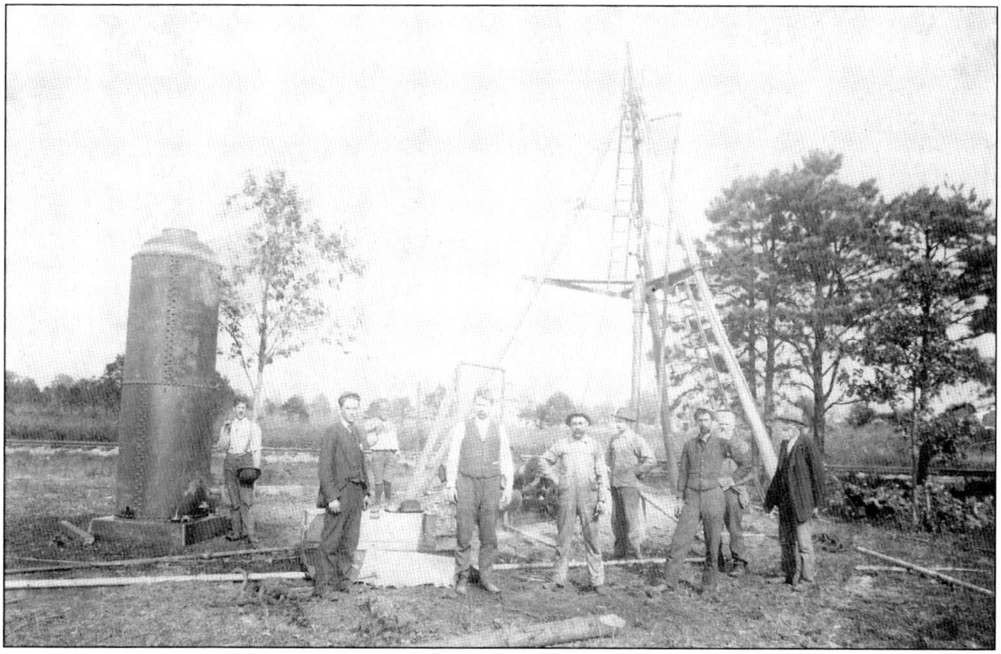

LAST WELL AT WATER WORKS, C. 1910. This picture shows the last well being dug at the Vineland Water Works on the corner of West Avenue and Plum Street. The workmen shown are, from left to right, R. McIntire, Victor Braidwood, Homer Lewis, Matthew Miller, Herb Lewis, George Becker, Mr. Fisher, and Mr. Aldrick. Third from left an unidentified young errand boy appears atop wooden boxes. (Photograph by Percy D. Darr of Vineland.)

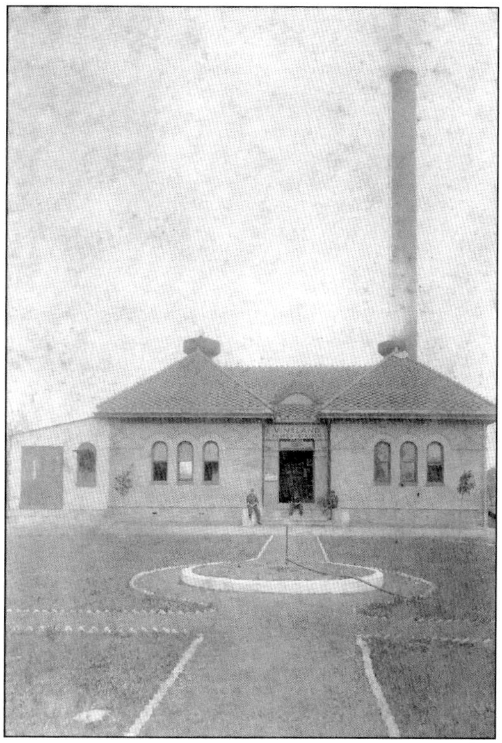

VINELAND POWER STATION. Like most towns during the late 1800s and early 1900s, electricity was first installed in Vineland by its local government. Over time, most municipalities elected to sell those lines to private utility companies. However, Vineland retained its electric utility and currently has the only municipally owned and operated power-generating station in the state of New Jersey.

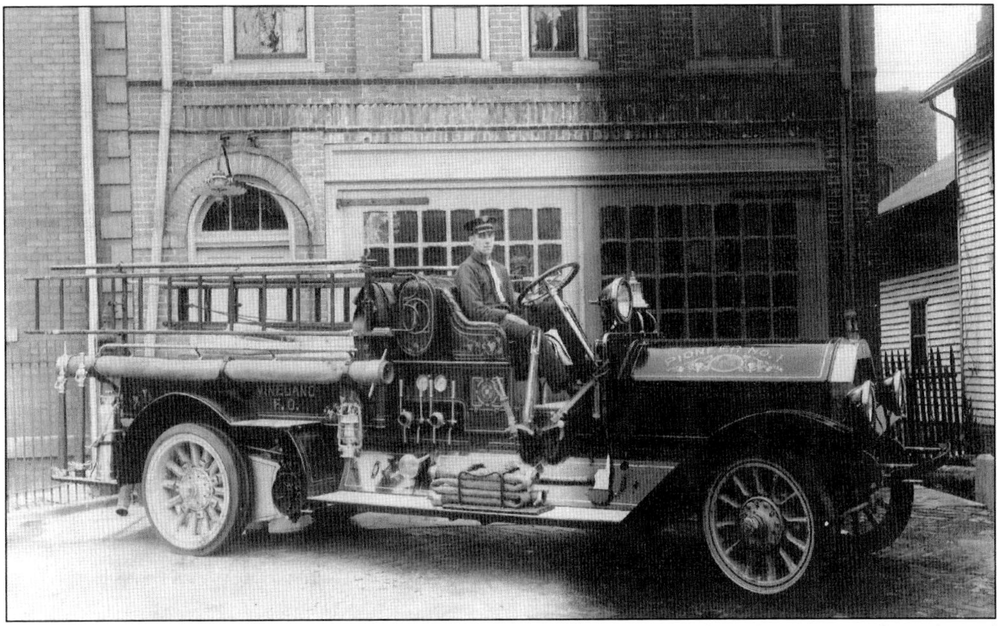

Pioneer Fire Company. In 1878, a brick building was constructed at the corner of Sixth and Wood Streets as the Vineland Fire Department's headquarters. When the first brick city hall building was constructed on Wood Street, it was located directly adjacent to the Pioneer Fire Hall. The company's members from about 1900 are shown below, with Chief Wallace Frost in the first row, third from left. In the picture above, Howard Garrison is shown at the Pioneer Fire Hall behind the wheel of a 1917 Seagrave Fire Engine, which was capable of providing a flow of over 1,000 gallons of water per minute. Garrison was the company's first paid driver. (Photograph by Roland G. Robbins of Vineland.)

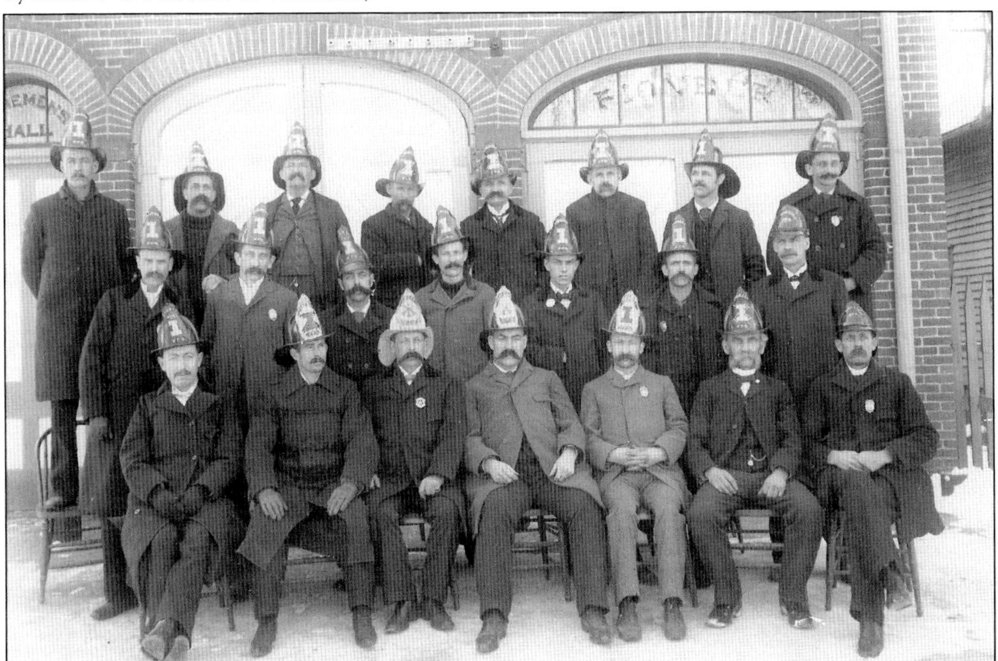

Reliance Fire Company. About 1915, members of the Reliance Fire Company raised funds to purchase new equipment and construct a building on Sixth Street, just south of Landis Avenue. The Reliance Fire Hall was used until 1962, when the company merged with the Pioneer Fire Company to form Company No. 1. In the picture below, Vineland's first motorized fire engine, a 1916 Brockway, is shown inside the Reliance Fire Hall. (Photograph by Roland G. Robbins of Vineland.)

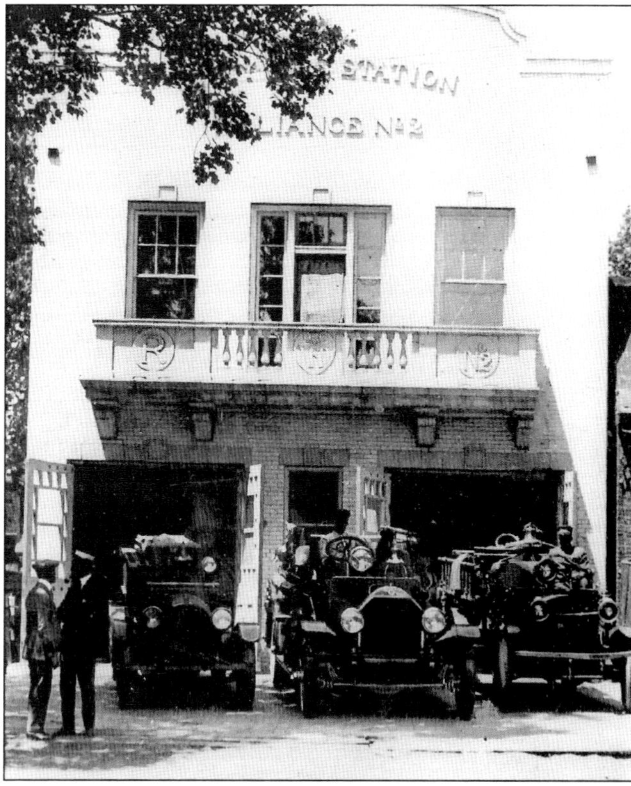

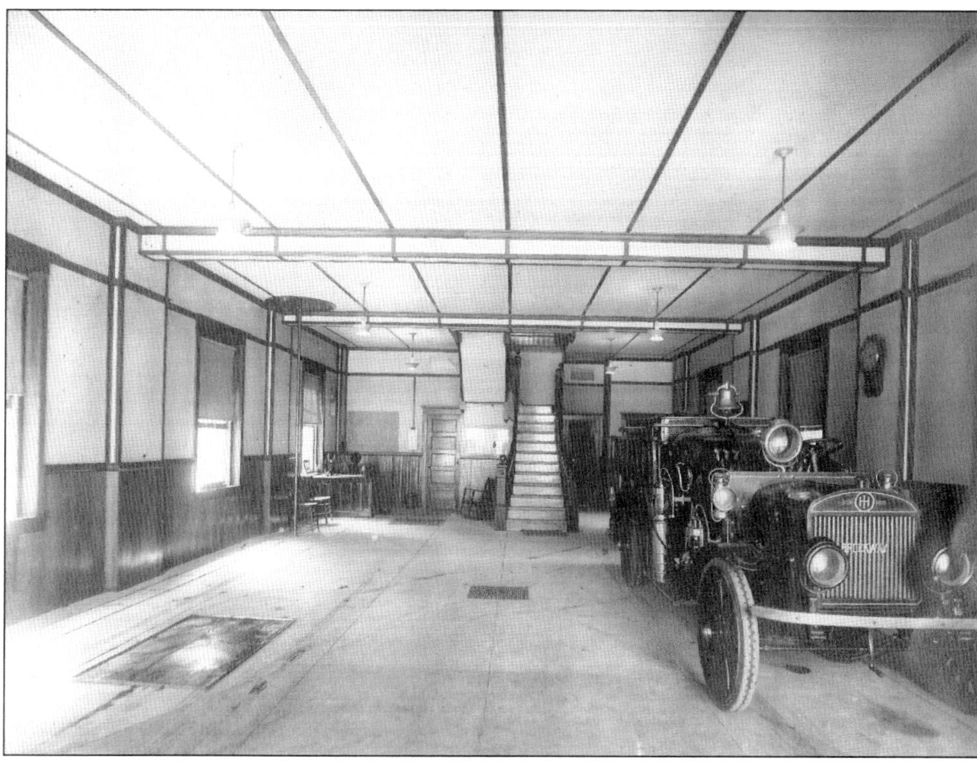

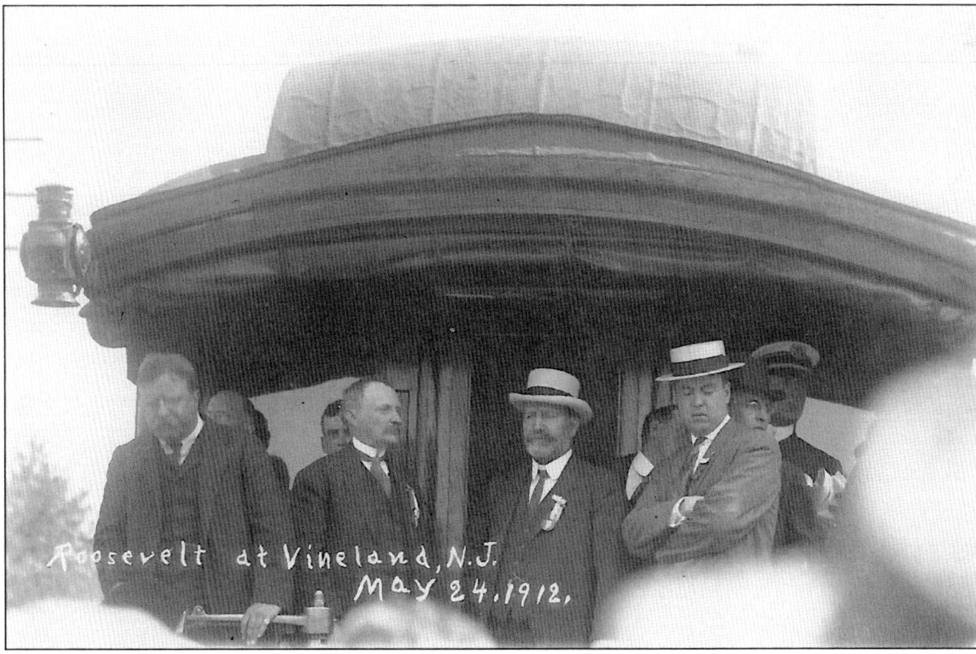

ROOSEVELT VISITS VINELAND, 1912. On May 24, 1912, Pres. Theodore Roosevelt visited Vineland. Although he only spoke from the back of a train, that did not stop a crowd of Vinelanders from forming around the railroad tracks to listen to his speech.

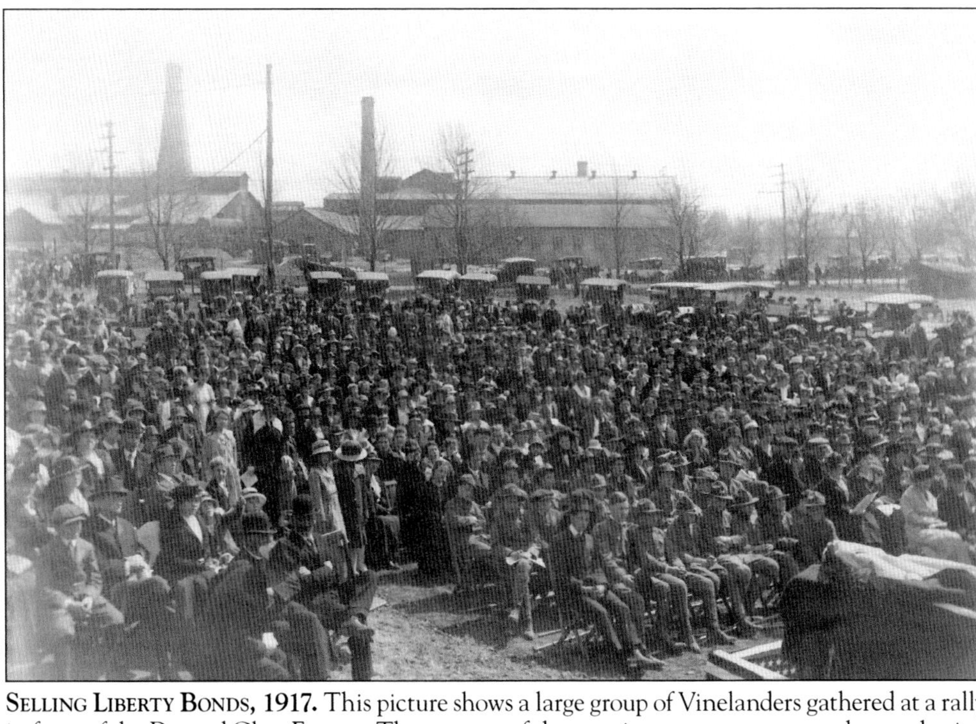

SELLING LIBERTY BONDS, 1917. This picture shows a large group of Vinelanders gathered at a rally in front of the Durand Glass Factory. The purpose of the meeting was to encourage the purchasing of Liberty Bonds. The patriotism of Vinelanders continued in the Second World War, and Sgt. Alvin York praised Vineland for purchasing almost 10 times its quota of war bonds.

Six

Entertainment in Vineland

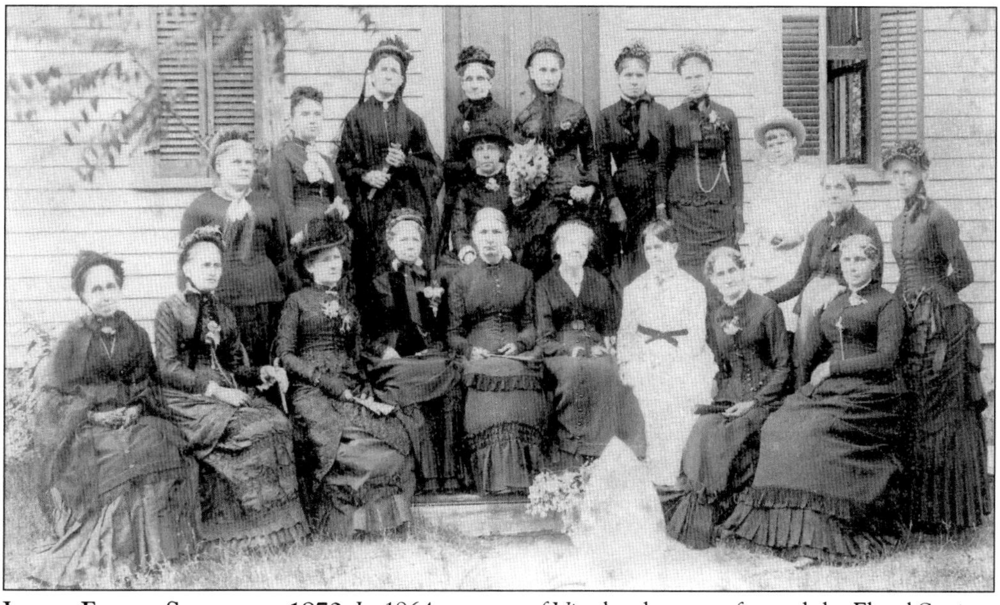

Ladies Floral Society, c. 1870. In 1864, a group of Vineland women formed the Floral Society for the encouragement of the cultivation of flowers and the improvement of its members in the study of botany. Only women were admitted to the society, although men were allowed to be honorary members. (Photograph by L. D. Johnson of Vineland.)

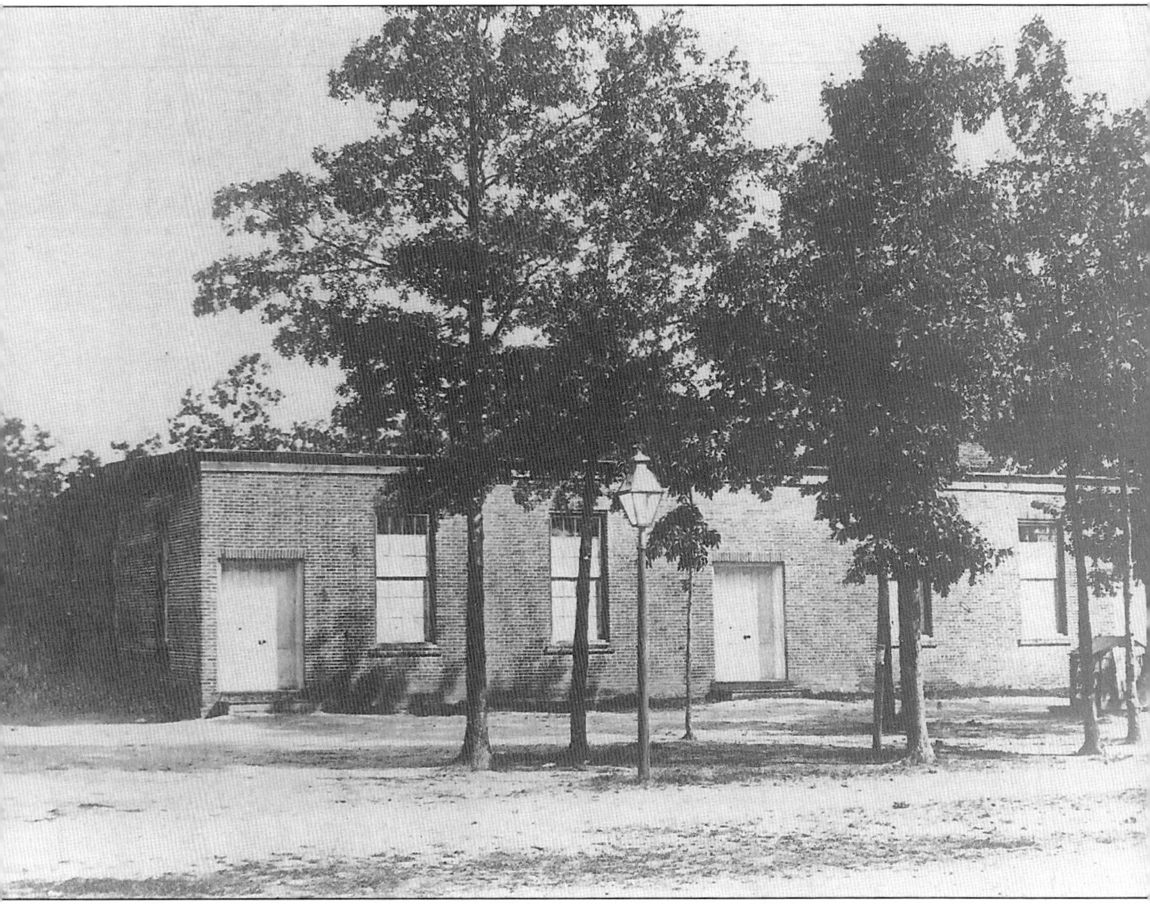

Plum Street Hall. In 1864, a group of liberal-minded Vinelanders formed an association called the Friends of Progress. This group included spiritualists, Quakers, atheists, and deists and was organized to promote the complete independence of thought, unattached to a single religion. A year later, they began construction of a building on Plum Street near Sixth Street on land donated to the association by Charles K. Landis. Upon its completion, the hall became a popular venue that hosted well-known lecturers and activists, including Sojourner Truth and Frederick Douglass. In 1867, a women's suffrage convention was held at Plum Street Hall and speakers included Lucy Stone Blackwell and Lucretia Mott. In 1875, the building was enlarged and became known as Cosmopolitan Hall.

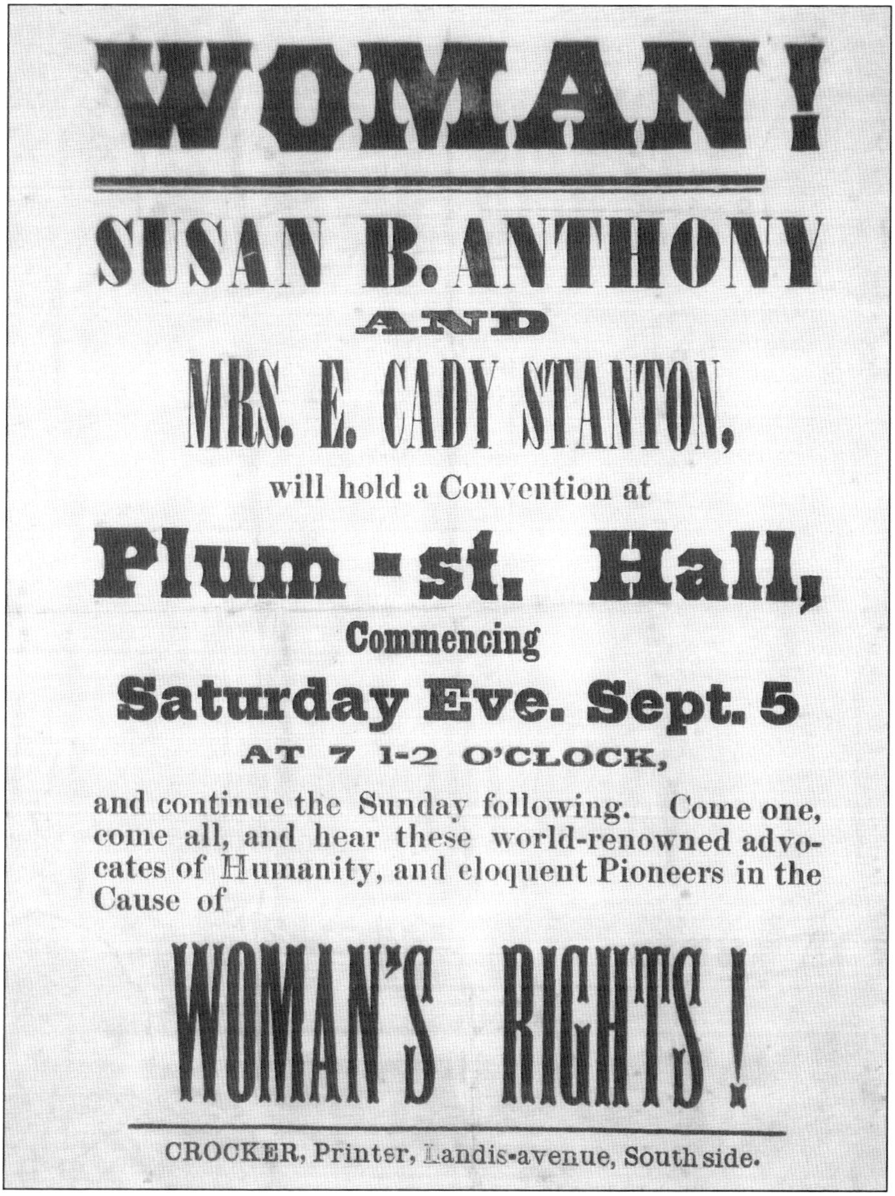

"WOMAN'S RIGHTS!" In this rare and perhaps unique broadside, notice is given of a convention to be held at Plum Street Hall on September 5 [1868], the participants to include Susan B. Anthony and Elizabeth Cady Stanton. Vineland had by then achieved some measure of renown in the national press as a community in which the women were politically active. In January 1867, also at Plum Street Hall, the Equal Rights and Universal Peace Associations of Vineland held a convention, at which numerous resolutions in support of equal rights were adopted, among them "that every argument in favor of white and male suffrage, is equally valid in favor of black and female suffrage" and "the ballot alike to the woman and the negro, means bread, education, intelligence, self-protection, self-reliance, and self respect; to the daughter—industrial freedom and diversified employment; to the wife, the control of her own person, property and earnings; to the mother, an equal, legal right to her children; to all it means social equality, colleges, and professions, profitable business, skilled labors, and intellectual development."

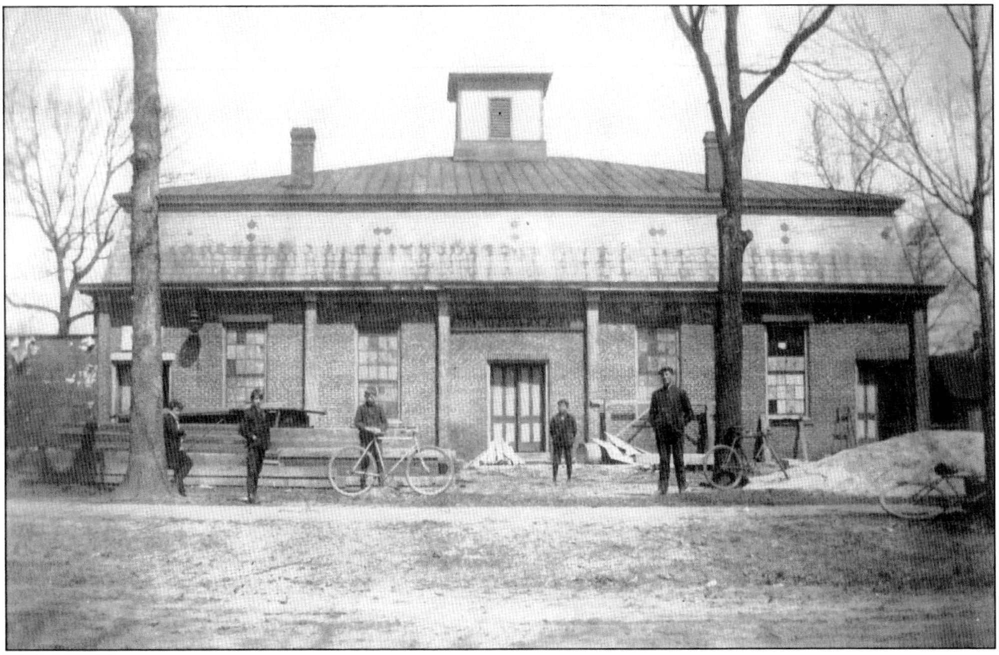

Cosmopolitan Hall. From 1875 to 1908, the Cosmopolitan Hall served as Vineland's most popular venue for community events, including lectures, plays, concerts, sermons, graduation exercises, and political meetings. By 1908, however, the town had outgrown the hall, and its owners agreed to remodel the building to better accommodate a larger, more sophisticated crowd. Philadelphia architect George E. Savage designed the renovations for the hall, which then became known as the Auditorium. The expanded interior is shown below. The Auditorium was used by the community as often as the old Plum Street Hall and the Cosmopolitan Hall, until it was destroyed by fire in 1918.

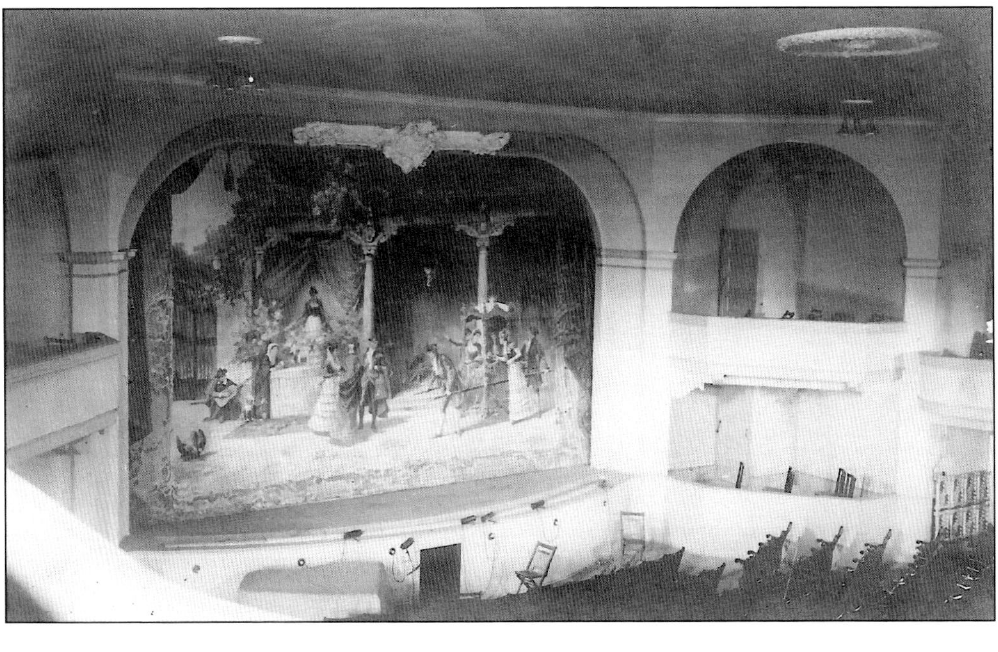

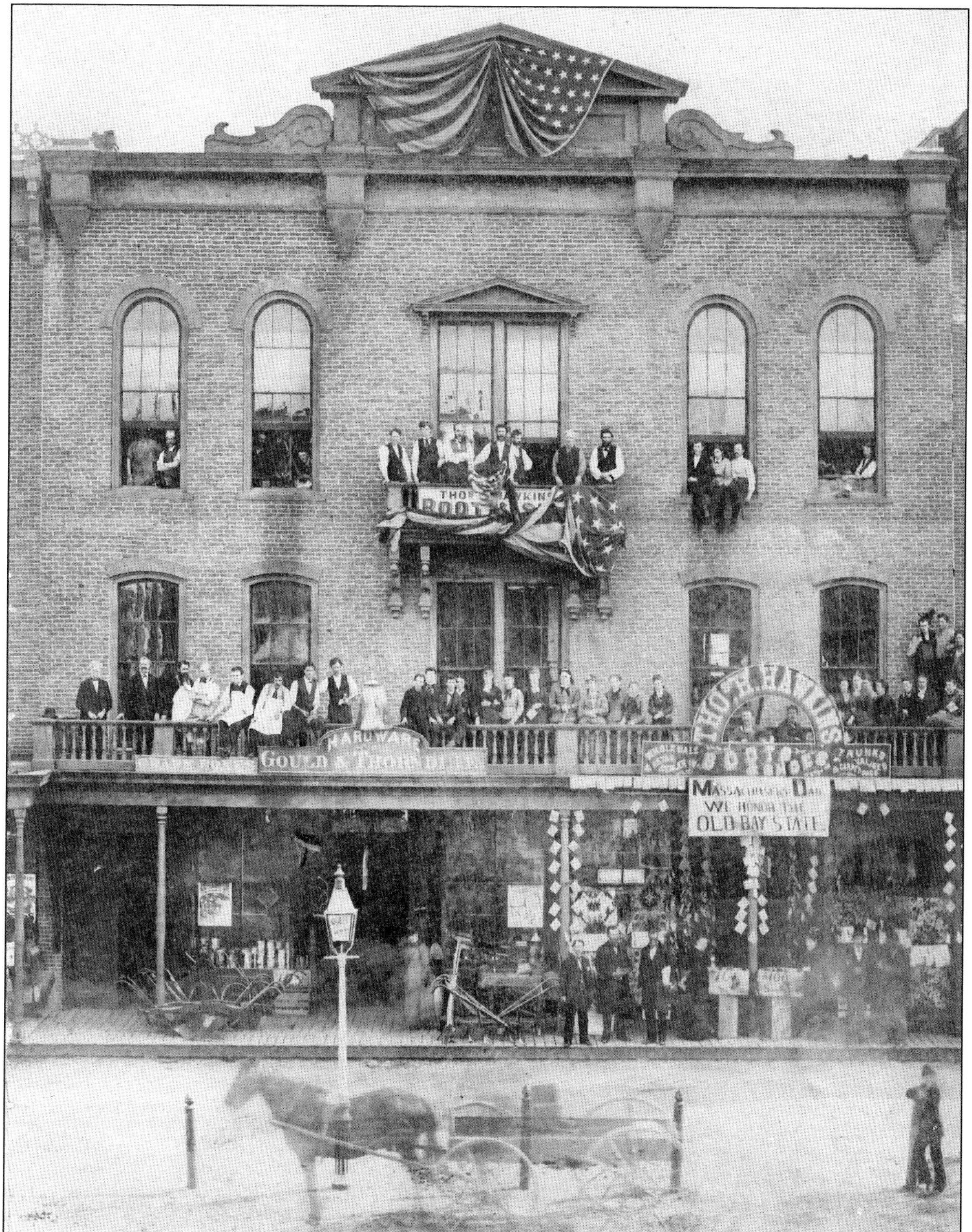

Natives of New England. This picture, taken in the 1880s, shows Vinelanders celebrating Massachusetts Day on Landis Avenue. Many early settlers of Vineland were from New England and retained a strong sense of connection with their original home states. In 1902, a large group of town residents formed the New England Society of Vineland, New Jersey, which met regularly and held an annual celebration.

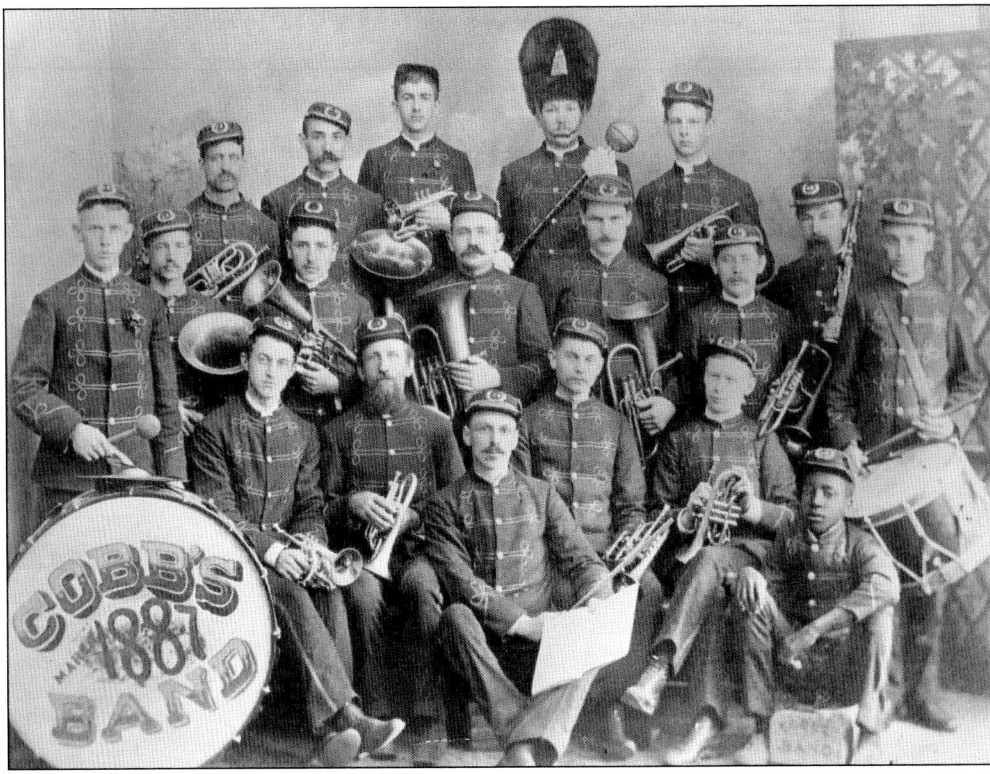

Cobb's Band, 1887. In 1879, a group of employees in the Keighley Shoe Factory formed a band, which included William B. Keighley, son of the factory's owner. It was known as the Keighley Band, and its members received personal lessons once a week from an instructor from Philadelphia. In 1887, a Mr. Cobb was made director, and its name changed to Cobb's Band. The band was later known as the Vineland City Band and then the Silver City Band.

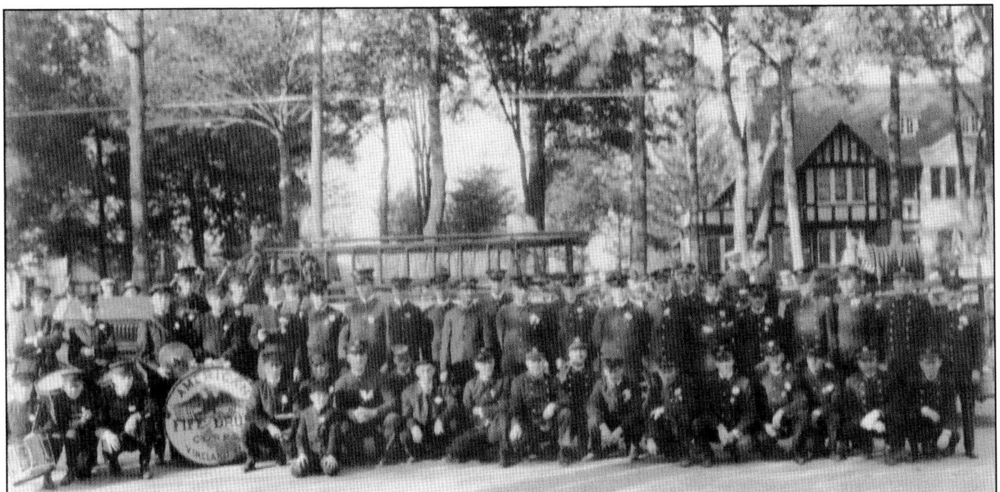

American Fife and Drum Corps of Vineland, c. 1900. This picture shows a large fife and drum corp in front of the Kimball House, which was built in 1895 and is currently used as the rectory of Vineland's Sacred Heart Church. This group could have been performing in a parade on Landis Avenue. (Photograph by Fred Hess of Atlantic City.)

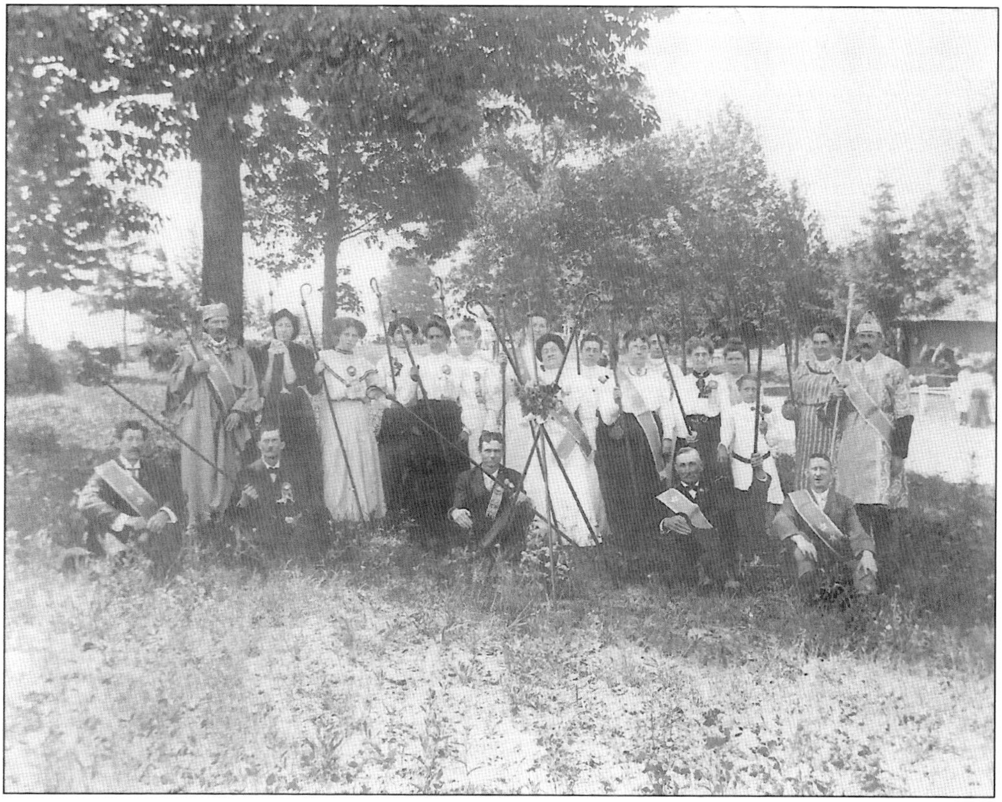

VINELAND SOCIETIES. The picture above shows the Order of the Shepherds of Bethlehem, a religious charitable organization. The picture below shows the Great Council of the Degree of Pocahontas, a society for women that was associated with the Improved Order of Red Men.

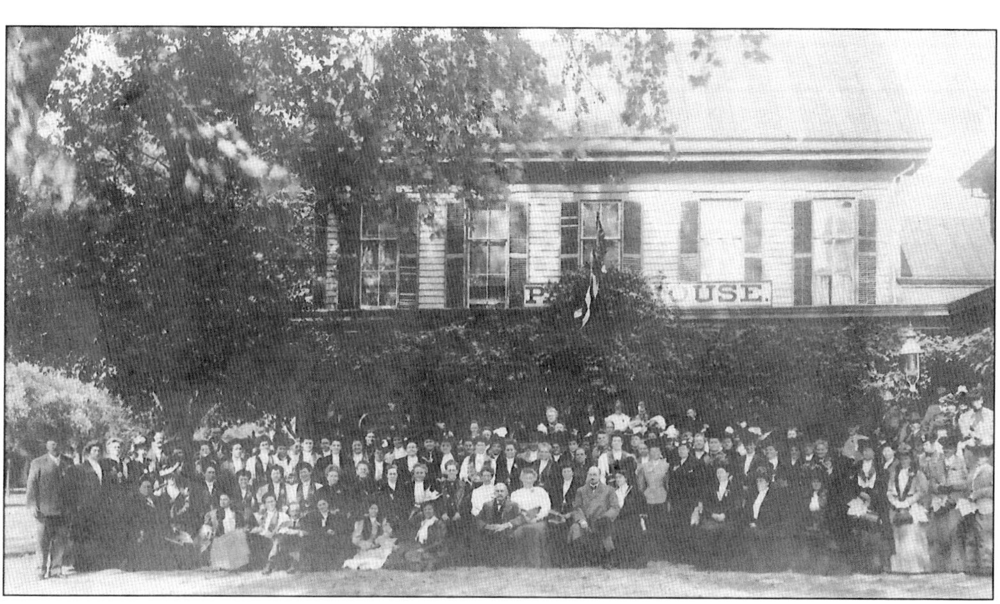

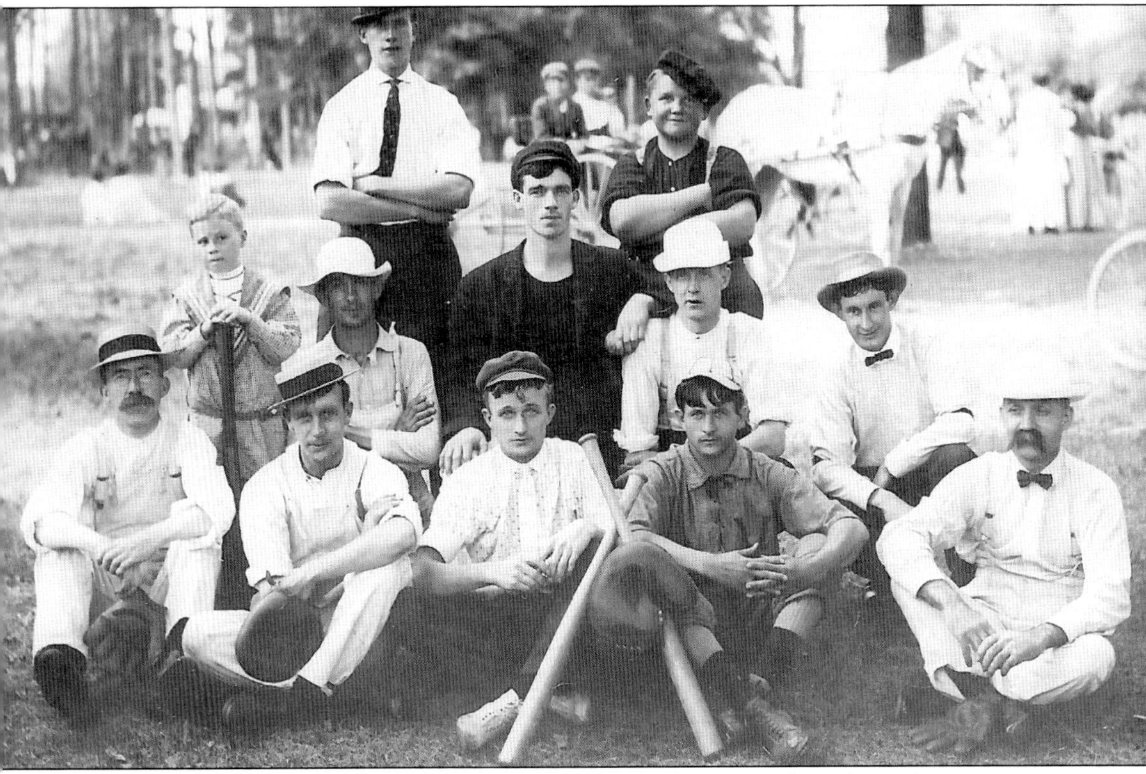

The Paper Hangers. From the earliest years of Vineland, town residents formed various groups to participate in intramural sporting competitions. This baseball team from about 1900 was known as the "Paper Hangers" because the men were all employed as wallpaper applicators.

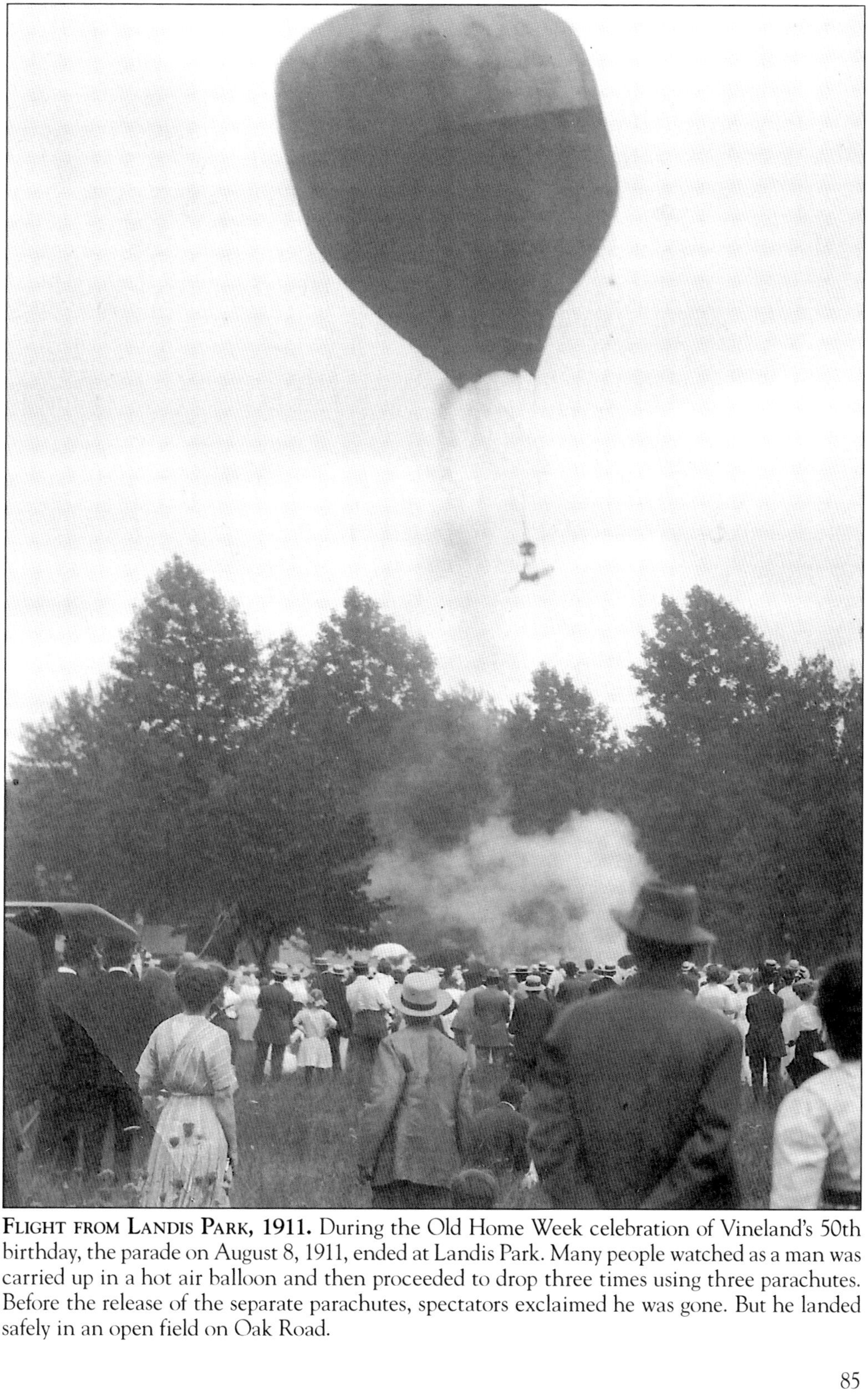

FLIGHT FROM LANDIS PARK, 1911. During the Old Home Week celebration of Vineland's 50th birthday, the parade on August 8, 1911, ended at Landis Park. Many people watched as a man was carried up in a hot air balloon and then proceeded to drop three times using three parachutes. Before the release of the separate parachutes, spectators exclaimed he was gone. But he landed safely in an open field on Oak Road.

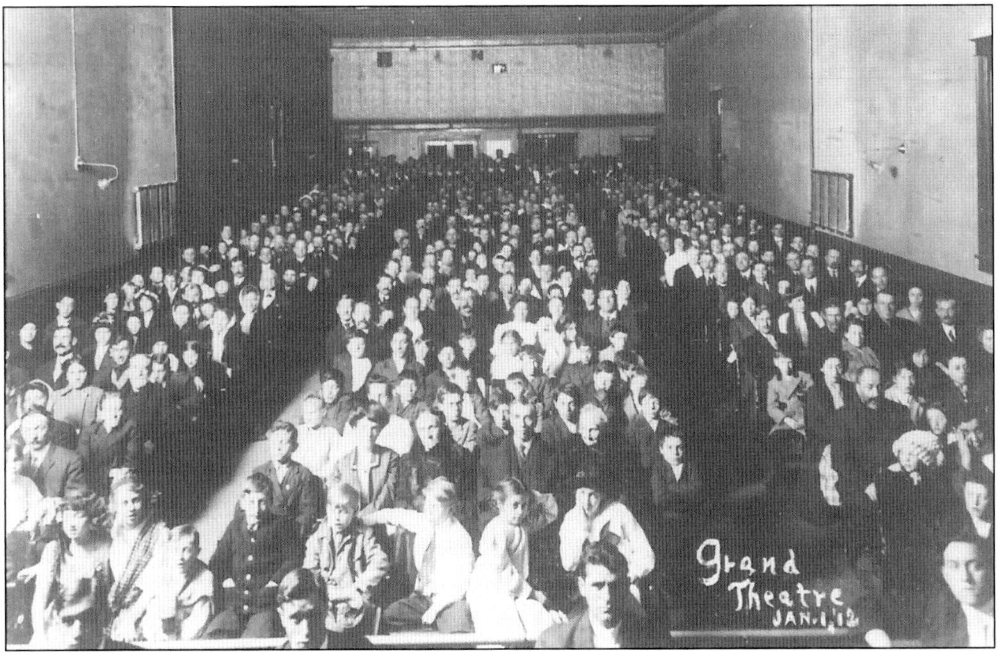

A Grand Theatre Audience, 1912. In 1912, the Grand Theatre opened on the 400 block of Landis Avenue. The original building could seat 400 people. In 1914, it was purchased by the Lubin Amusement Corporation, which expanded it several times to its largest capacity of 1,500 seats. The theater was closed and demolished in the 1960s.

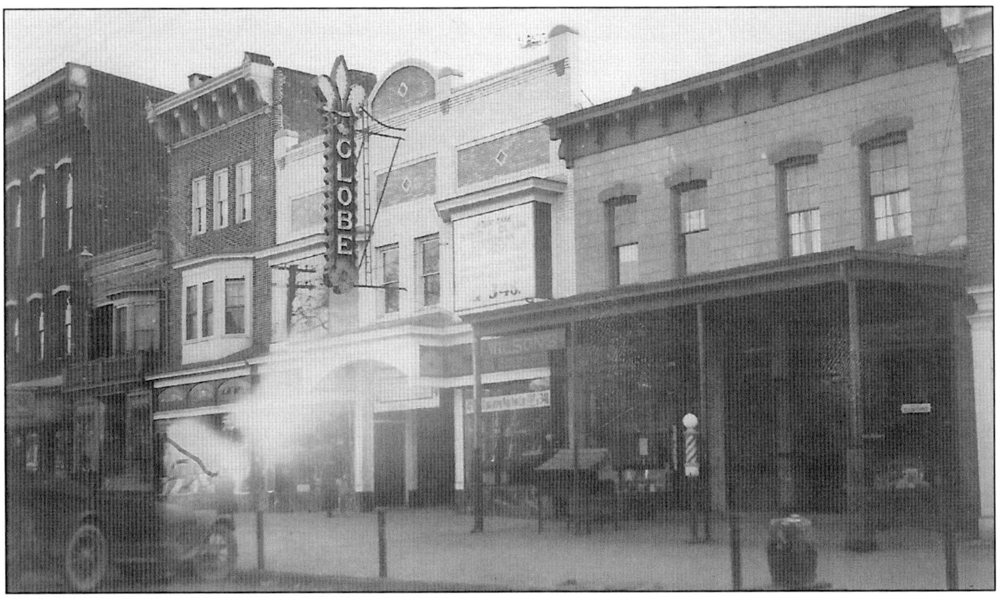

The Globe Theater. This theater was located on the south side of Landis Avenue between the Boulevard and Sixth Street. When it was first established, it was open only a few days a week and had a low admission price of about 10¢. With double features and matinees, it became a popular place for young people to spend all afternoon. The theater's most played films were westerns. In the 1930s, the Globe began opening its doors seven days a week. The building was demolished in the 1960s.

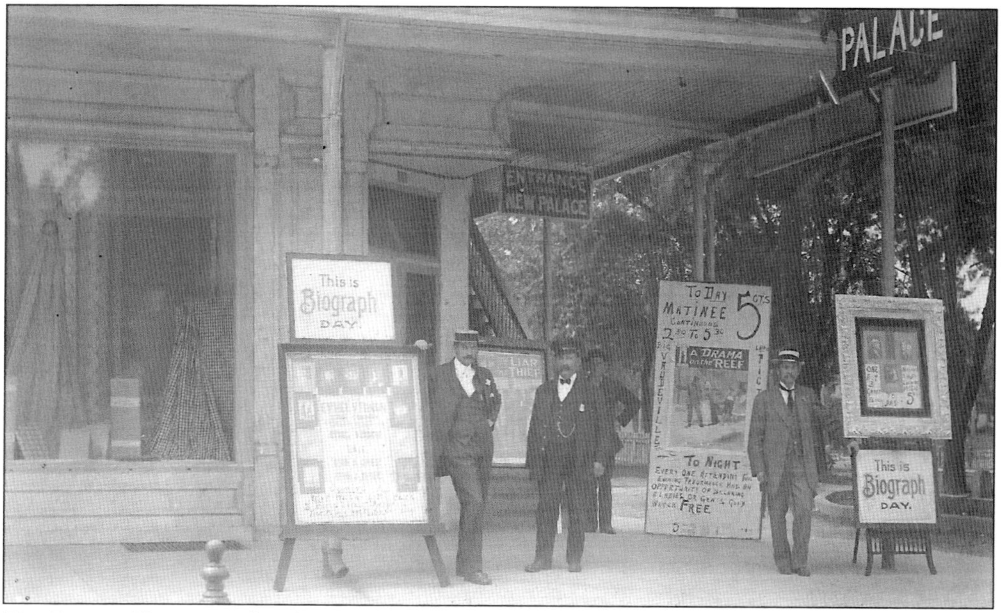

The Palace Theater. This theater was located on the corner of Landis Avenue and the Boulevard, on land previously occupied by the home of Charles K. Landis. The theater was operated by Leon Cassidy. A sign in this picture promotes that day's matinee, *A Drama on the Reef*, admission 5¢.

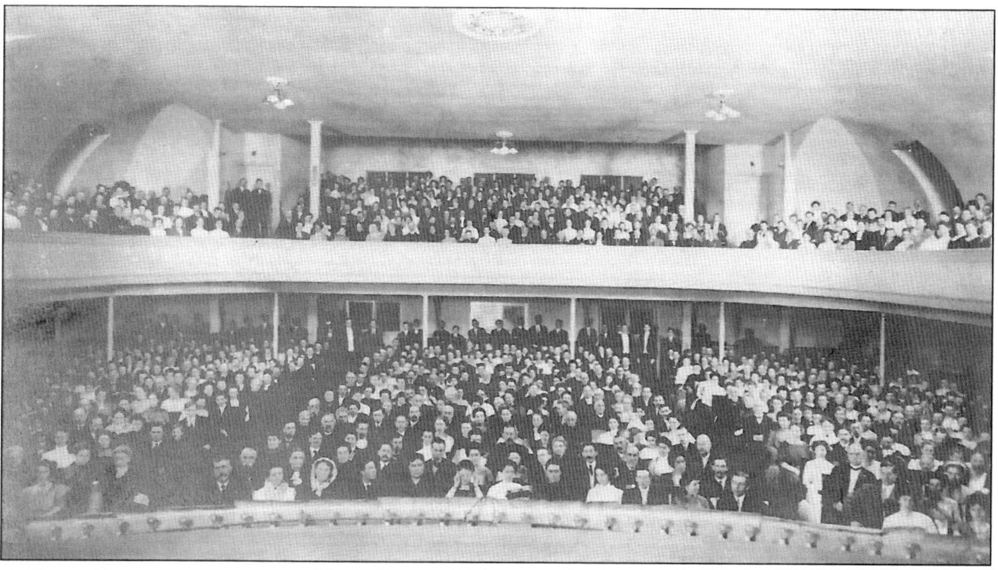

A Star Course Audience, 1910. From 1888 to 1915, Vinelanders participated in a national movement known as the "Lyceum Movement," a series of lectures, debates, concerts, and other entertainments. It was originally conducted in Cosmopolitan Hall and continued in the Auditorium, where the above picture was taken. In 1915, the least expensive ticket for the year was $1 per seat. The purpose of the lyceum was both to entertain and to enlighten.

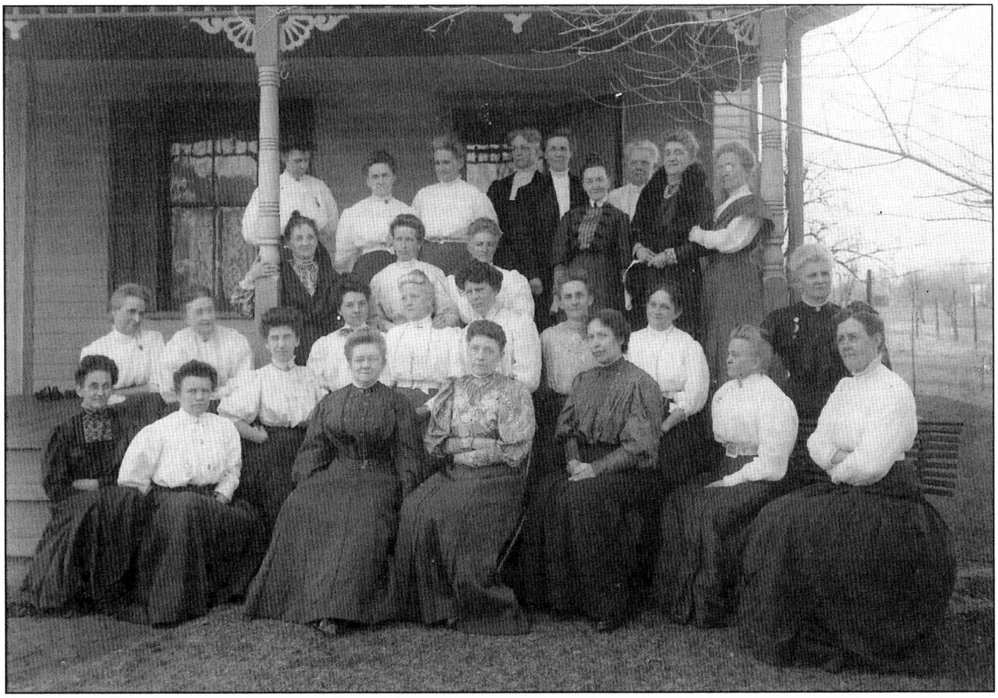

Wallsholm Club. In 1897, about 20 Vineland women formed the Tuesday Afternoon Club, a group that met every Tuesday at the home of Dr. and Mrs. Frank Walls on Myrtle Street. The object of the group was the study of literature and the culinary arts. After two years, the name was changed to Walls' Home Reading Club and later shortened to the Wallsholm Club. The club survived until the turn of the 21st century, when it disbanded due to a lack of members.

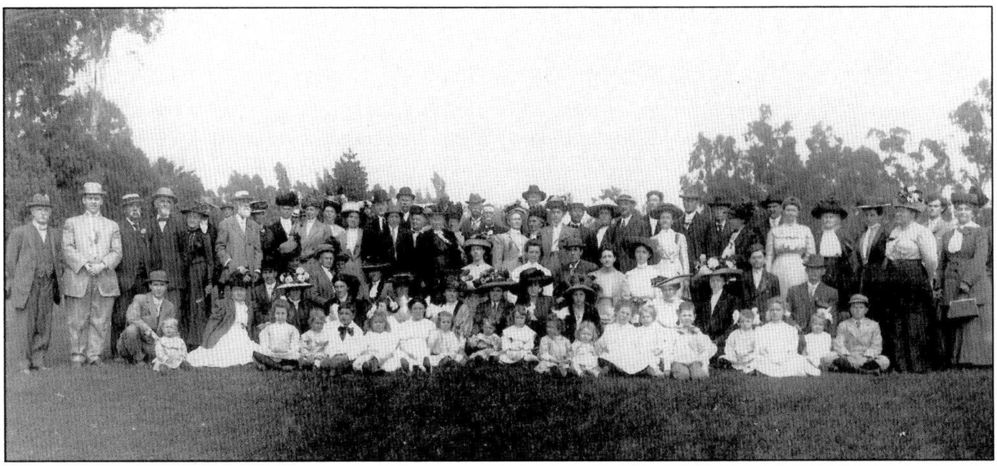

Vineland, New Jersey Association, 1911. To honor the 50th birthday of Vineland, former residents of the town who lived in California arranged a picnic reunion to be held at East Lake Park in Los Angeles. About 90 people attended this first reunion, which resulted in the organization of the "Vineland, New Jersey Association." The group continued to meet annually for many years. The families represented here are Aiken, Allen, Avis, Bartlett, Buerkle, Cornell, Curtis, Gifford, Goodwin, Hammond, Hayes, Herdeg, Hirst, Keyser, Learned, Linnekin, Lush, Martin, Mayo, Parker, Rath, Ray, Read, Righter, Sherer, Smith, Stearns, Sullivan, Townsend, Wells, Witham, and York. (Photograph by Hilyard of Orange, California.)

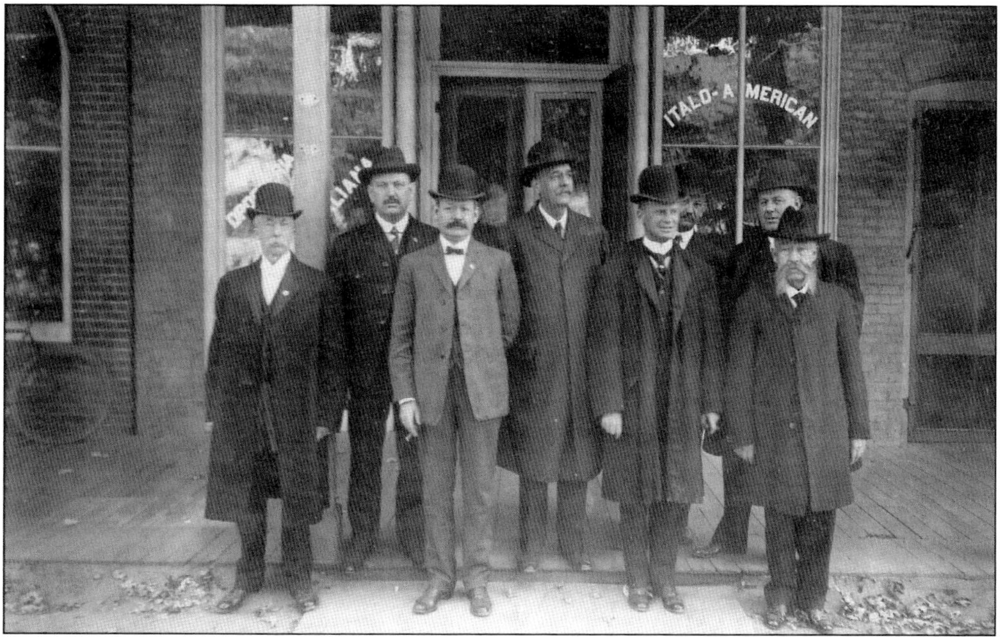

Italo-American Club, c. 1900. In the 1870s, Charles K. Landis traveled to Italy to attract Italians to the growing prosperity found in Vineland. He was successful in doing so, and soon after, hundreds of Italian families immigrated to the town as farmers and merchants. In 1885, Landis purchased 3,500 acres of land near Panther Creek and annexed it to Vineland under the name of New Italy. This land, which is now known as East Vineland, was dedicated to Italian colonization.

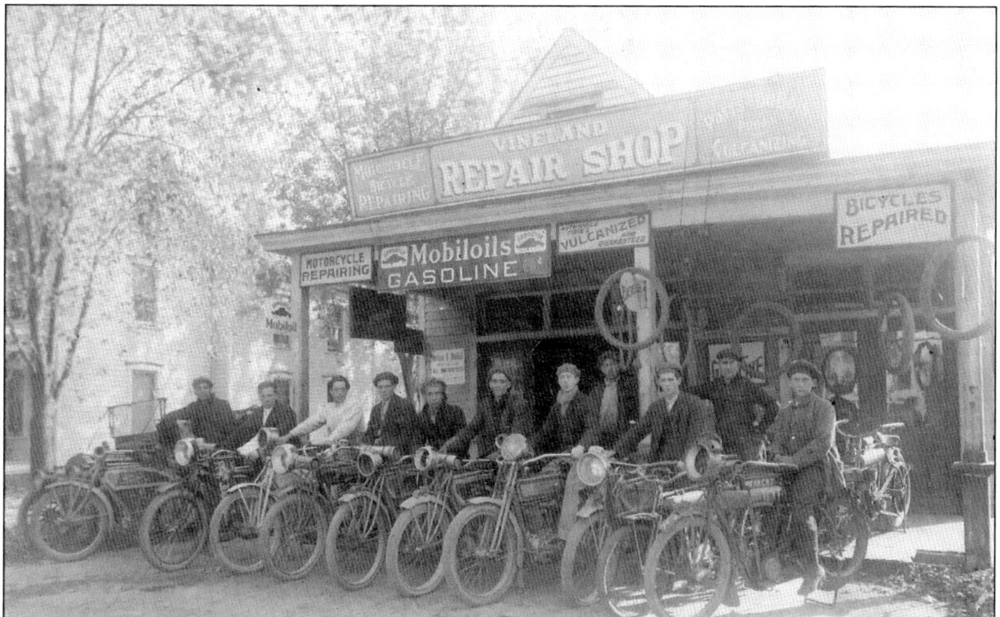

Motorcycle Club, c. 1915. This picture shows Vineland's Motorcycle Club in front of J. U. DuBois and John W. Potts's Vineland Repair Shop, located on the 300 block of Landis Avenue. DuBois (left) and Potts (right) are seen standing behind the group of motorcyclists.

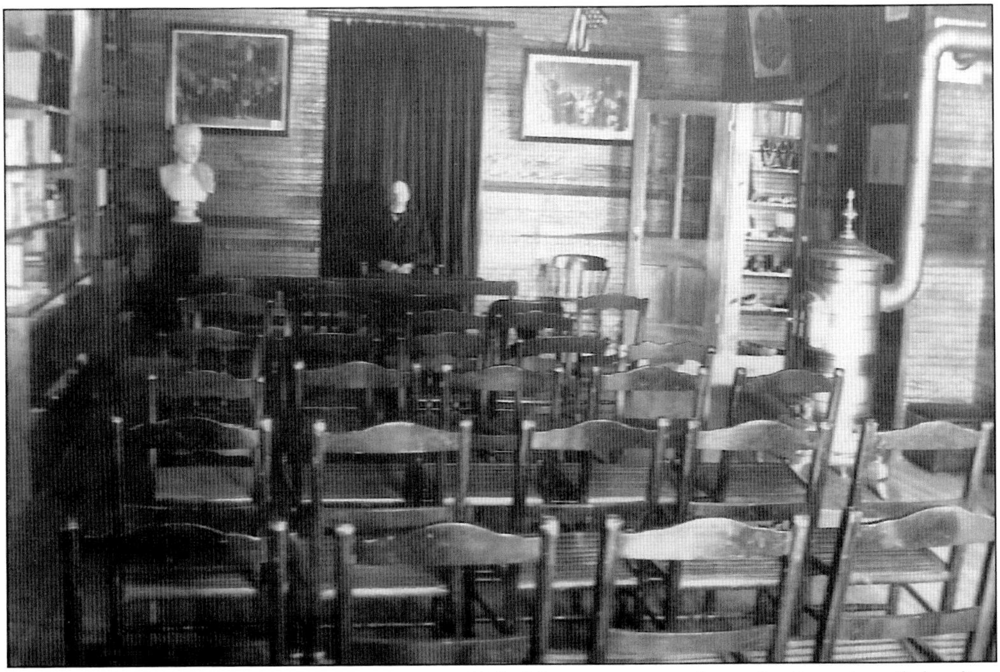

First Historical Society Interior, c. 1895. These pictures show the interior of the first building of the Vineland Historical and Antiquarian Society, located on South Seventh Street near the corner of Elmer Street. The building was used by the society for about 17 years, until the larger building it currently occupies was constructed next to it. In the picture above, Frank D. Andrews, longtime trustee of the society, is shown seated at the front of the room. The stove in the picture above was preserved and remains on display in the Vineland Historical and Antiquarian Society Museum.

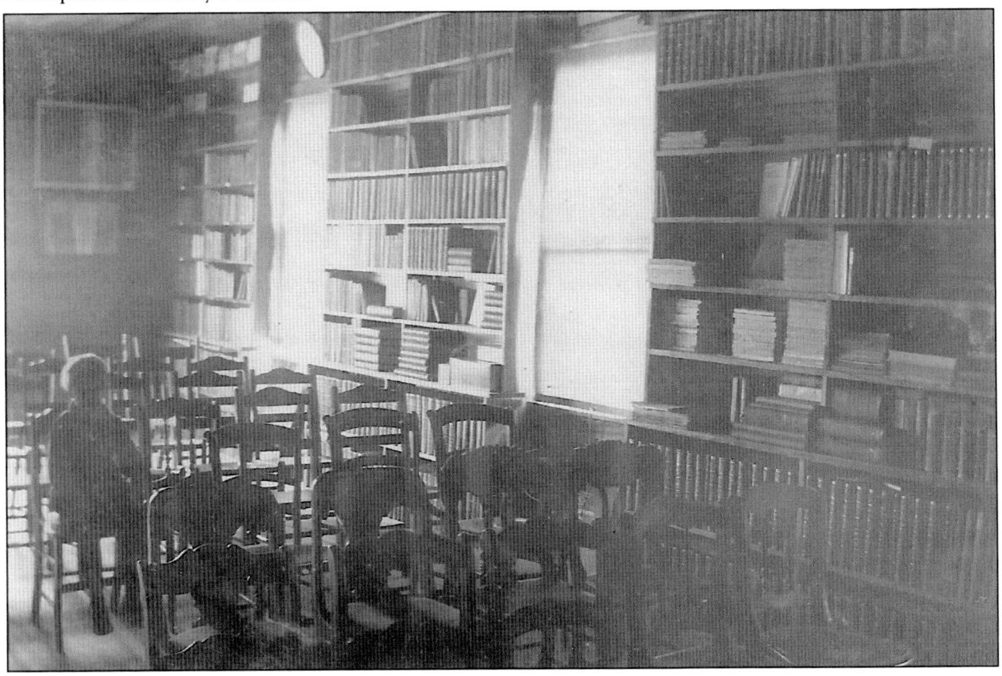

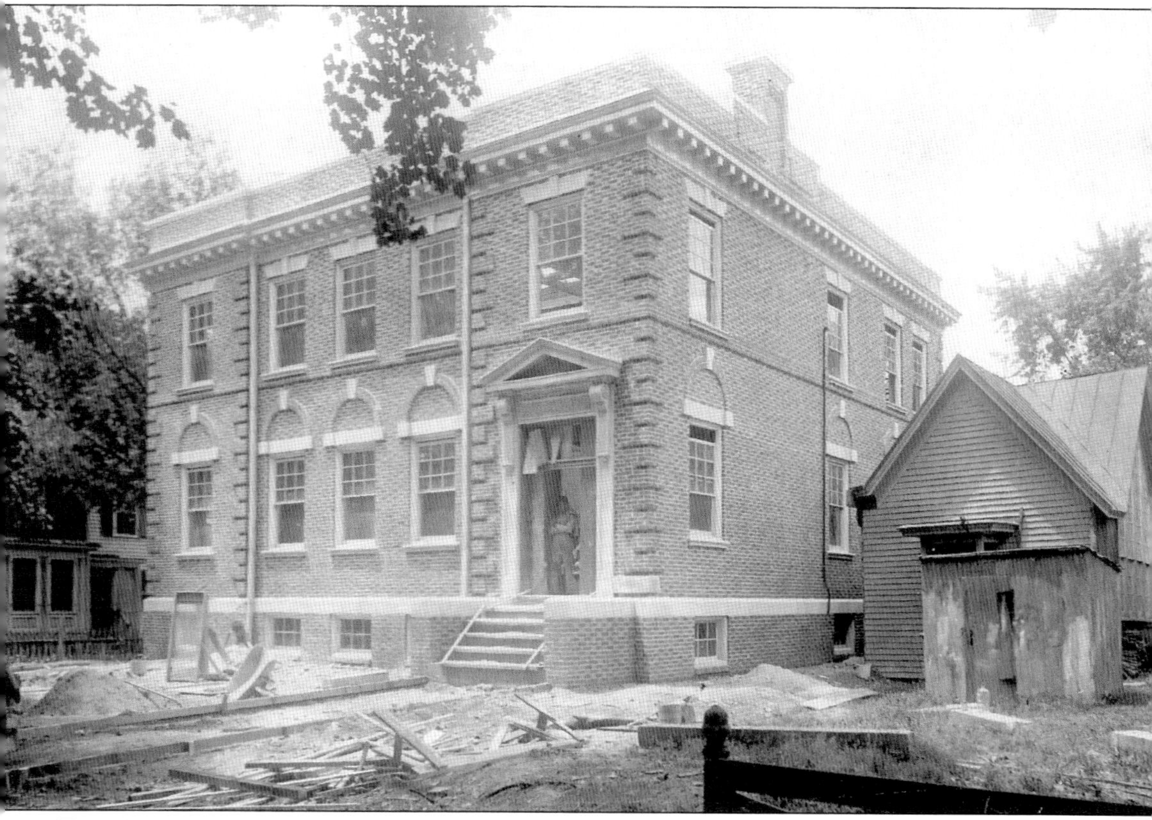

THE VINELAND HISTORICAL AND ANTIQUARIUN SOCIETY, 1910. The Vineland Historical and Antiquarian Society was founded in 1864, just three years after the establishment of the town of Vineland. It is the second oldest historical society in New Jersey, second only to the New Jersey Historical Society. In 1893, John S. Shepard and Daniel F. Morrill donated money for the society to secure a lot and building on South Seventh Street, and through the efforts of Frank D. Andrews, Charles K. Landis included a substantial bequest to the society in his last will. In 1910, with this funding, the society began construction of its current building, which was completed the following year. The building continues to retain a high degree of historical integrity. The above picture shows the new building during its construction, next to the building it replaced.

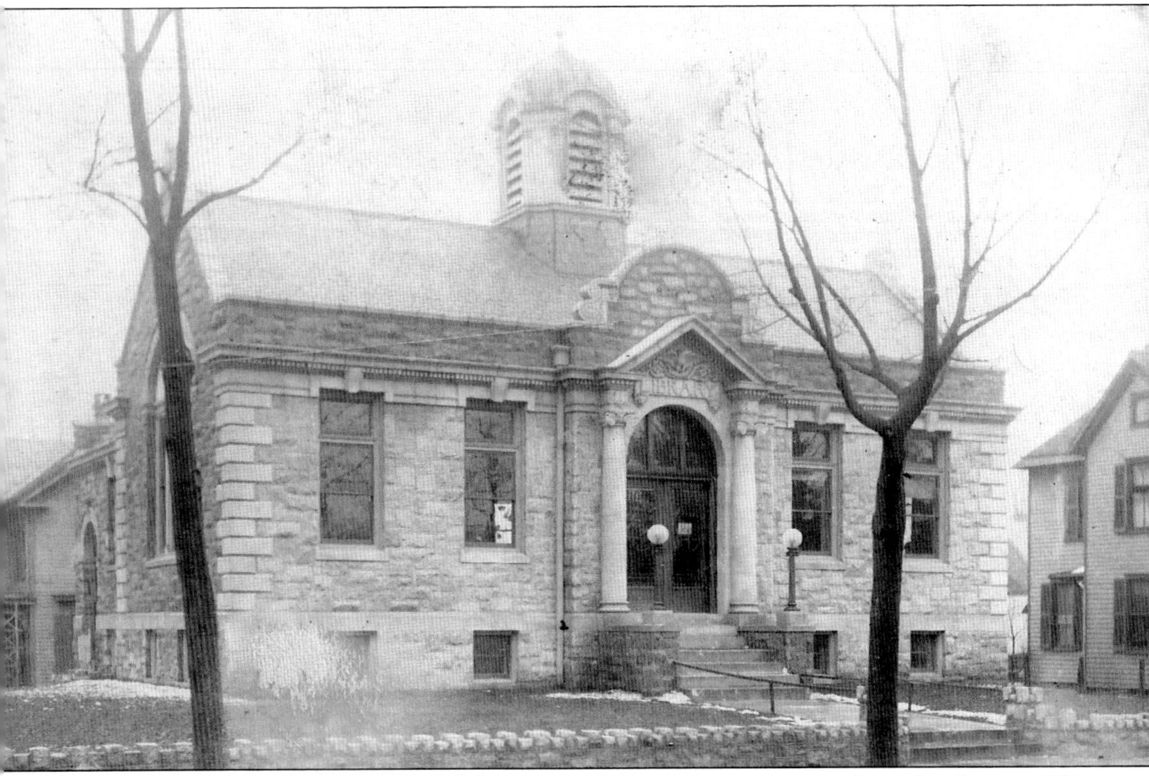

VINELAND PUBLIC LIBRARY. In 1866, the Vineland Library Association was formed and counted 150 members during its first year. In 1868, the library was moved to the post office and the postmaster was appointed librarian. In 1872, after years of disinterest, the library's books were sold at an auction. However, in 1875, Thomas W. Braidwood, founder of Vineland's first art school, sought to establish a free public library for the community. He successfully lobbied Andrew Carnegie of New York for funds to construct a library building. Vineland's first public library building, shown above, is now a senior center.

Seven

Schools in Vineland

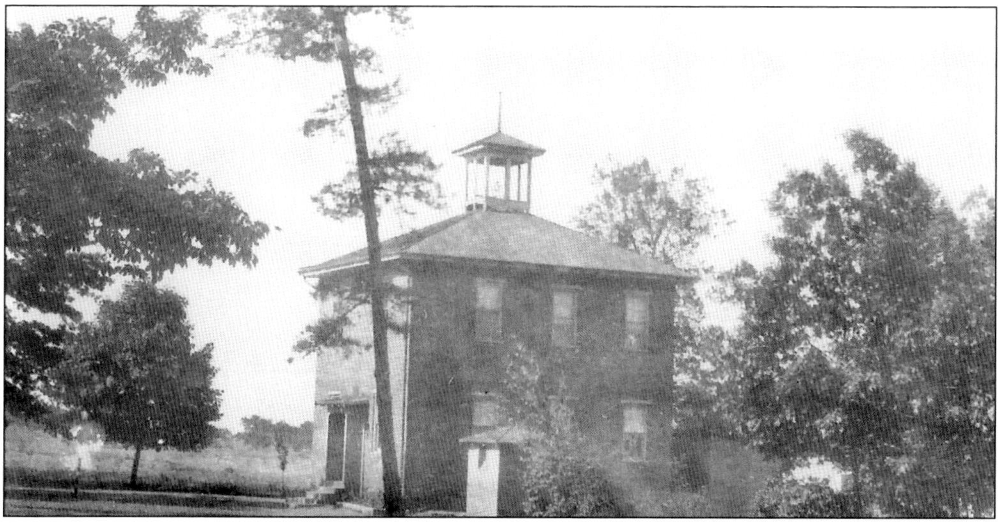

Orchard Road School. In 1870, the Orchard Road School was constructed on Orchard Road on an acre of land donated by John Gage. The erection of this school and others like it marked an upstart in Vineland's devotion to early education. The building was destroyed by fire before World War II.

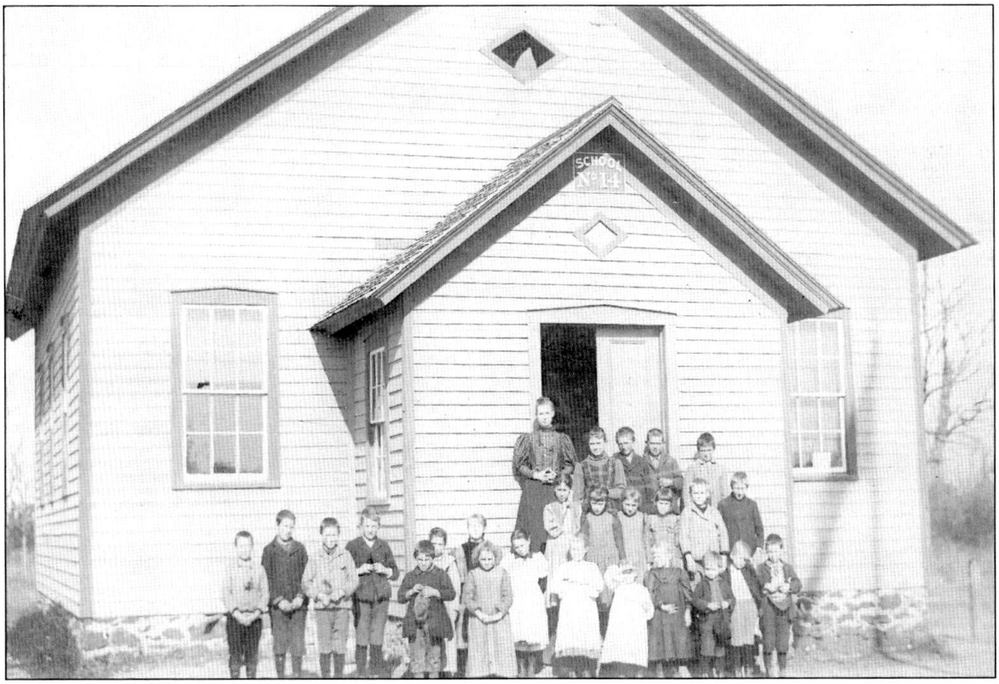

COOPER MILL SCHOOL, C. 1898. In 1868, a one-room schoolhouse was built at the corner of Chestnut and Lincoln Avenues. In this picture, the teacher standing at the door is Eunice A. Richardson, who taught at Cooper Mill School for several years. She would tell her students that she was born in the same year as the school. The school is no longer in use but remains standing as one of the oldest buildings in Vineland.

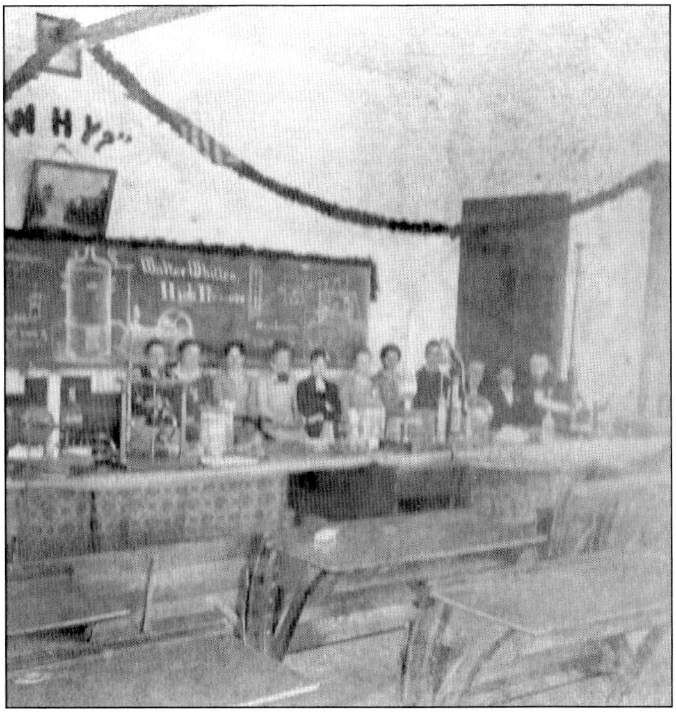

EARLIEST SCHOOLROOM, C. 1876. This photograph is perhaps the earliest to depict a classroom in Vineland. It shows a class studying the sciences.

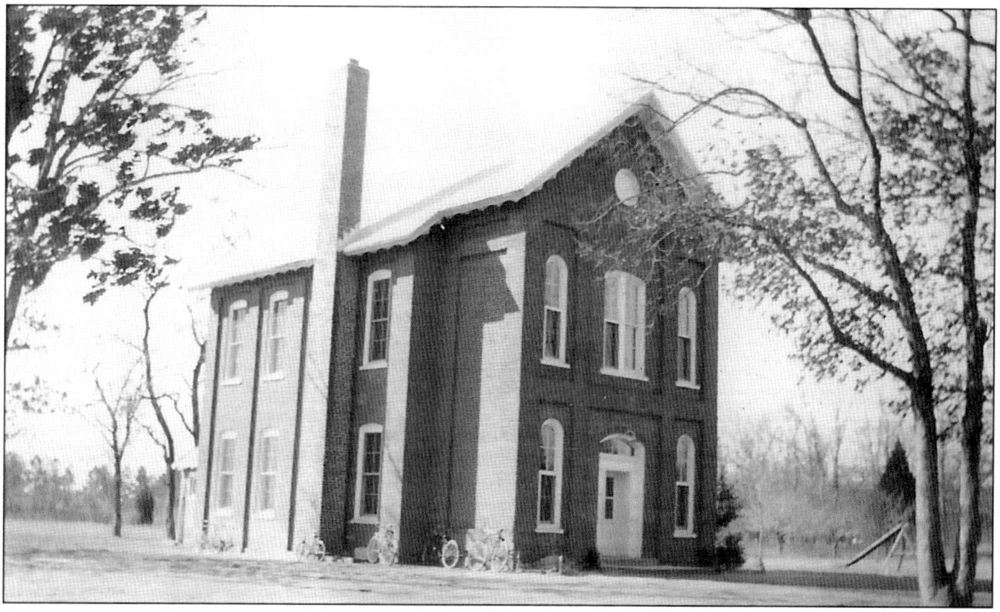

Spring Road and Landis Avenue School. This schoolhouse, built in 1870, was located on Landis Avenue and Spring Road. It had two classrooms and a capacity of 60 students. In 1957, the school was closed but reopened in 1958. It was torn down after the 1970s.

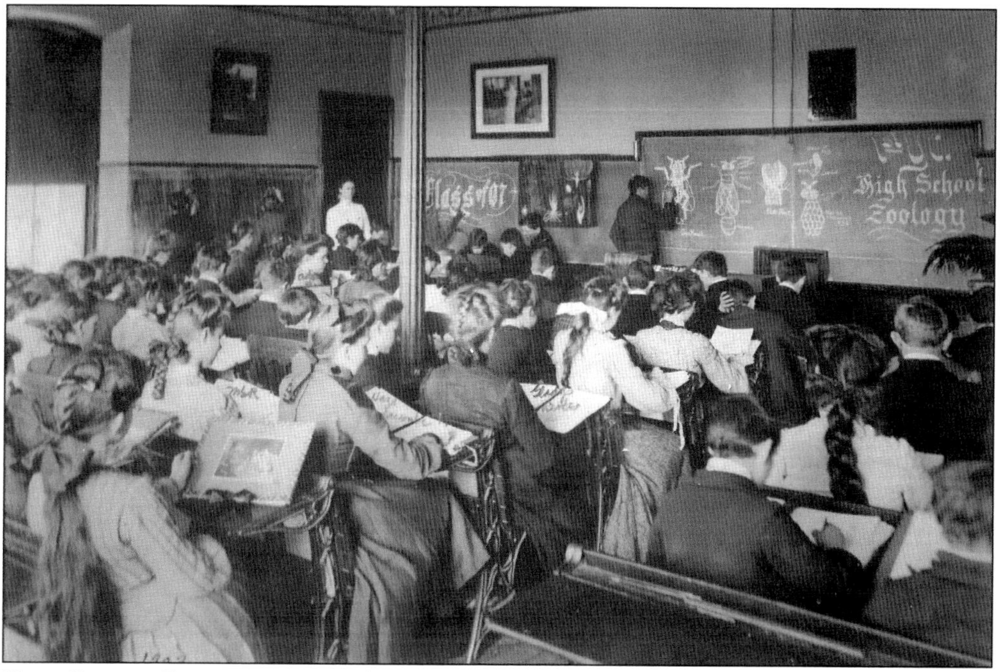

High School Zoology, 1903. This picture shows a class of high school freshmen studying zoology and a student creating an intricate chalk drawing of a bug. During that time, students in the Vineland public school system took courses that are no longer part of the school curriculum. Elementary students took classes in iron working, mat weaving, and pose drawing. High school students took classes in cast drawing and manual training, where they were taught to construct book covers, frames, tables, and so on.

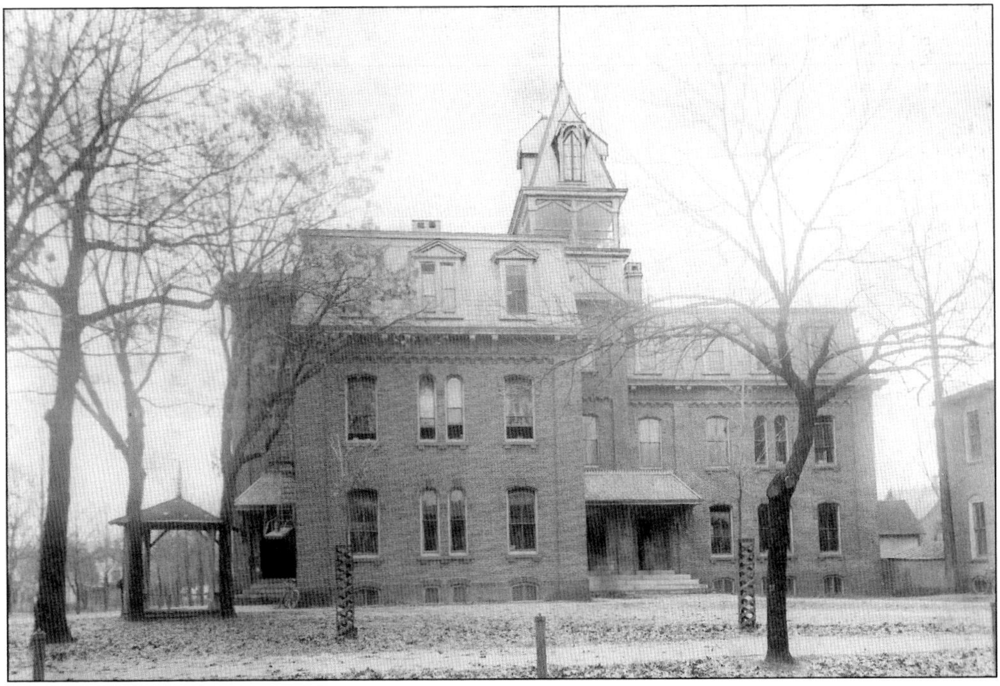

VINELAND'S FIRST HIGH SCHOOL. In 1873, Vineland's first high school was constructed on Sixth Street between Wood and Plum Streets. On August 22, 1874, Pres. Ulysses S. Grant visited Vineland and dedicated the opening of the building. The original building was used for a two-year high school program until an addition in 1895 allowed for a four-year program. When a new high school was built, this school became Central School and was used as an elementary school. In 1954, it was closed and, four years later, torn down.

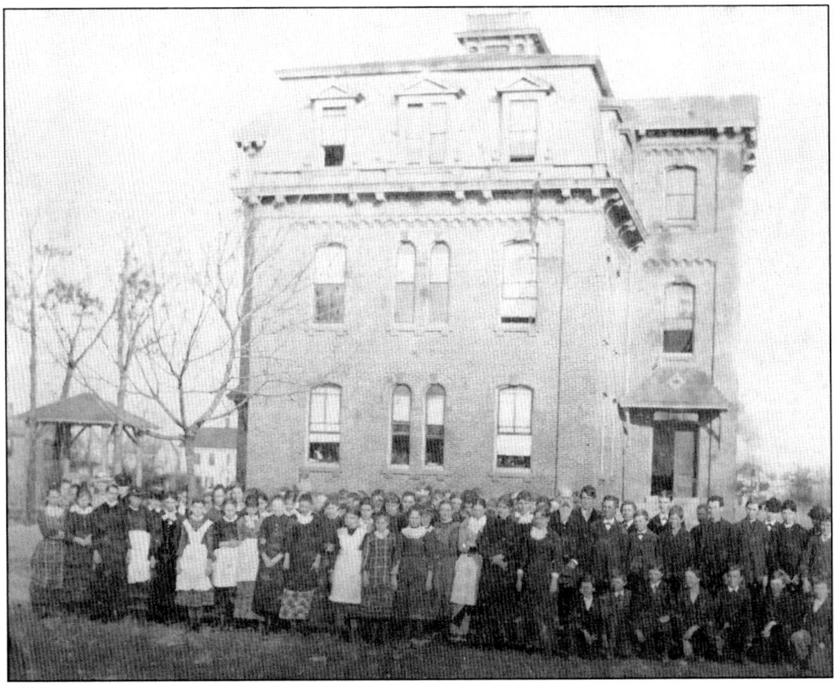

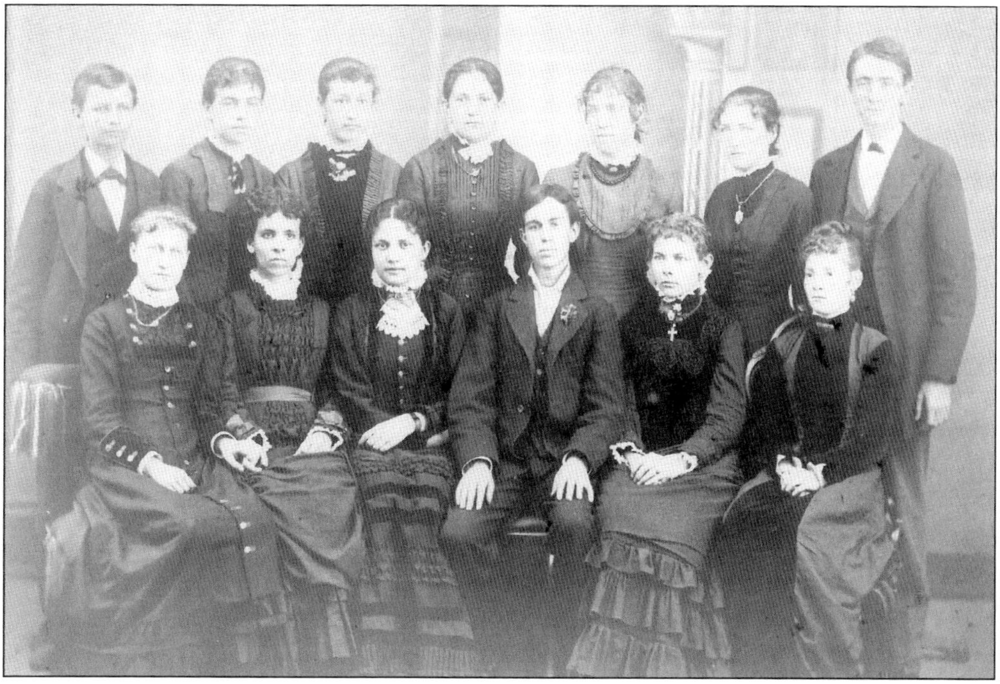

Class of 1879. This picture shows Vineland's graduating high school class of 1879 as they posed for their formal class picture. This class was the first to have gone all through high school at the building on Sixth Street.

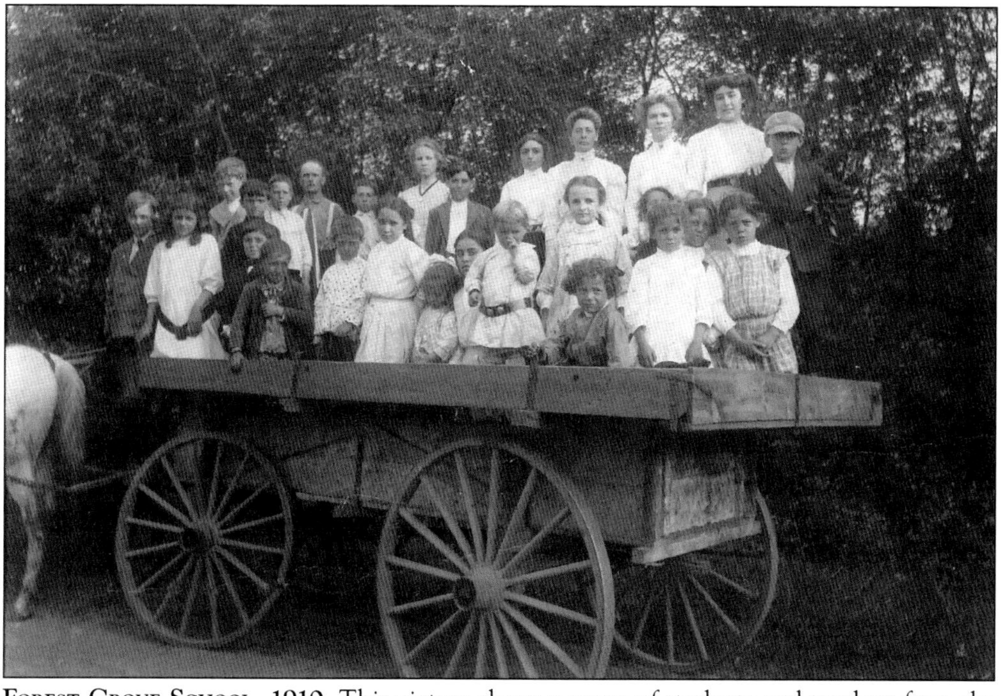

Forest Grove School, 1910. This picture shows a group of students and teachers from the Forest Grove School standing in a tomato wagon. The teachers at the far right include Mrs. Grossman and Mrs. Wolfe.

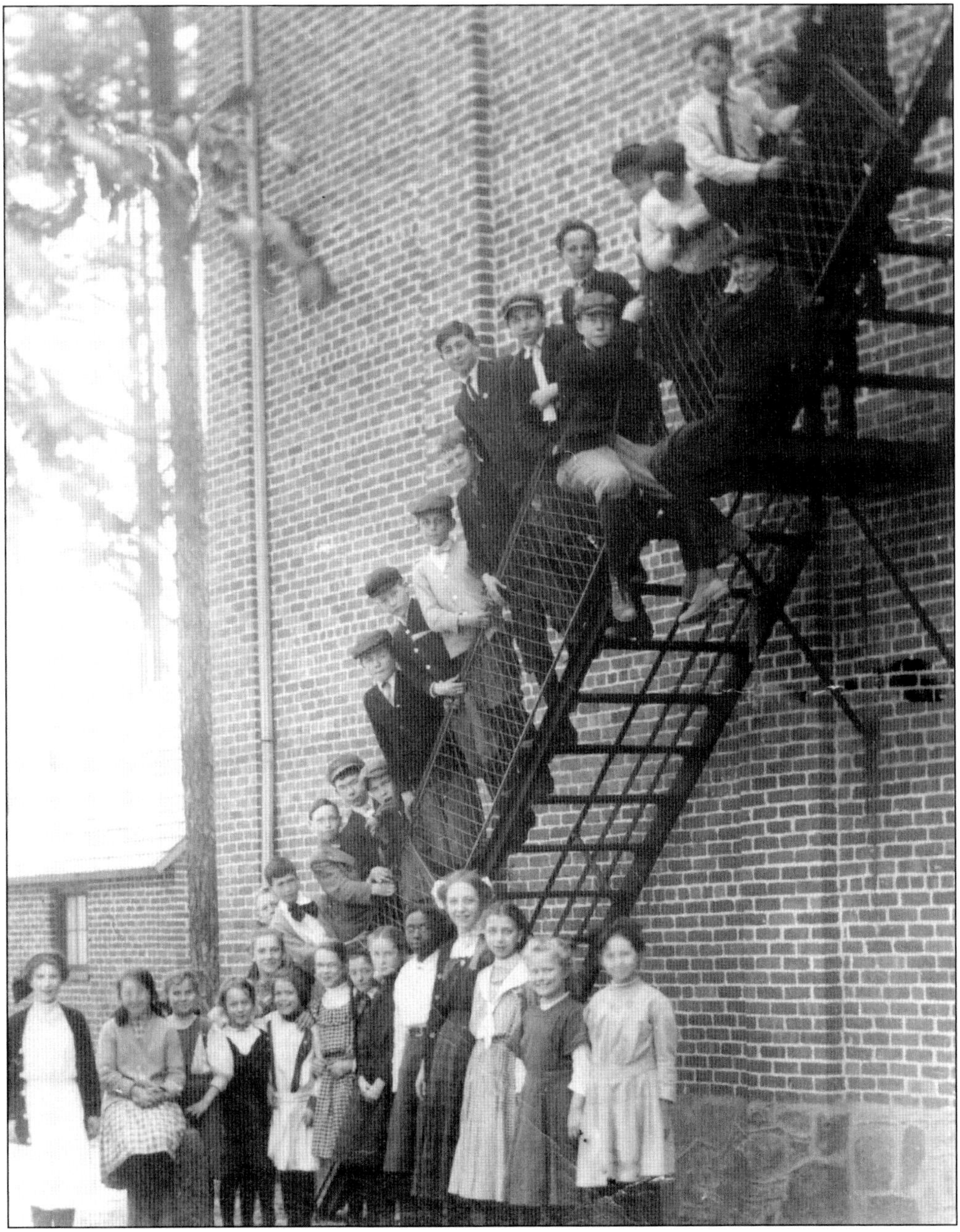

PARK AND EAST SCHOOL, C. 1910. A class gathers on the fire escape for their moment before the camera at Park and East School, which was built in 1899 as a four-room schoolhouse. The interiors of this all-brick building contained rich wood floors and oak desks. A huge school yard oak tree was surrounded by a wooden bench seldom used, since the students usually enjoyed the freedom and activity of recess and play. Until recently, the Park and East School continued to be used for educational purposes.

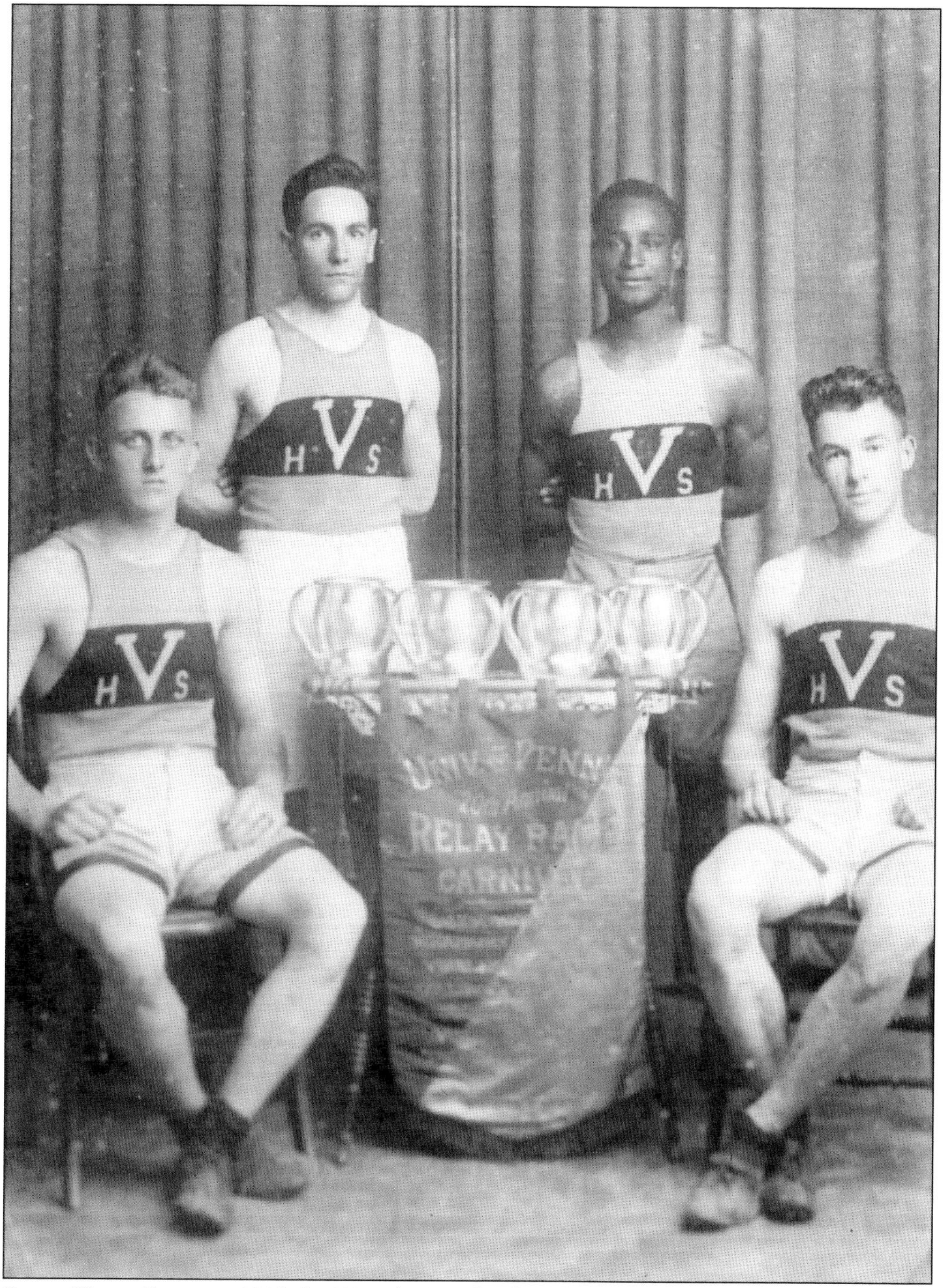

Relay Team Champs, 1914. In 1914, the Vineland High School relay team became the first from the town to win the championship at the famous Penn Relays, held at the University of Pennsylvania in Philadelphia. The team members were, from left to right, Walther "Bud" Weylman, Charles "Chuck" Finch, "Smiling Sammy" Robinson, and Fred "Hamfoot" Snell. The banner shown above has been preserved and is on display in the administration building of the Vineland public schools.

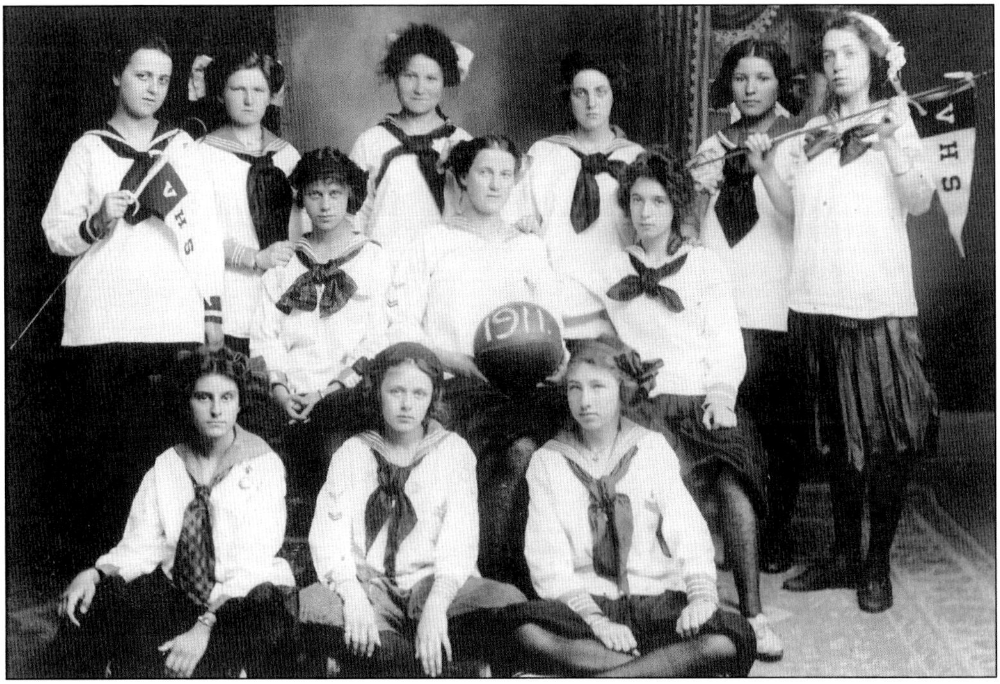

VHS Girls' Basketball Team, 1911. From left to right, this team's members are as follows: (first row) Ethel Bradwater, Eleanor Jones, and Bessie Turner; (second row) Naomi Bishoff, Sovey Koetz, and Charlotte Rule; (third row) Adelnia Gillette, Sottie Barber, Mary Gallea, two unidentified, and Matilda Knoll.

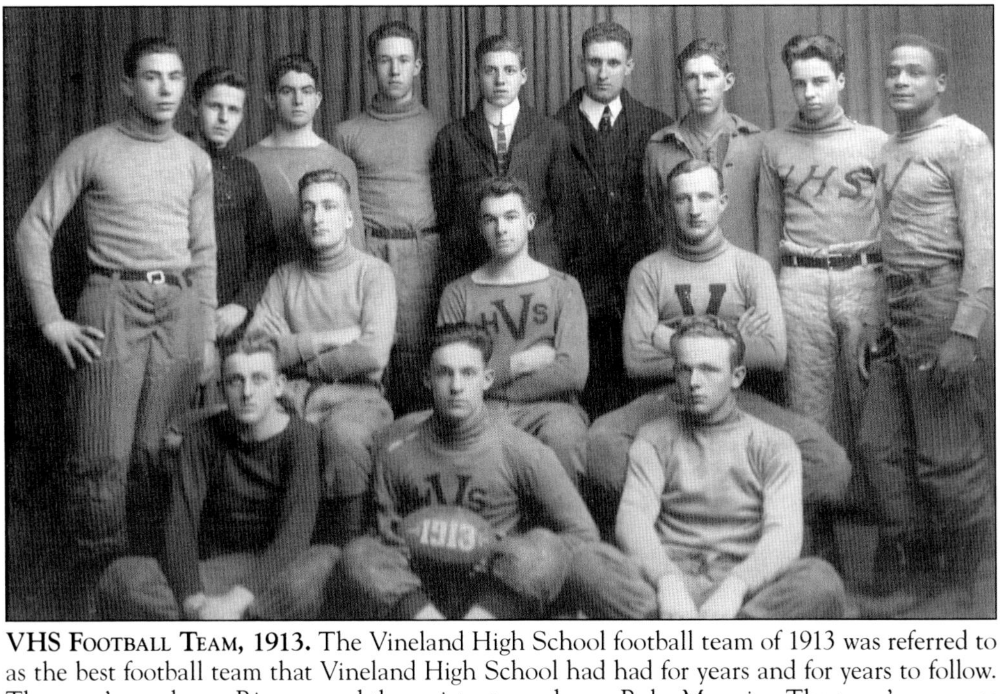

VHS Football Team, 1913. The Vineland High School football team of 1913 was referred to as the best football team that Vineland High School had had for years and for years to follow. The team's coach was Rieman and the assistant coach was Rube Mennies. The team's manager was called Pinhead Adams.

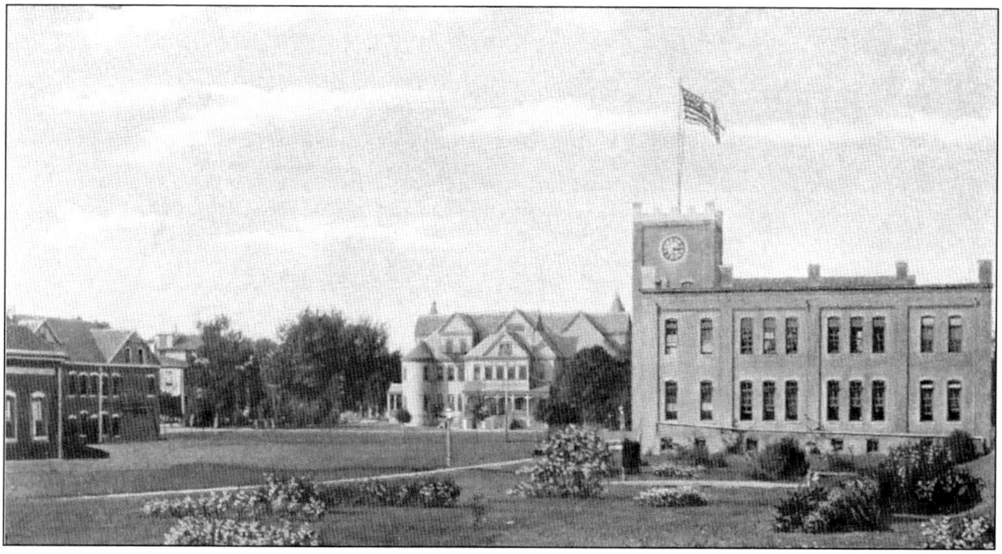

VINELAND TRAINING SCHOOL. In 1888, Rev. S. Olin Garrison established the Vineland Training School on a large plot of land that spanned from present-day Main Road to Spring Road and Landis Avenue to Chestnut Avenue. The school housed both females and males, who stayed in same-sex cottages with a house mother. It was also home to famous author Pearl S. Buck's daughter Carol Buck. The school led the research field with new tests and groundbreaking research. The picture below shows a farm located on the school's grounds, which was used to feed the students.

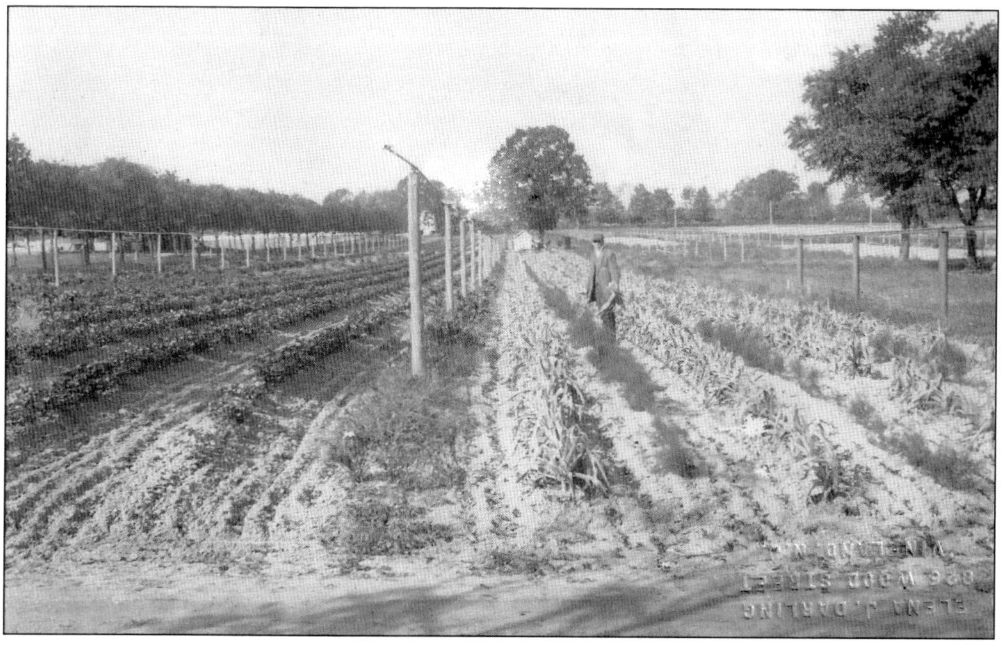

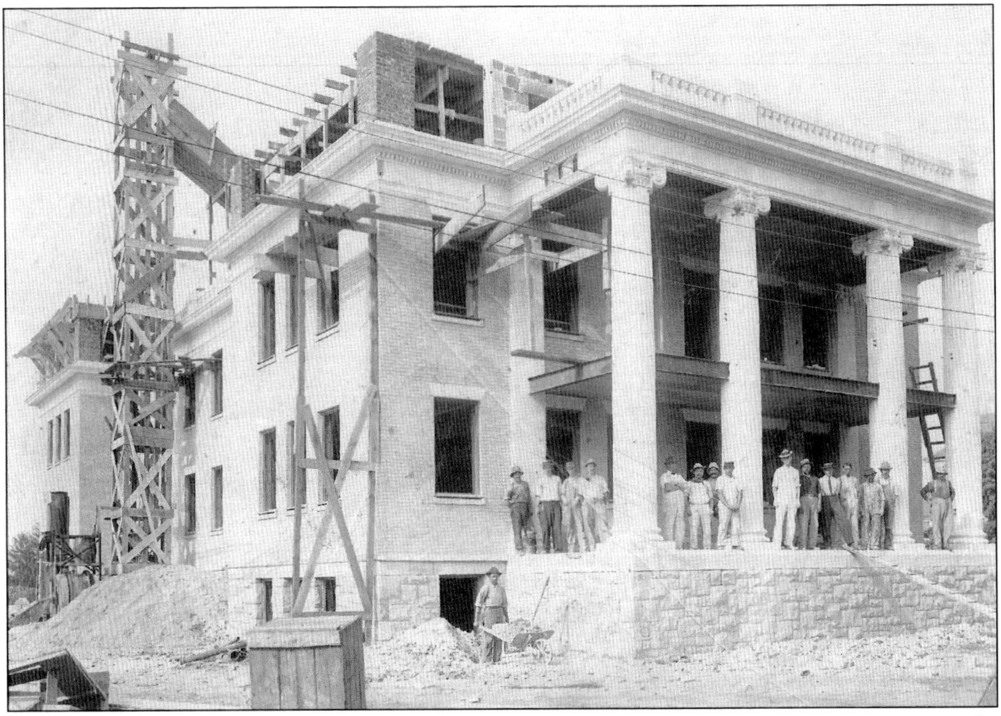

STATE INSTITUTION FOR FEEBLE-MINDED WOMEN. In 1888, the New Jersey State Institution for Feeble-Minded Women, which is now called the Vineland Developmental Center, was opened on Main Road across the street from the Vineland Training School. The picture above shows the institution's main building under construction. The building is currently used as the center's administration offices. The picture below shows a class of women from the institution's early years. The center maintains its original purpose of providing care and training for persons with developmental disabilities.

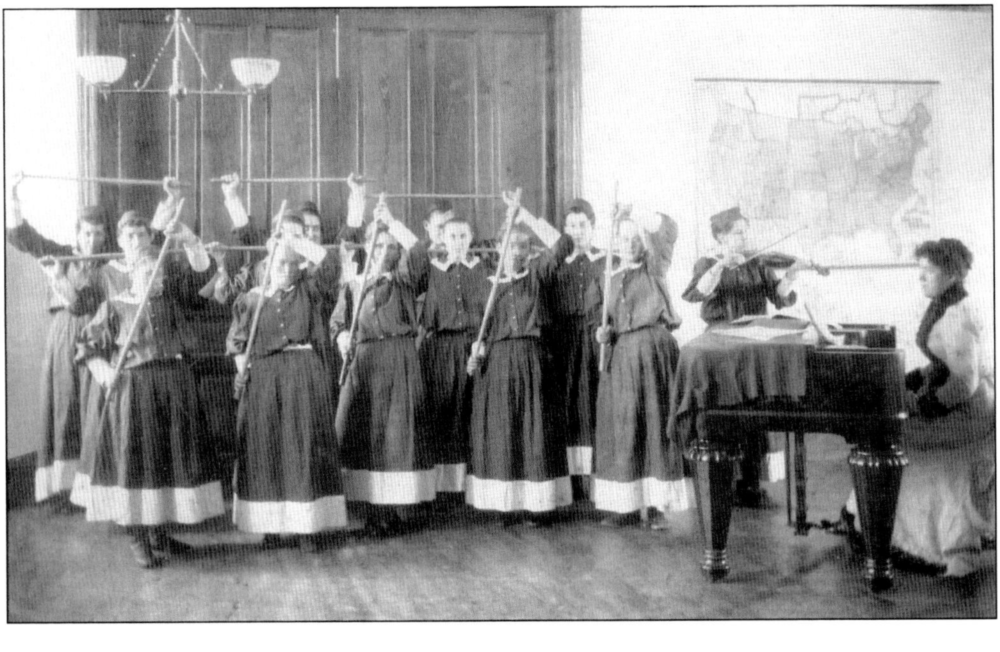

Eight

Churches in Vineland

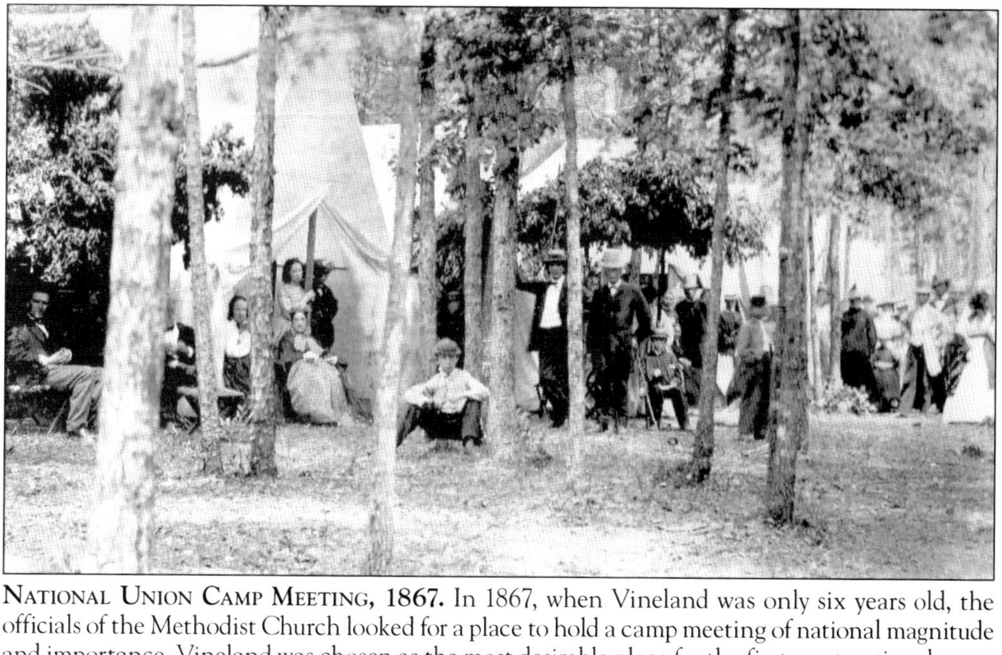

National Union Camp Meeting, 1867. In 1867, when Vineland was only six years old, the officials of the Methodist Church looked for a place to hold a camp meeting of national magnitude and importance. Vineland was chosen as the most desirable place for the first great national camp meeting to be held in America. For 10 days in July, the Methodist Church held the camp meeting in Landis Park, where tents were pitched and a tabernacle for preaching was constructed. Approximately 12,000 people from all over the country attended the revival meeting. Hotels, boardinghouses, and many private residences were crowded with guests. Temporary dormitories were also built to accommodate visitors. The following year, the success of the camp meeting in Vineland led to the establishment of Ocean Grove as a permanent national camp meeting ground.

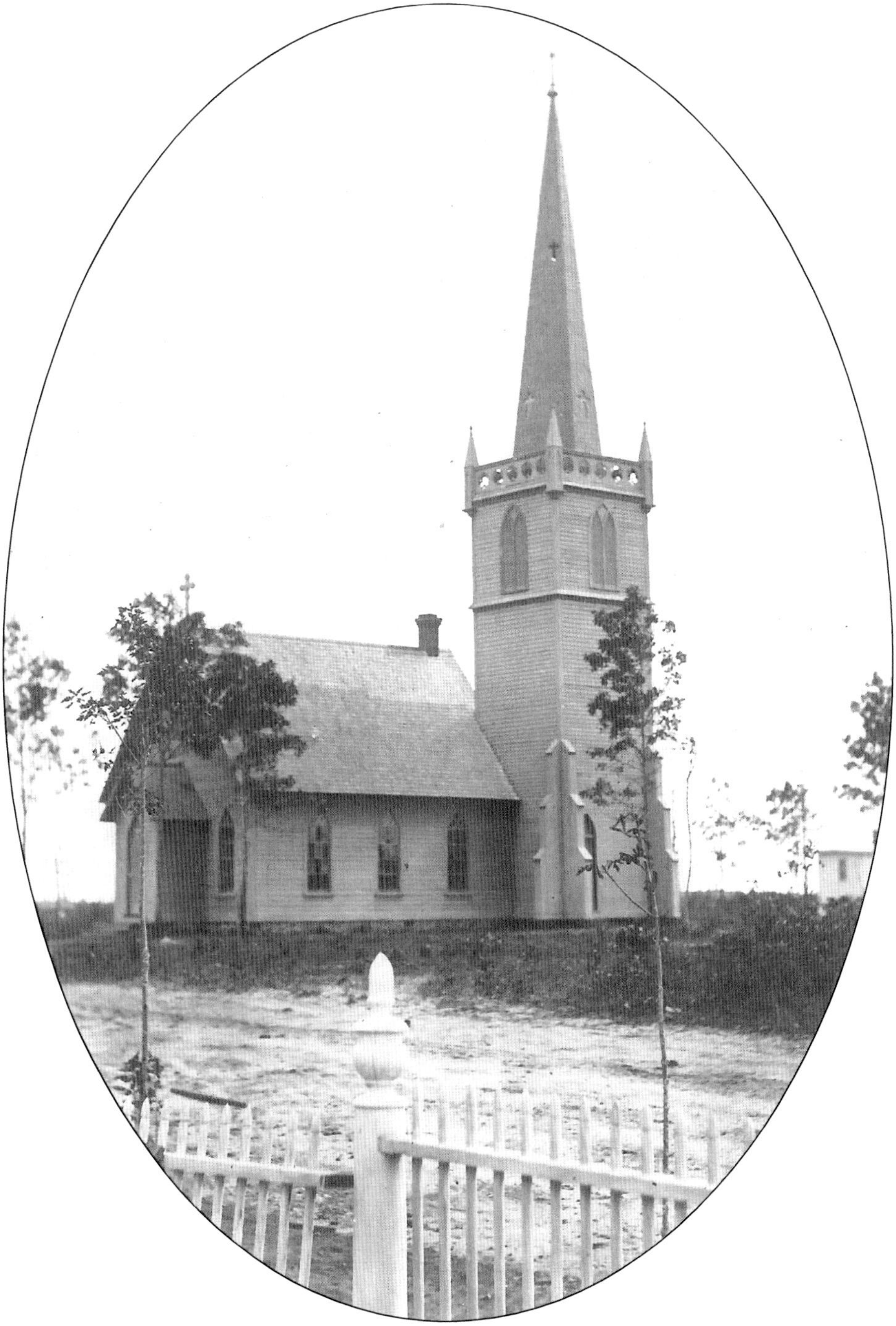

Trinity Episcopal Church, 1865. In November 1864, the Trinity Episcopal Church on Elmer Street was the first church building completed on the tract of Vineland. The land on which it was built was donated by Charles K. Landis, who gave land to any church that would erect a structure on it. In 1865, the church was enlarged and it added a steeple in which a bell, also a gift from Landis, was placed. In 1871, a tornado struck and destroyed the church. The congregation rebuilt the church on the corner of Wood and Eighth Streets.

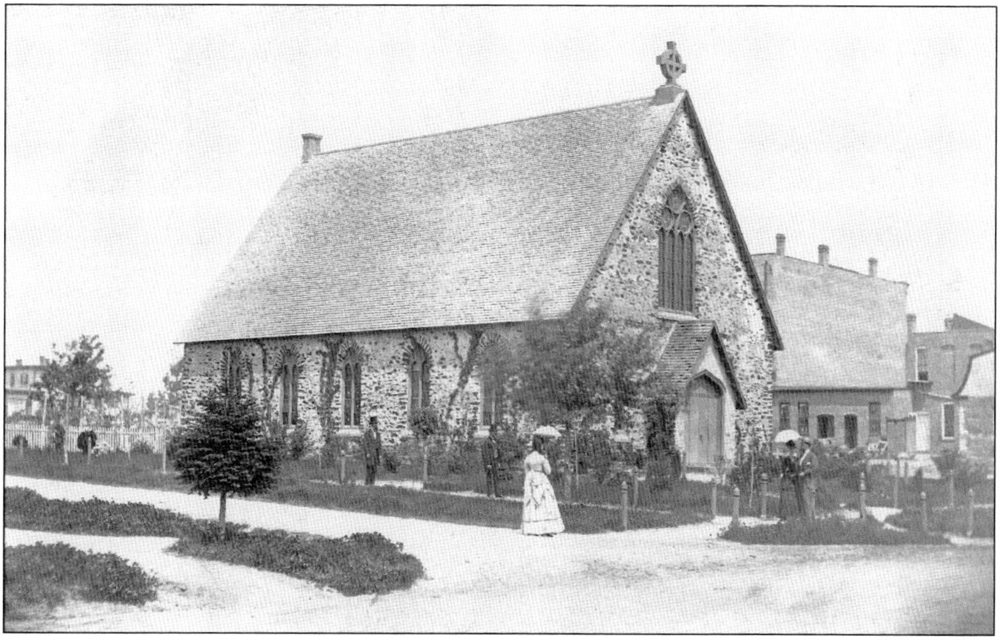

FIRST CONGREGATIONAL UNITARIAN CHURCH. In 1865, a group of Vineland residents who were natives of New England formed a religious society that would embody the liberal Christian thought with which they were familiar. In 1868, they completed construction of a church building made from Vineland sandstone on the corner of Sixth and Elmer Streets. From 1887 to 1916, Rev. William M. Gilbert served as pastor of the church and was an active voice in community affairs. The picture below shows several female parishioners painting the fence around the church property about 1890. The church building was destroyed by fire in the 1930s and was not rebuilt.

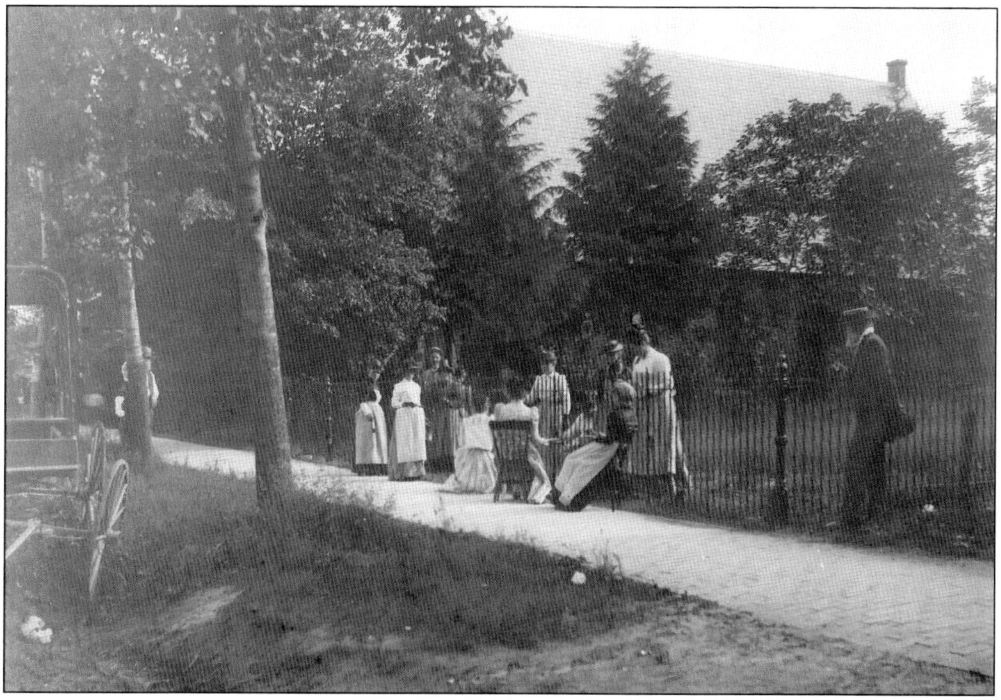

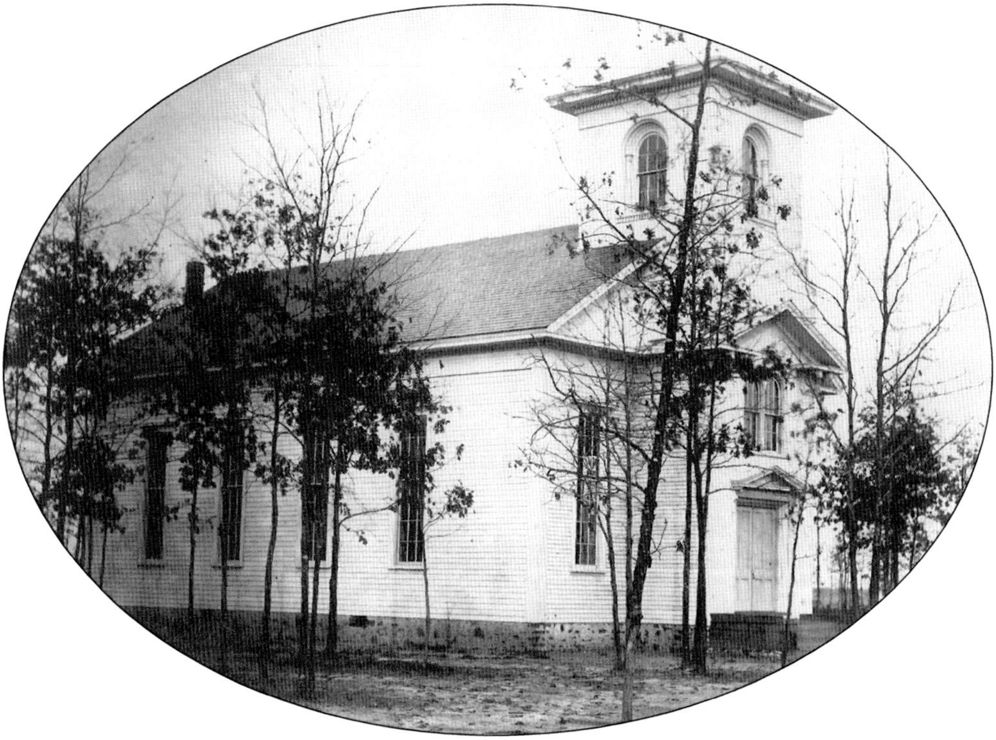

First Presbyterian Church. In 1863, Presbyterians in Vineland formed a church under the Presbytery of Philadelphia. In December of that year, the congregation held the first communion to be given in the town. The church's first pastor was Rev. Samuel Loomis. In 1865, a church building was constructed on the 700 block of Landis Avenue.

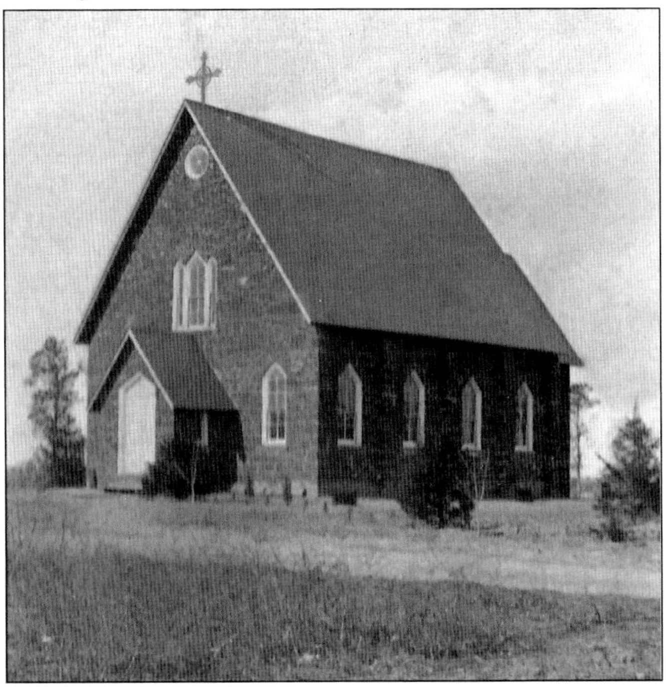

Sacred Heart Church. In 1874, the Catholic congregation in Vineland constructed a small church building on South Eighth Street on land donated by Charles K. Landis. The building was made from sandstone gathered from the surrounding woods. It served as the main church building until 1927, when a new stone building was erected on the corner of Landis Avenue and Myrtle Street.

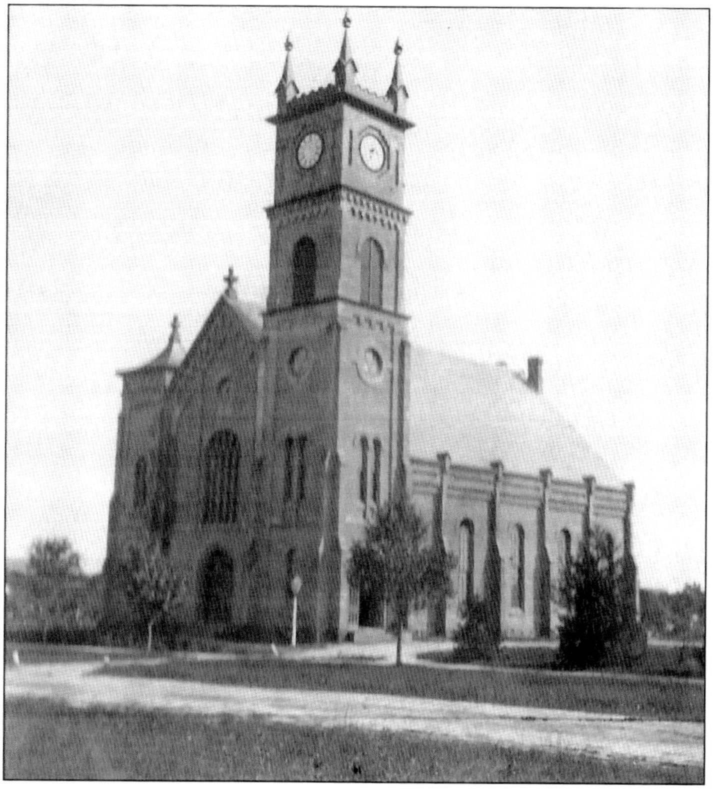

First Baptist Church, 1873. In 1865, a Baptist congregation was formed in Vineland whose first pastor was Rev. Lyman Chase. In 1868, they began construction of a brick church on Landis Avenue near East Avenue. At that time, it was the largest church edifice in the town, and its auditorium could seat over 500 people. In 1873, the clock tower was completed. That same year, the picture below was taken after a Sunday school picnic. Although no longer used as a church, it stands today as one of the oldest buildings in Vineland.

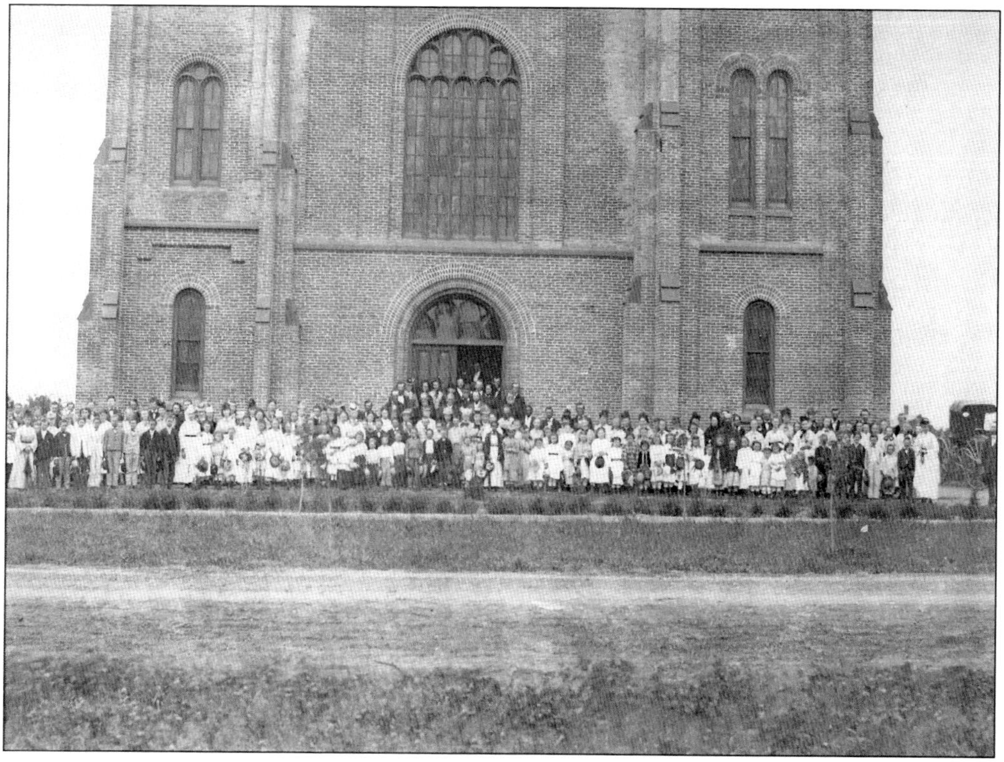

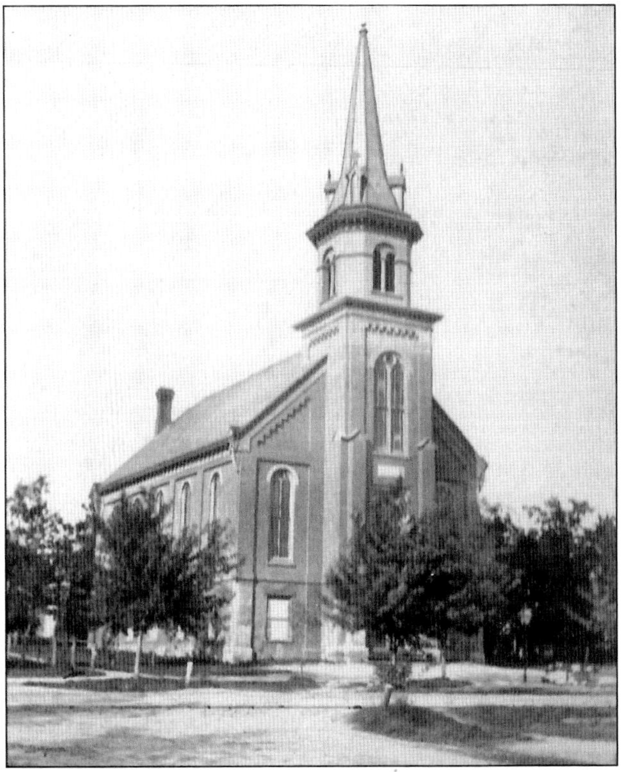

First United Methodist Church. In 1863, the Methodist Episcopal Church was formed in Vineland. The following year, a church building was constructed on the corner of Landis Avenue and Seventh Street, on land donated by Charles K. Landis. In 1867, it hosted the first National Camp Meeting of the Methodist Church. In 1931, the church building shown at left was destroyed by fire. Shown below is the inside of that original building, the altar decorated in celebration of the autumn harvest. In 1932, the church was rebuilt on the site. The congregation included several prominent Vinelanders, including Dr. Thomas B. Welch, inventor of Welch's Grape Juice, and Thomas O. Chisholm, a hymn writer.

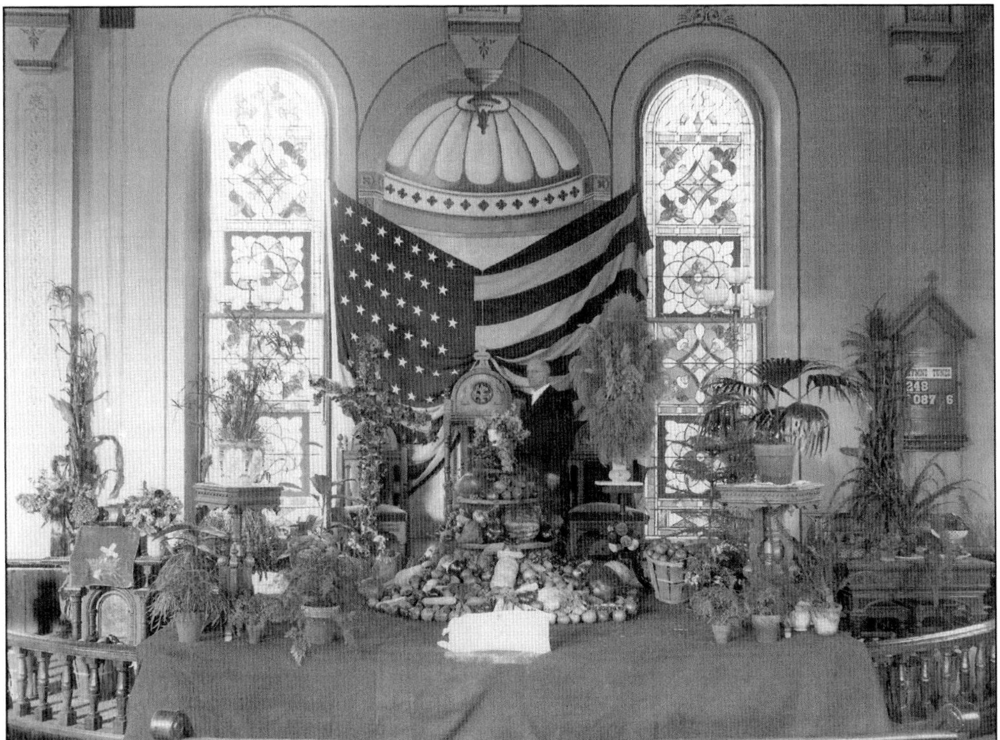

WEST BAPTIST CHURCH. In 1895, several members of the First Baptist Church of Vineland withdrew from the church to establish a church of like faith on the west side of town. Rev. John Bourne was the first pastor of this new congregation. The building shown at right was constructed in 1898 on the 400 block of Landis Avenue, where the church continued to operate until about 1957.

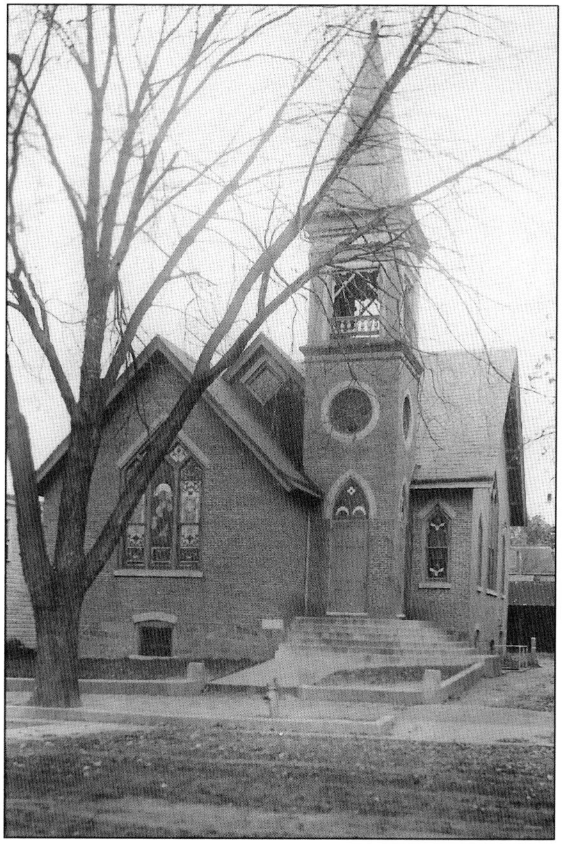

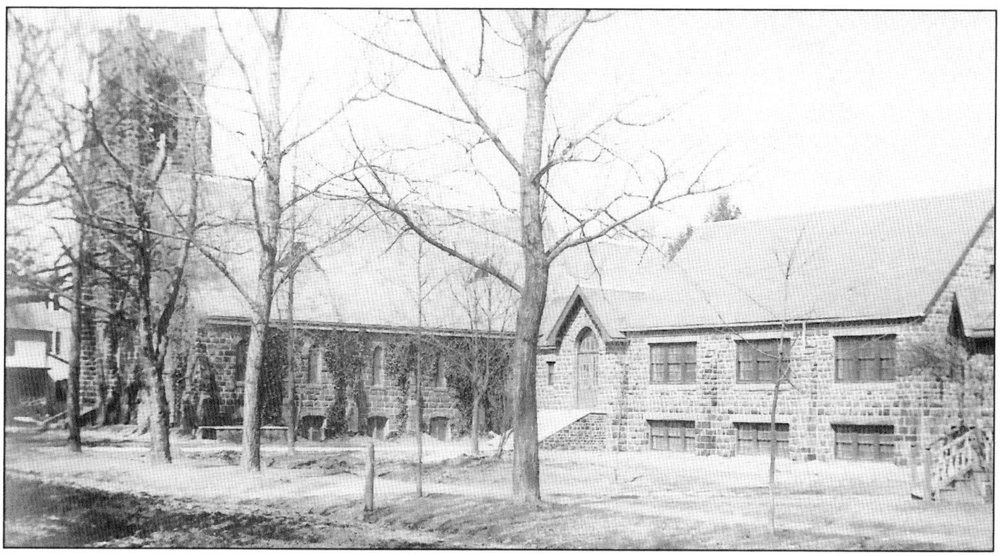

TRINITY EPISCOPAL CHURCH. In 1863, the Trinity Episcopal Church of Vineland was officially formed. That same year, a church building was constructed on Elmer Street on land donated by Charles K. Landis. In 1871, a tornado struck and demolished the building. In 1878, a new building, shown above, was constructed at the corner of Eighth and Wood Streets. In 1902, bells were added to the bell tower.

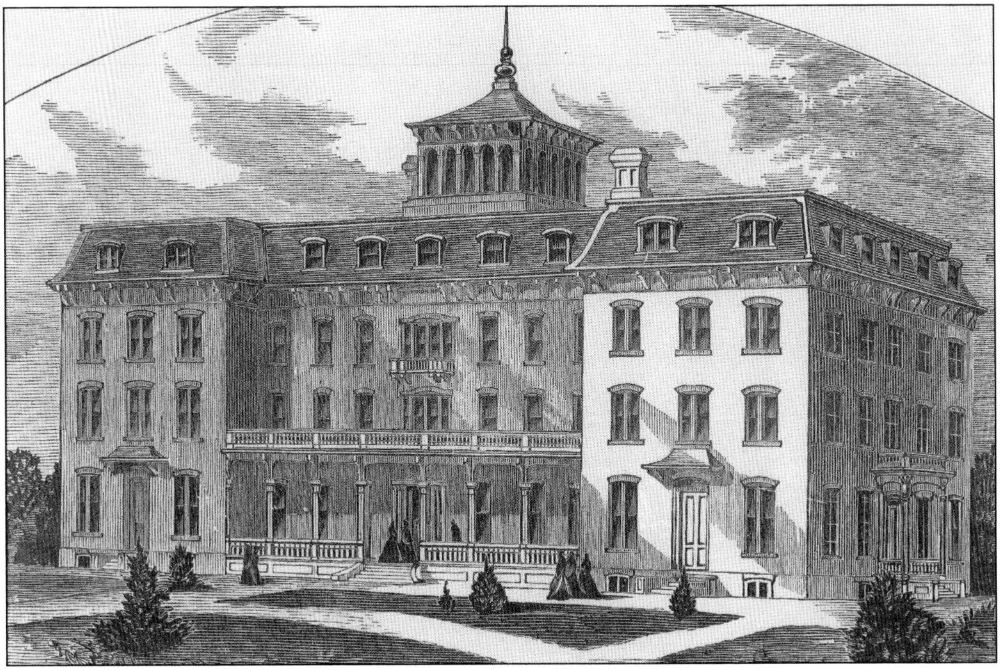

FROM SEMINARY TO SOLDIERS' HOME. In 1868, the Methodists of South Jersey began construction of a seminary in Vineland, shown above. However, lack of funds caused the building to be sold by foreclosure. From 1884 to 1893, it served as the College of the Sacred Heart, a school preparatory to Catholic priesthood. Many prominent Vinelanders attended the college, including Charles K. Landis Jr. In 1898, the property was purchased by the State of New Jersey and reopened as the New Jersey Home for Disabled Soldiers, Sailors, or Marines and their Wives. In about 1920, its administration was changed from military to civil. In 1990, the Soldiers' Home shown below was torn down and its present building constructed on the site.

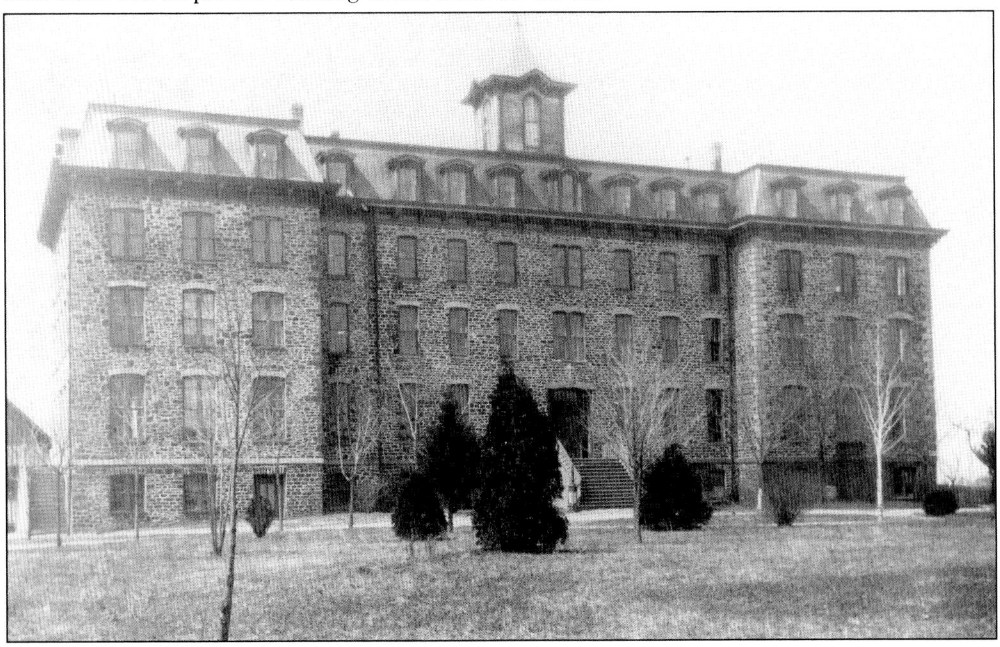

Nine

VINELAND HOMES AND VINELANDERS

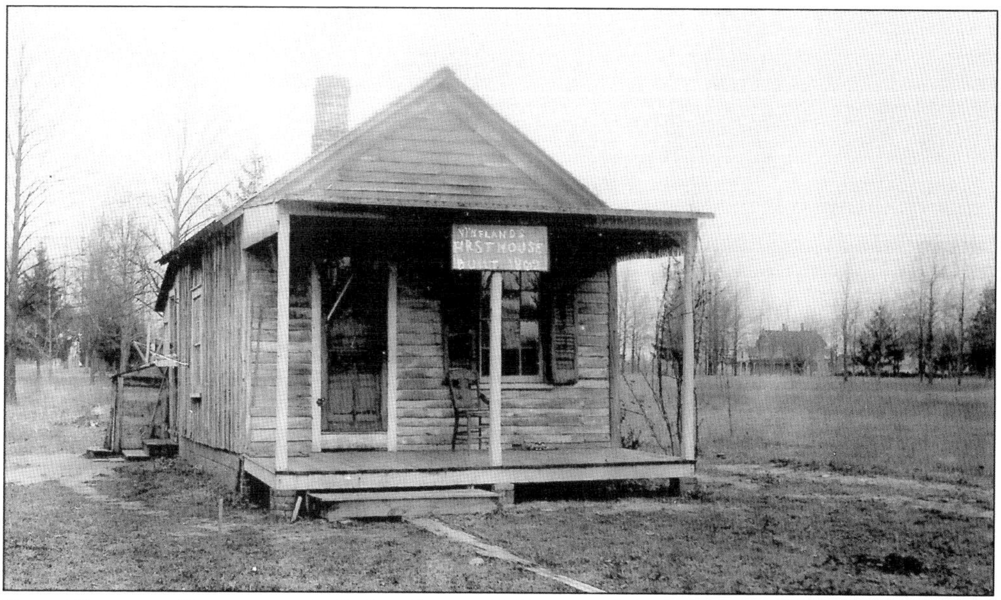

FIRST HOUSE IN VINELAND. In 1862, Chester P. Davis and Lester Richardson constructed the first house built in the borough of Vineland. It was located on the north corner of the Boulevard and Landis Avenue. It was called a "stipulation house" because the deed transfer from Charles K. Landis required that a building be erected within a year of purchasing the land. The lumber used to build the house was hauled in one load from the Forest Grove Mill. About 1900, the house, then owned by the Borough of Vineland, was moved to Landis Park, where it continued to be used as a dwelling. In 1961, it was moved to the grounds of the Vineland Historical and Antiquarian Society.

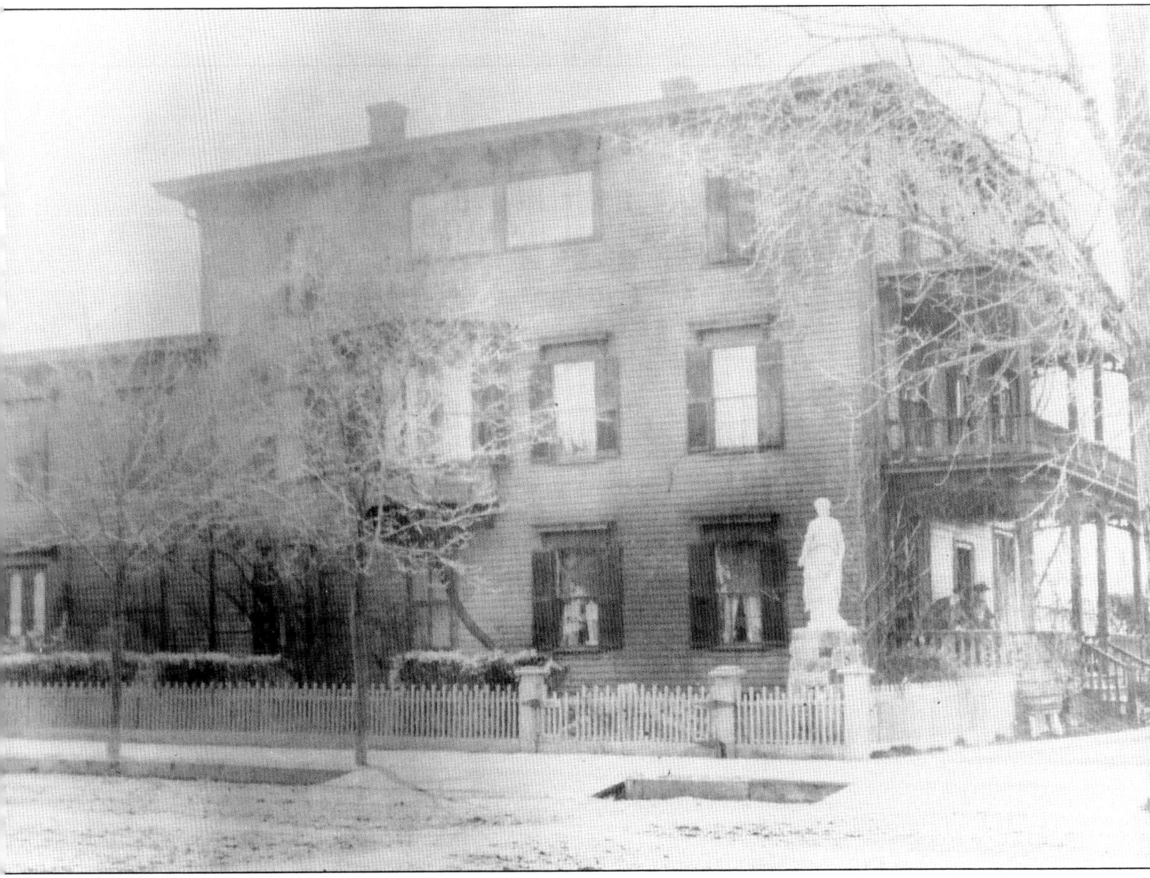

HOME OF CHARLES K. LANDIS, C. 1890. This picture shows the home of Charles K. Landis, at the corner of the Boulevard and Landis Avenue. This large three-story structure, which was originally the Magnolia House Hotel, was filled with artifacts that Landis collected on his travels in Europe. Landis lived in this home at the time of his death in 1900. After his death, the building was converted into a store but was later demolished.

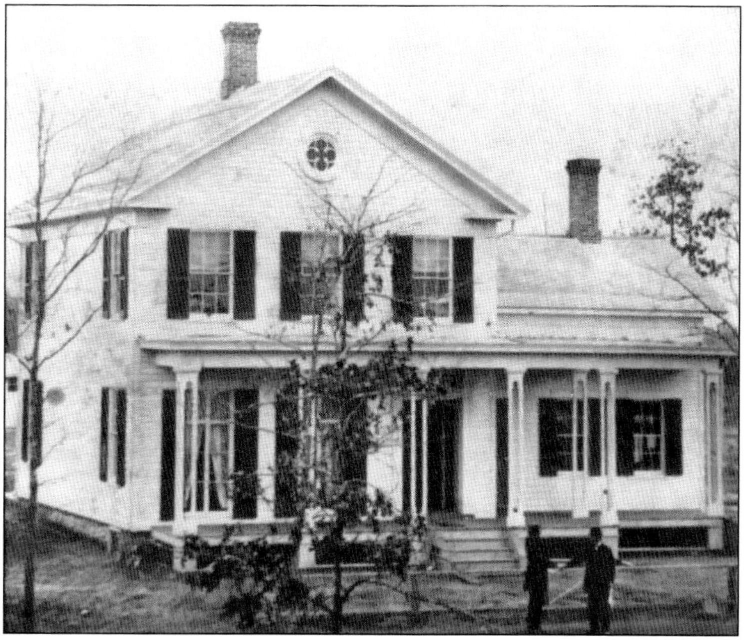

Home of Henry Clay Work. In 1867, Work moved to Vineland with his family and purchased hundreds of acres of land to establish a fruit farm. Work authored several songs that became popular during and after the Civil War, including "Marching Through Georgia" and "Grandfather's Clock."

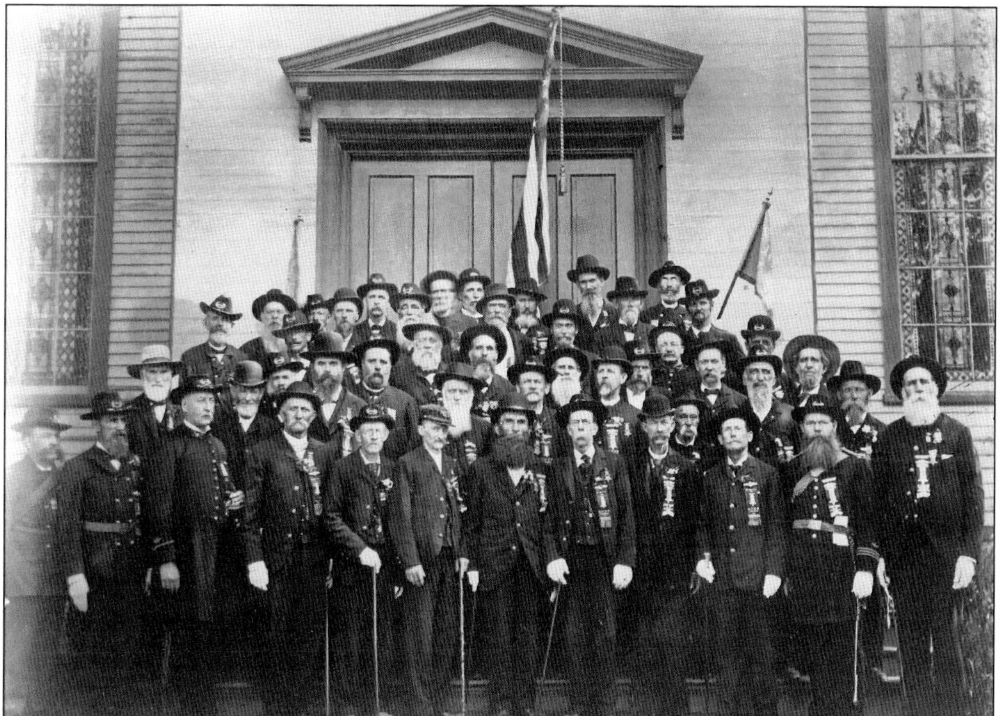

Vineland Lyon Post. In 1875, several Civil War veterans living in Vineland organized Lyon Post 10, Grand Army of the Republic, named after Maj. Gen. Nathaniel Lyon. The post's most active member, Walter H. Blake, shown at the far right, was the driving force behind the erection of the GAR monument on Landis Avenue. Blake also authored a book entitled *Hand Grips: the Story of the Great Gettysburg Reunion, July 1913.*

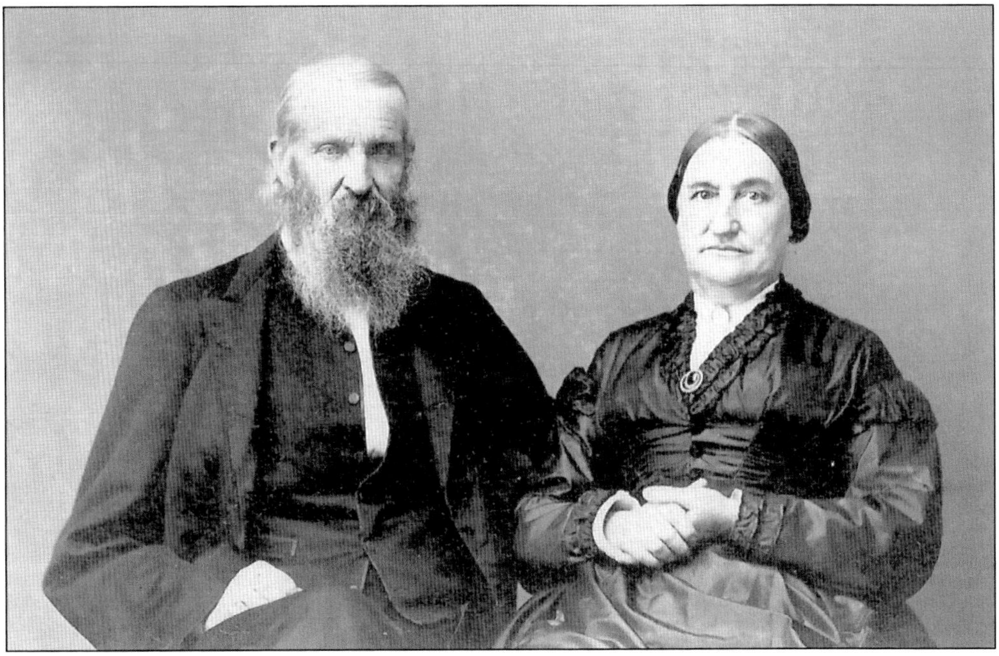

Gage Family Home. In 1868, John and Portia Gage, shown above, moved to Vineland with their children and immediately immersed themselves in the town's progressive atmosphere. Portia was one of the 172 Vineland women who voted ceremoniously in the 1868 U.S. presidential election. Their son John Portius Gage invented the Gage Self-Setting Plane, an improvement on the standard wooden plane. He received patents from several countries and manufactured the planes in Vineland until he sold the invention to the Stanley Tool Company.

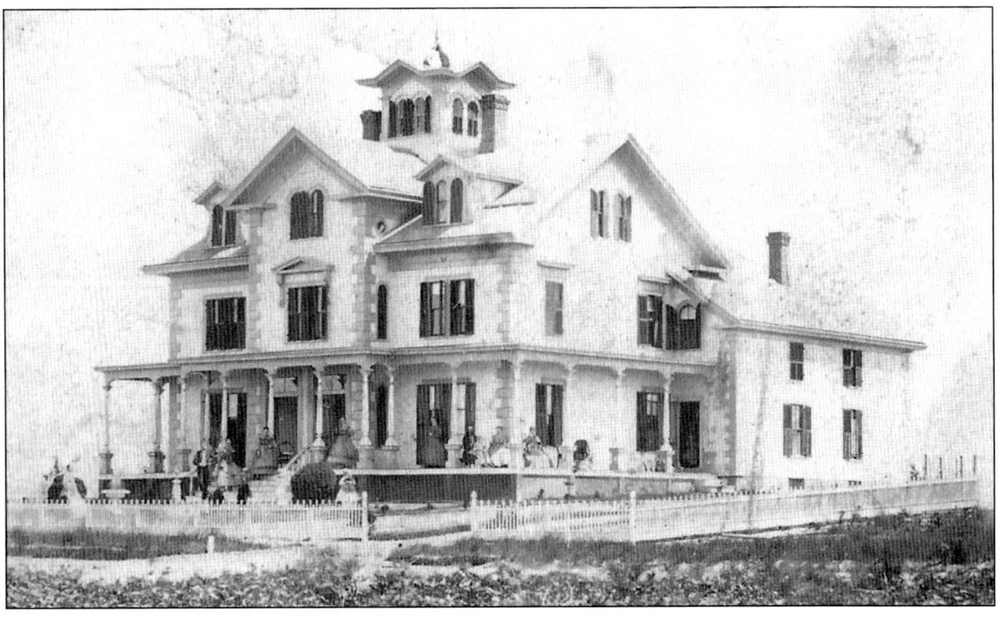

Mary E. Tillotson. In 1864, Tillotson moved to Vineland with her son. She was an advocate of dress reform, a movement that asserted that women were slaves to fashion, and the weight of their clothes sustained by their hips was injurious to health. Her attire consisted of a one-piece dress reaching slightly below the knees, worn over pants. In 1874, she was instrumental in organizing a Dress Reform Convention held in Vineland.

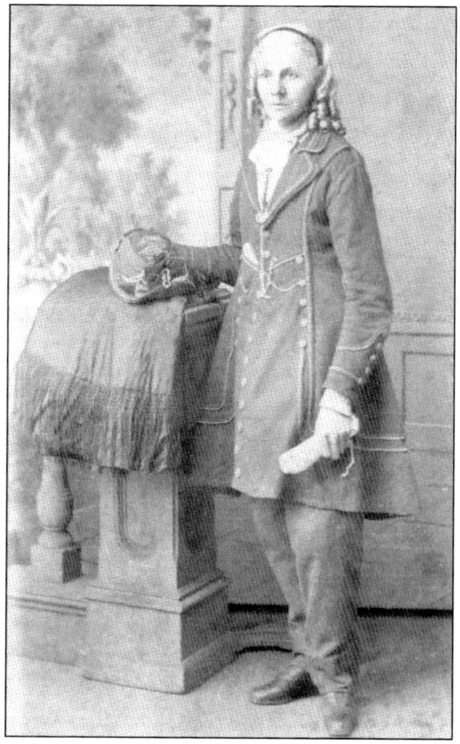

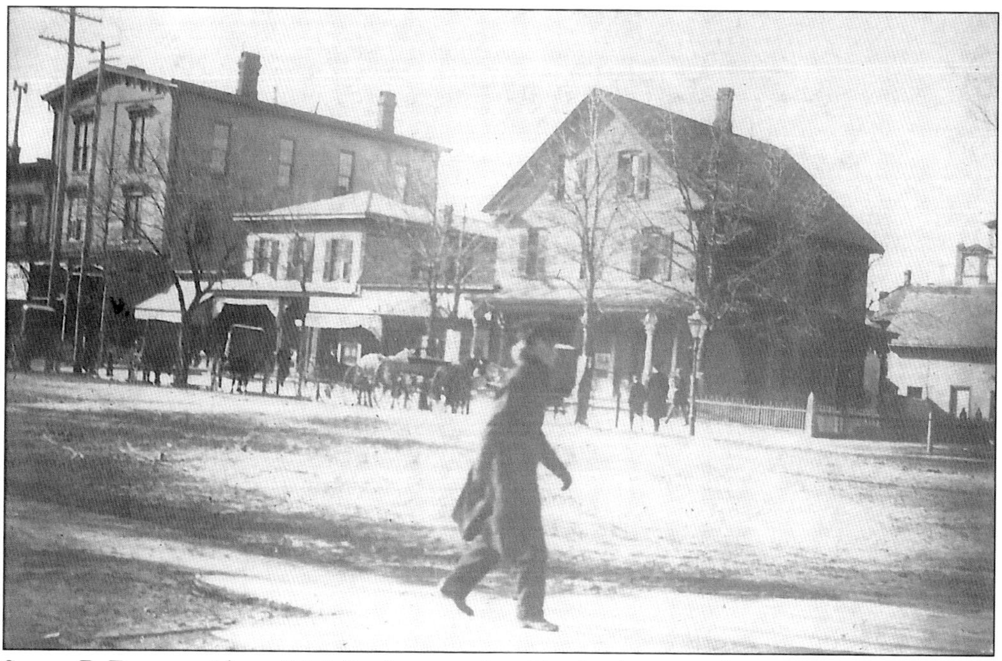

Susan P. Fowler. About 1870, Fowler moved to Vineland as a single woman and established a farm in Landis Township. Fowler was an advocate of dress reform and wore what was called "bloomer fashions," as seen in this picture of her crossing Landis Avenue. She sent many letters of protest to newspapers that advocated equal suffrage for women and protested the taxation of women without representation.

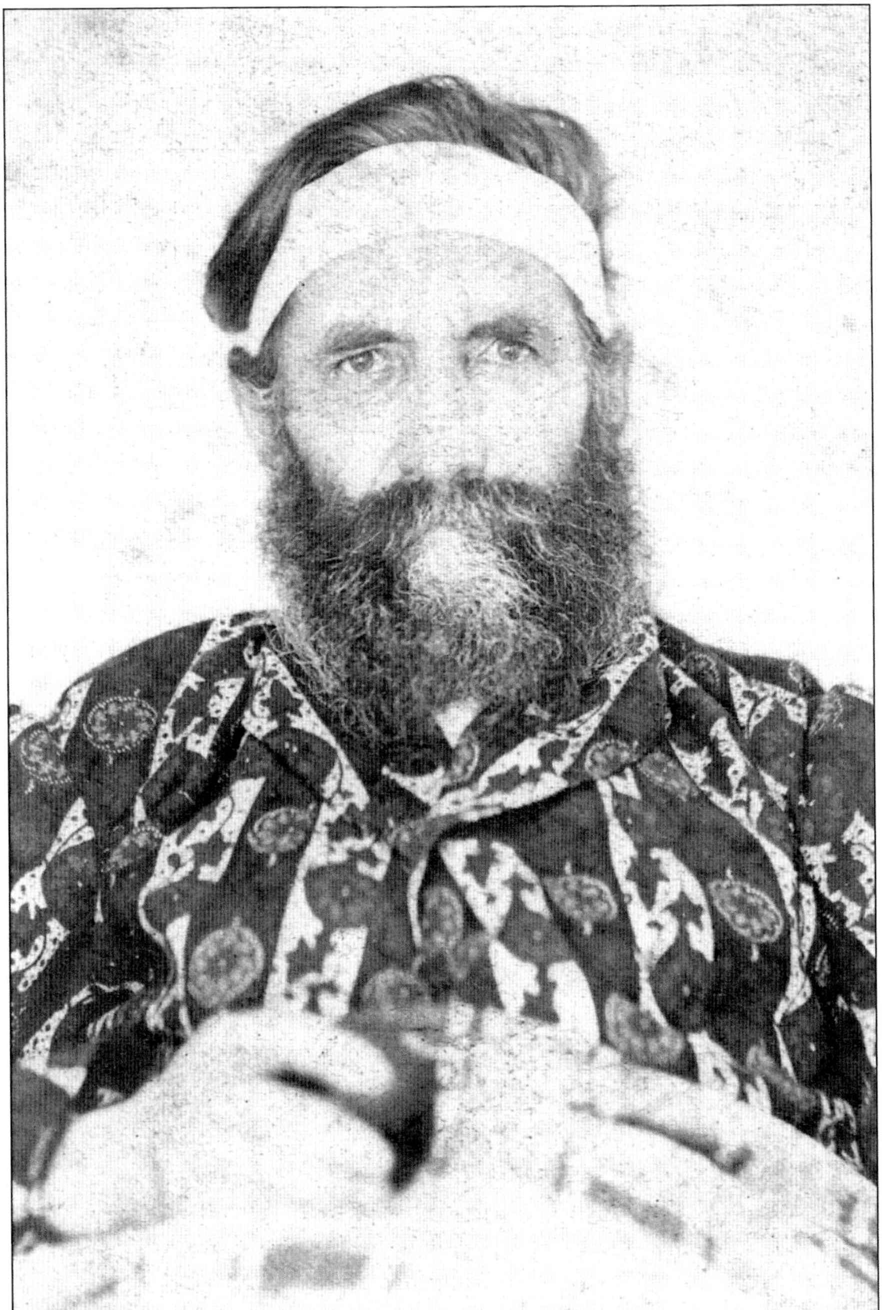

Uri Carruth. In 1867, Carruth moved to Vineland and purchased land on the Boulevard and Walnut Road. In 1870, he purchased the *Vineland Independent*, a newspaper established three years earlier as a means of voicing the dissatisfaction of a group of townspeople with the manner in which Charles K. Landis was involved in the town. Carruth continued that style of writing against Landis, using the paper as an opportunity to deliberately and personally attack him, often referring to Landis as the "King." While his writing was clever and comical, the five-year affair took a toll on Landis.

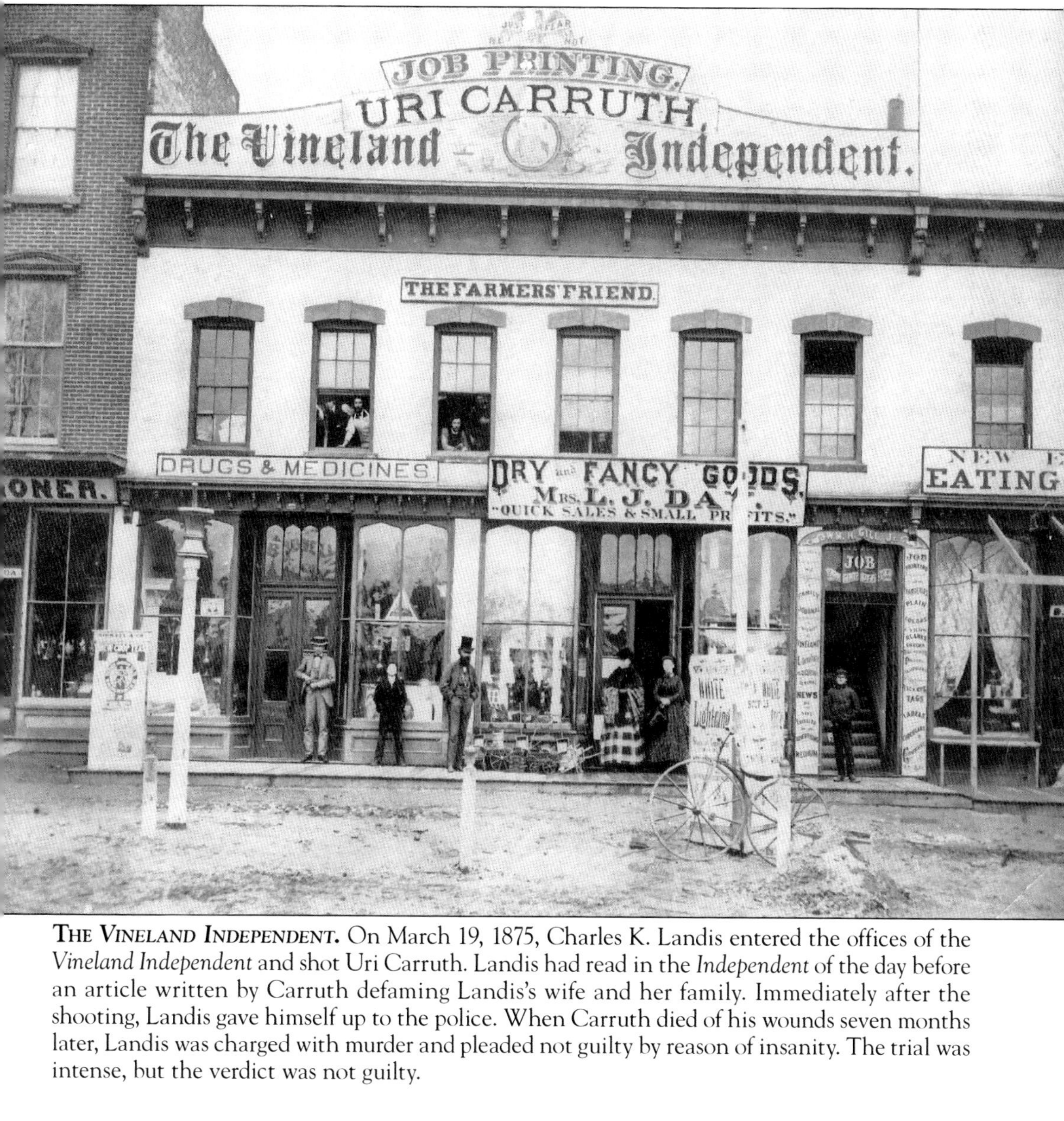

THE *VINELAND INDEPENDENT*. On March 19, 1875, Charles K. Landis entered the offices of the *Vineland Independent* and shot Uri Carruth. Landis had read in the *Independent* of the day before an article written by Carruth defaming Landis's wife and her family. Immediately after the shooting, Landis gave himself up to the police. When Carruth died of his wounds seven months later, Landis was charged with murder and pleaded not guilty by reason of insanity. The trial was intense, but the verdict was not guilty.

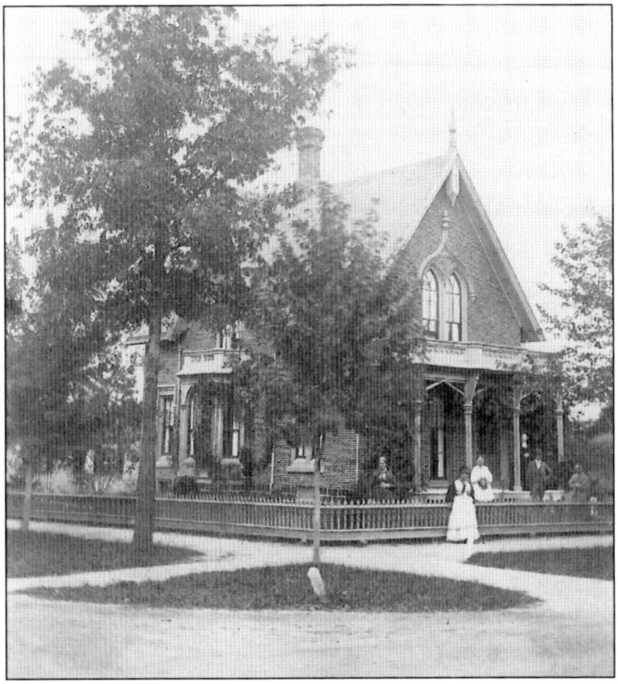

Hartson House, 1876. In 1870, Henry Hartson built this home on the northeast corner of Seventh and Wood Streets. It was the first house constructed in Vineland to be designed by an architect. In 1874, when Pres. Ulysses S. Grant visited Vineland to dedicate the new high school building, he stayed at this home. It was later owned by the Parkinson family and became known as the Thelma Parkinson Sharp house. Sharp, shown at left (in front of the fence), with her husband, Judge Howard P. Sharp, was the youngest delegate to the 1924 Democratic National Convention, the first national political convention held after the United States extended suffrage to women.

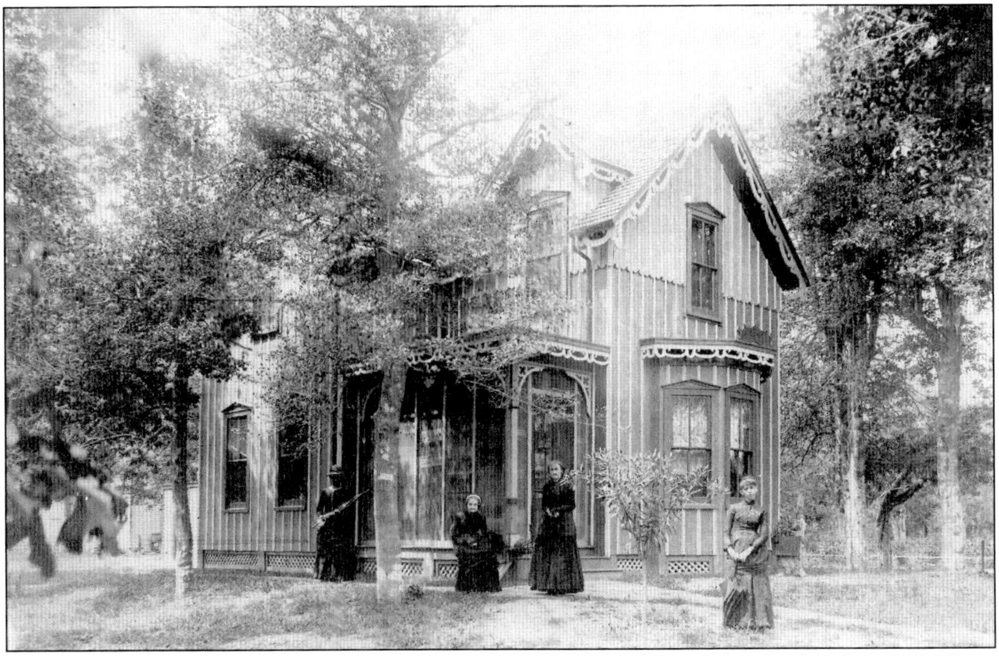

Augusta Cooper Bristol. In 1872, Bristol moved to Vineland with her husband and children. Their home, shown above, was located on Main Road. Bristol was a nationally recognized lecturer, writer, and advocate of progressive thinking. In 1880, she attended the International Convention of Freethinkers as a delegate from the United States. She was elected state lecturer of New Jersey by the Order of the Patrons of Husbandry and delivered hundreds of lectures in several states. In 1884, at the Greenback Party Convention, she gave the address to place Benjamin F. Butler in nomination as a candidate for president of the United States.

HOME OF PROF. MARCIUS WILLSON. Willson moved to Vineland in the 1880s after learning of the advertised health benefits of the town. He had been forced to give up his profession as a lawyer due to a bronchial disease and had begun his career as a writer before moving to Vineland. Willson authored *School and Family Readers*, a series of textbooks published by Harper's and used in schools throughout the country.

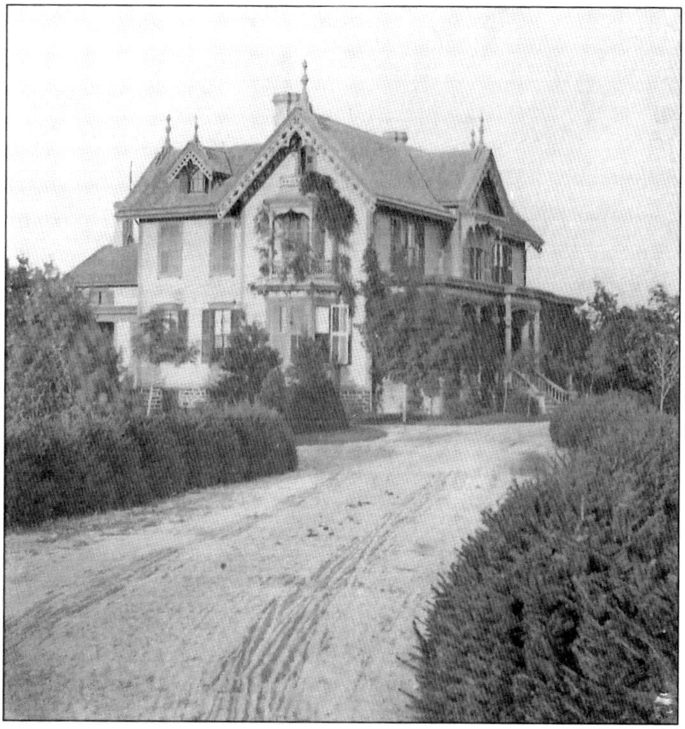

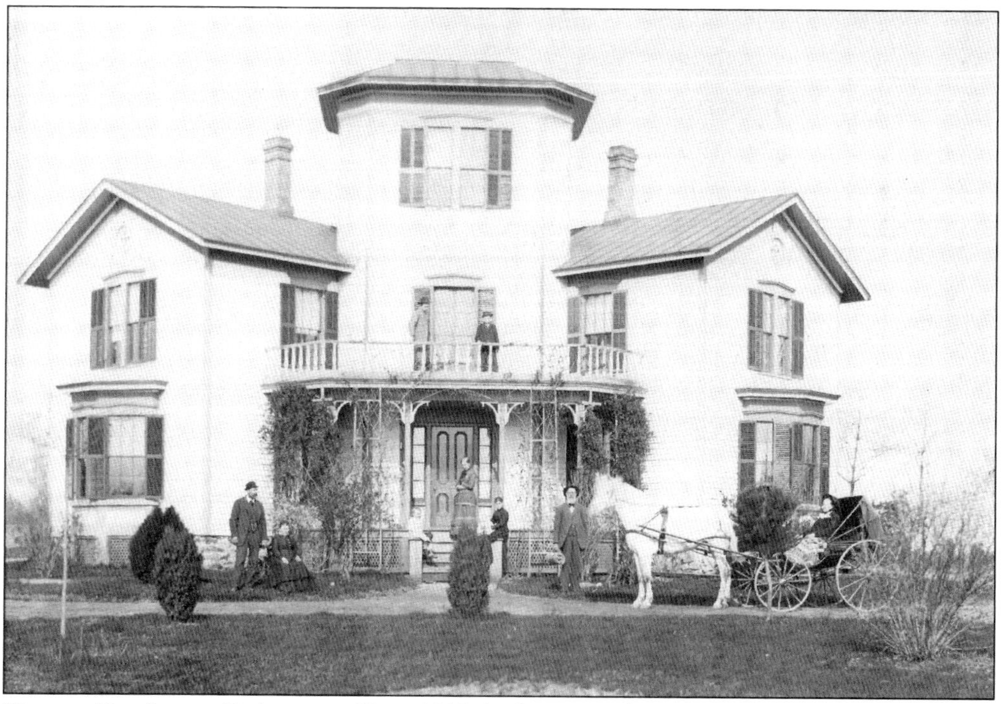

HOME OF DR. AARON C. ANDREW. About 1866, Andrew moved to Vineland with his family and built this house on West Grape Street. His wife, Sarah Brigham Andrew, is shown seated in the buggy in front of their home. Upon Andrew's death in 1908, the house passed through several owners before being occupied by Vineland's American Legion Post. About 1950, the house was demolished.

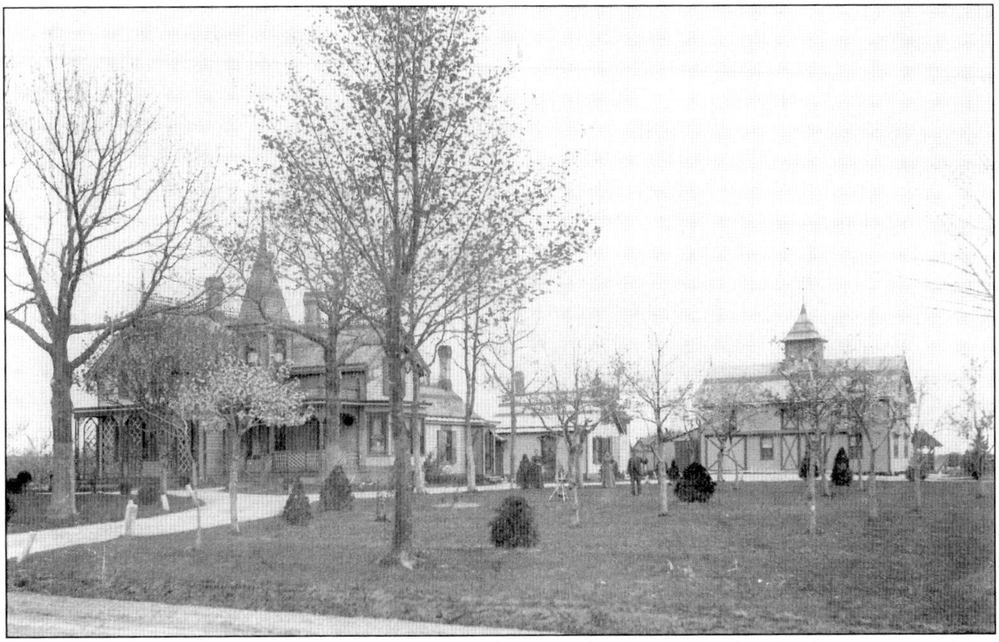

Gifford Home. In 1862, Pardon Gifford moved to Vineland with his family. He was one of the Vineland Pioneers, a group formed of the first settlers of Vineland. In 1863, he helped organize the First Methodist Episcopal Church in Vineland. Gifford was one of the town's first blacksmiths and continued in that business for many years. After his retirement, he settled in the home shown above on the corner of Main Road and Park Avenue.

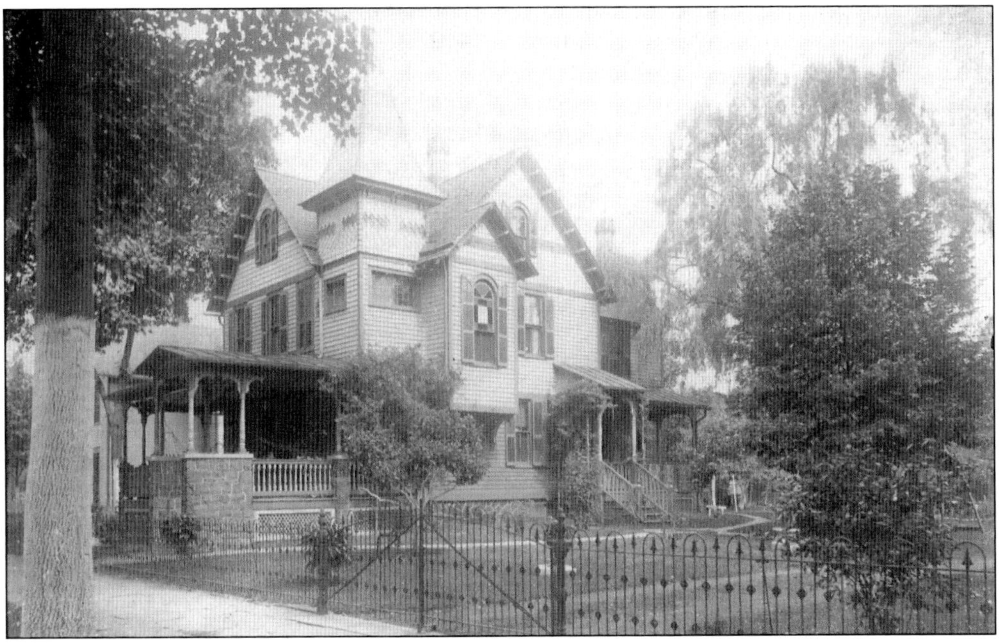

Ackley Home. In 1881, John A. Ackley moved to Vineland and worked as a farmer and as an employee in Keighley's Shoe Factory. In 1884, he became an auctioneer, dealing first in furniture and eventually also in houses. Ackley conducted large sales of real estate with the slogan, "If You Buy It of Ackley, It's a Bargain." His business continued until his death in 1933.

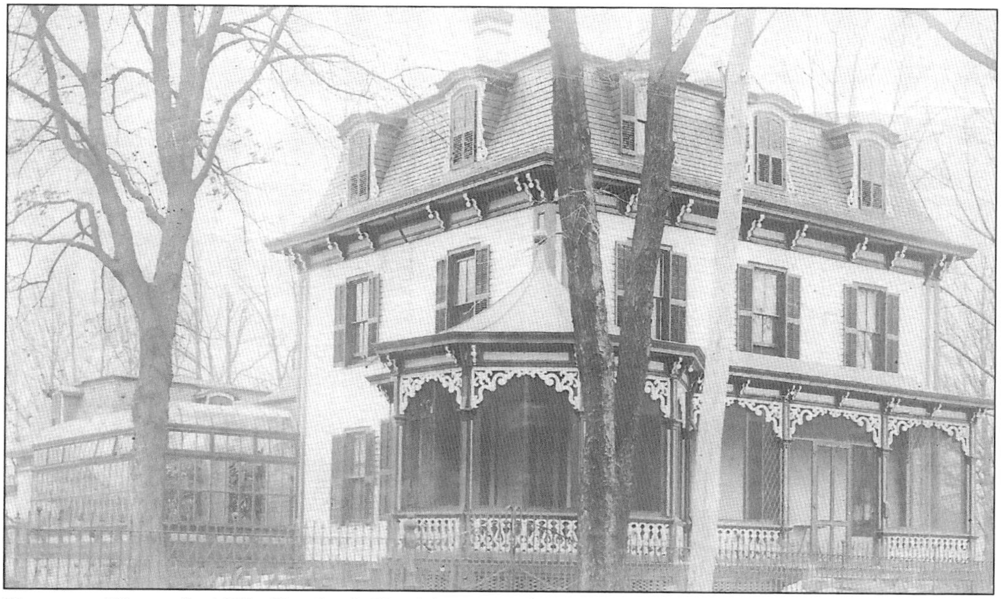

Keighley Home. In 1873, Charles P. Keighley moved to Vineland with his family. Two years earlier, the family had moved to Philadelphia from England, where Keighley learned the shoemaking trade by working in his grandfather's shoe factory. After making Vineland his home, he engaged in the cultivation of a farm for one year before finding employment in a shoe factory. In 1875, Keighley opened his own shoe factory, which became the largest factory of its kind in Vineland. The goods manufactured in his factory were sold all over the United States. In 1890, Keighley organized the Vineland Water Works Company. His wife, Martha Bottomly Keighley, shown below in their home on Almond Street, was also active in the town, serving as president of the Women's Christian Temperance Union and as a board member of the State Institution for Feeble-Minded Women.

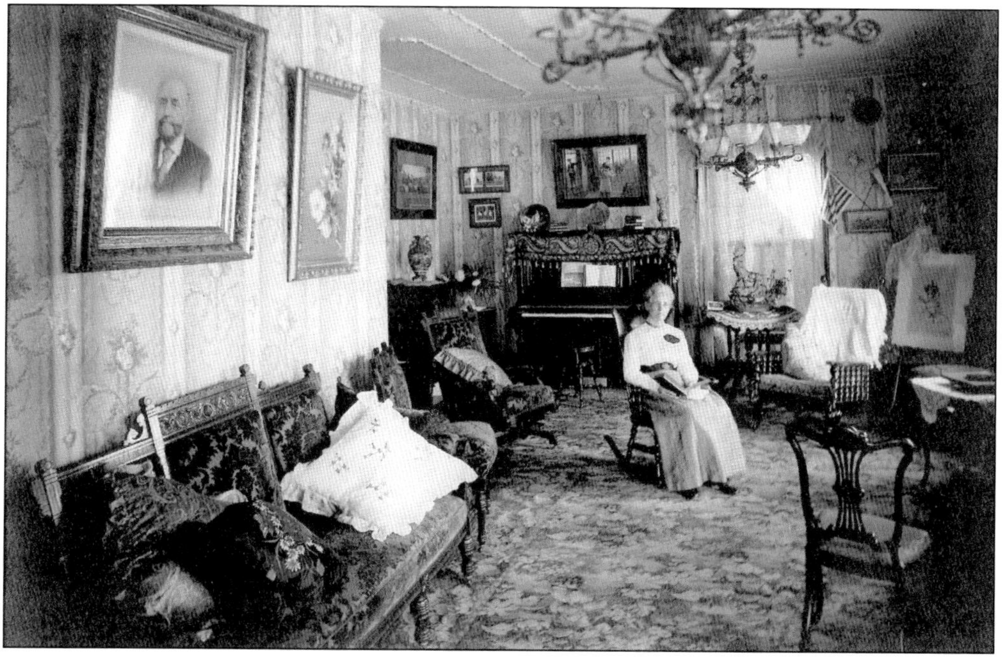

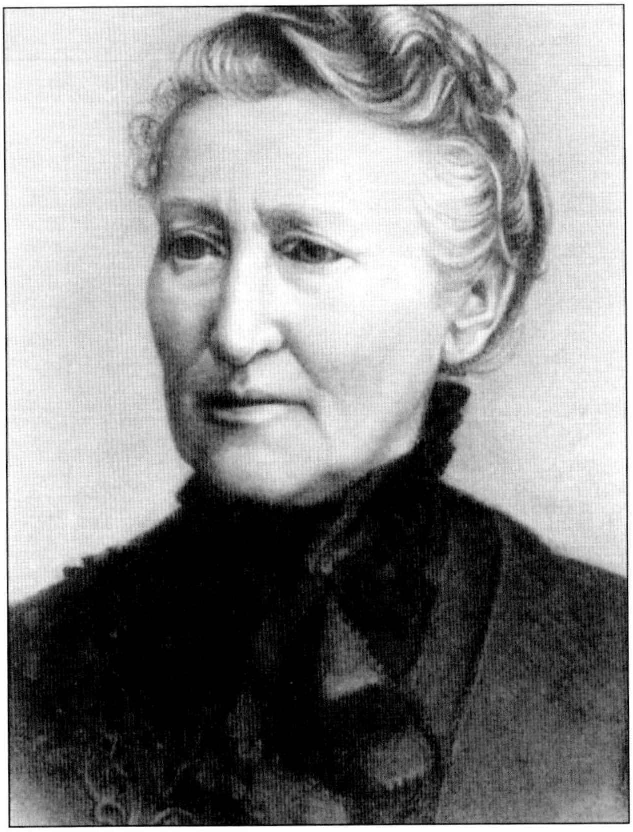

Mary Adelia Davis Treat. In 1868, Treat moved to Vineland with her husband to be involved with the intellectual and cultural movement happening in the town. As a naturalist, botanist, and entomologist, she conducted studies on specimens in the area, often collected from around her home on Park Avenue, shown below. She wrote numerous articles, which were published in professional journals and newspapers. Treat collaborated with Prof. Asa Gray of Harvard University and, in 1874, began corresponding with Charles Darwin. Darwin asked her to conduct various experiments and to tell him of her findings, and as she did, she was mentioned in one of his books. Treat maintained an active life in Vineland until her death in 1923.

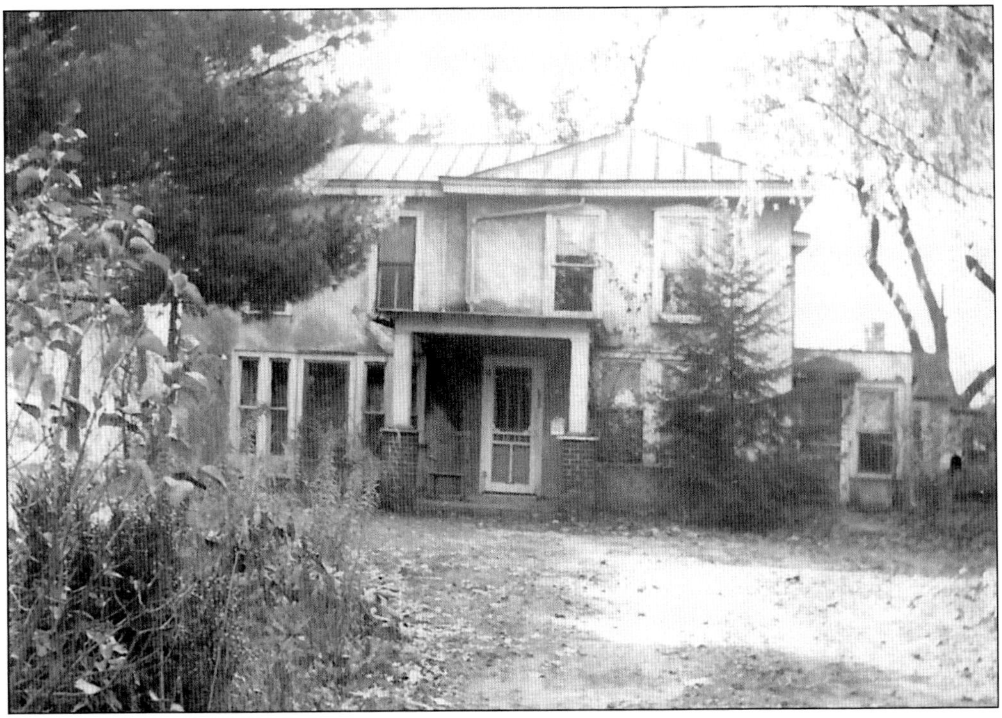

Leverett Newcomb. In 1870, Newcomb moved to Vineland and began practicing law in the office of the late Edwin M. Turner. He was one of the original incorporators and stockholders of the Vineland National Bank and the Vineland Trust Company. In 1922, Newcomb gave $200,000 for the building of a hospital in Vineland and also donated land on Chestnut Avenue for its construction. In 1923, the hospital opened as the Newcomb Hospital. Newcomb, one of Vineland's greatest philanthropists, died three years later.

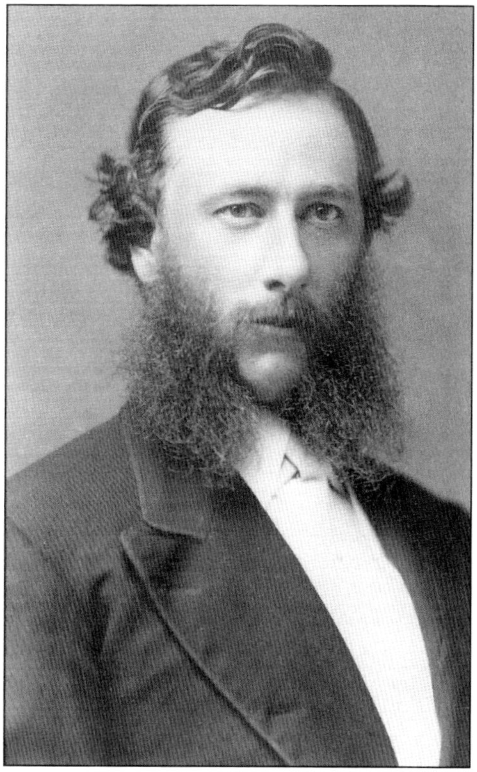

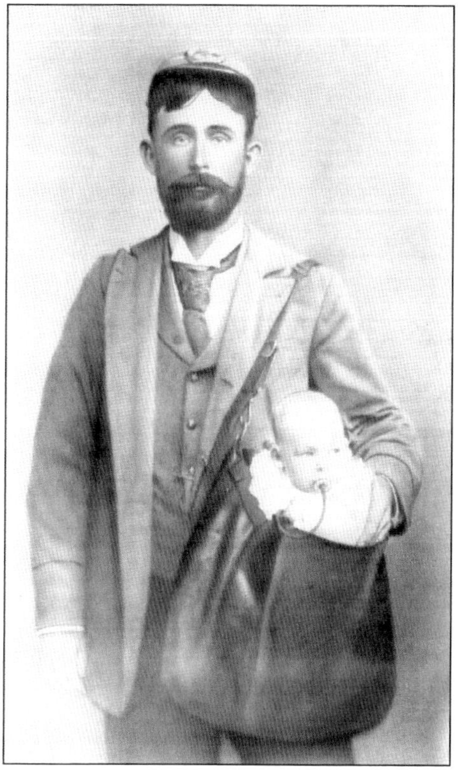

Veteran Mail Carrier. In 1893, William M. Gutterson became a delivery clerk for the Vineland Post Office, three years after the establishment of the Rural Free Delivery system. Mail carriers were equipped with a small shaded lantern attached to their coats, as they often delivered mail late into the evening. Gutterson continued as a carrier for about 40 years, until his death in the 1930s. He is shown here with a special delivery, most likely his own child.

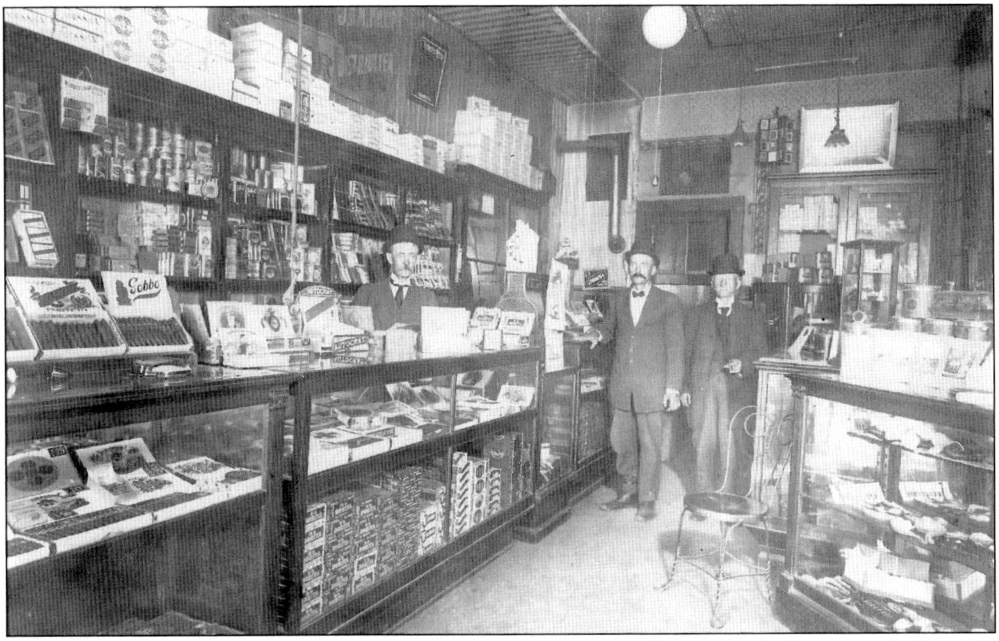

Joseph Hooker McKillip. At the age of 13, Joseph H. McKillip started a business for himself selling fruit on excursion trains from Vineland to the shore, in which he employed 20 other boys. His entrepreneurial spirit continued into adulthood, and he shifted careers several times after graduating from school. In the 1880s, he operated a grocery store, which he sold to John R. Potts, owner of a large shoe factory in town. In 1890, he opened a bakery, which he sold three years later, and afterwards he became a real estate agent. About 1907, he purchased a manufacturing and retail cigar business, shown in the picture above.

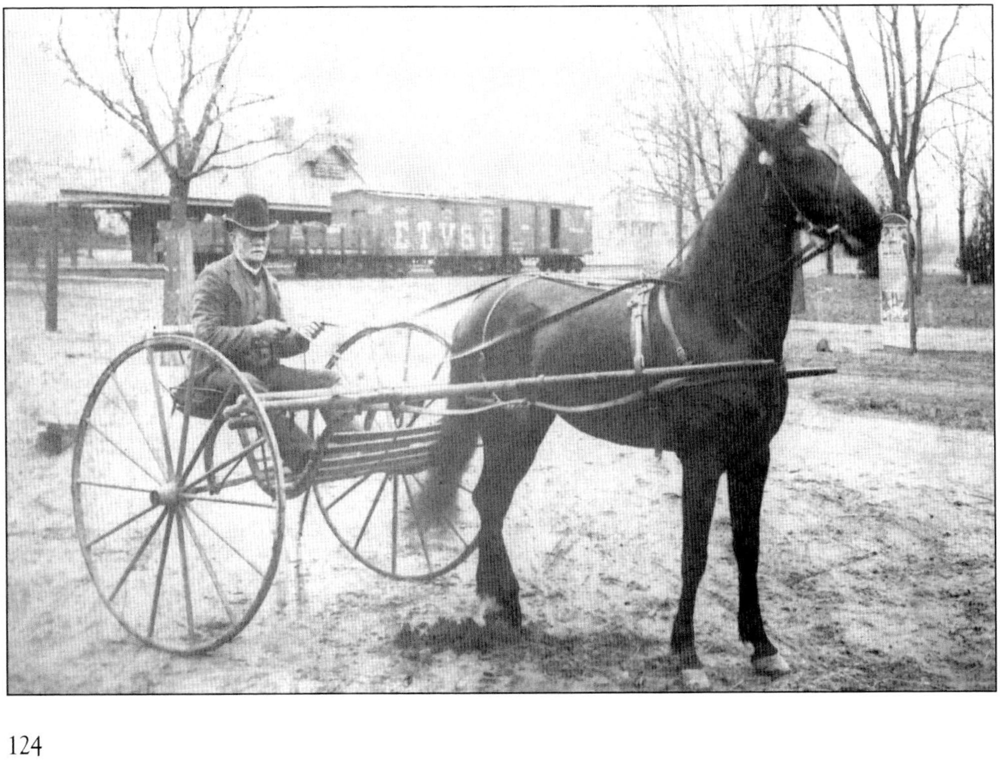

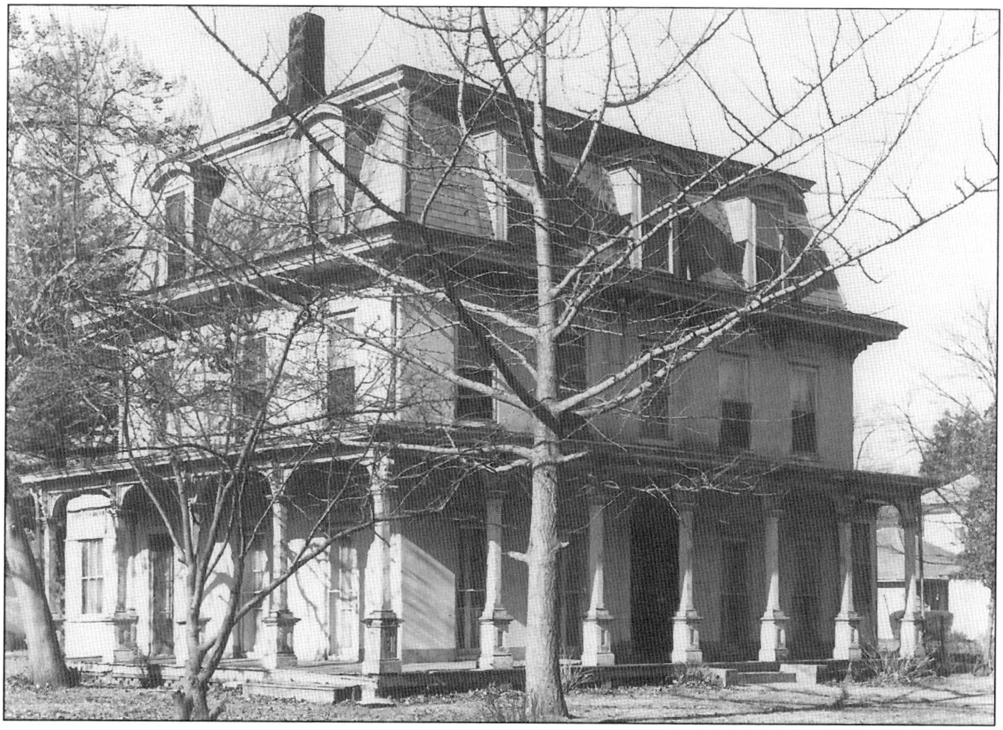

Home Hospitals. In 1910, five Vineland men formed the Vineland Hospital Association to provide means for the free care and treatment of the sick or injured. The association's office was located at the corner of Sixth and Plum Streets, where the first hospital was opened. Before the construction of Newcomb Hospital in 1922–1923, there were five "Home Hospitals" throughout the town where doctors conducted practices in buildings that once had been homes. The Vineland Hospital, shown above, was built by Edwin M. Turner on the corner of Eighth and Plum Streets. The Physicians Hospital, shown below, was located on the corner of Sixth and Pear Streets and, by 1914, had a total of 27 beds.

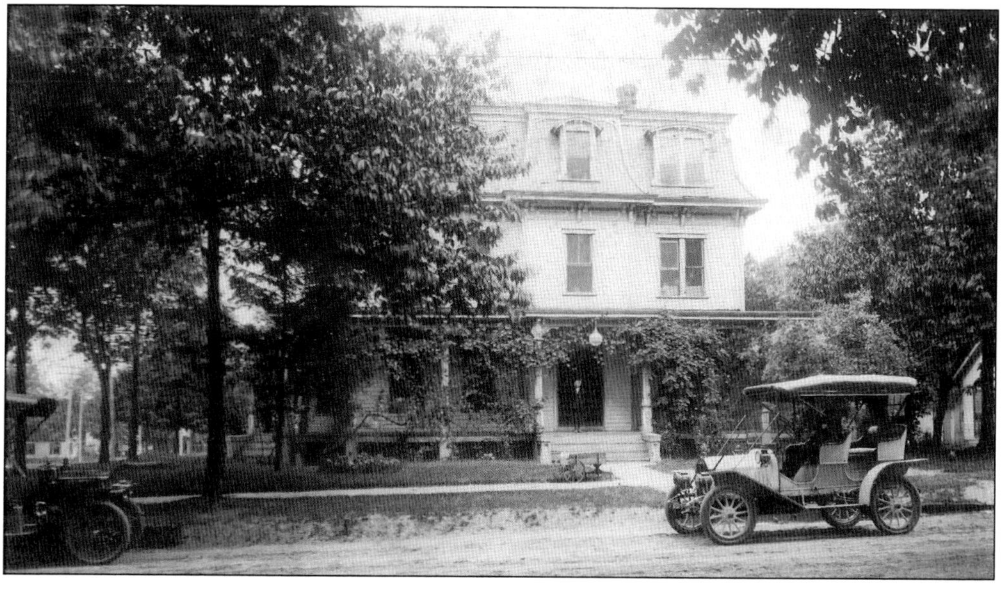

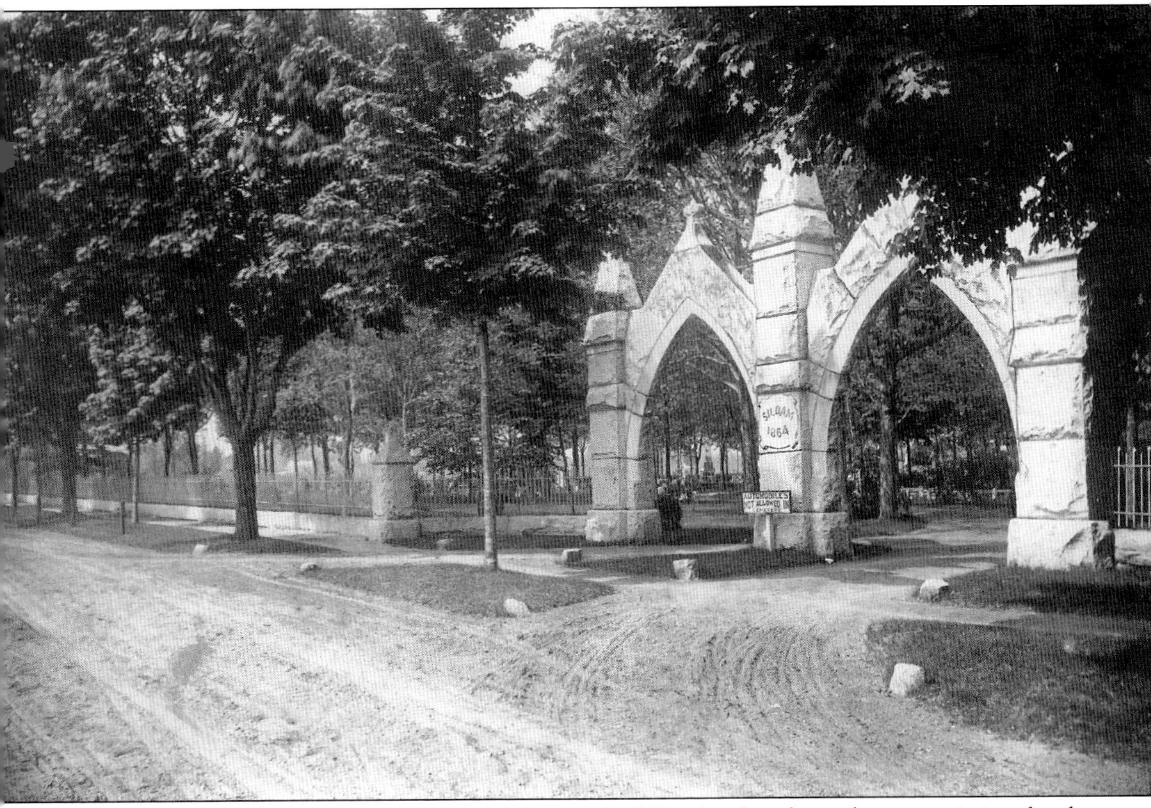

Beautiful City of the Dead. In 1864, a group of Vinelanders formed an association for the establishment of a nonsectarian cemetery. Charles K. Landis donated 14 acres of wooded land to the association, which then opened Siloam Cemetery on Valley Avenue. In this picture, a sign on the granite arch, which was completed in 1900, reads, "Automobiles not allowed in cemetery." Many of Vineland's most prominent citizens are buried in Siloam Cemetery, including the Landis family, Mary Treat, Frank D. Andrews, and Capt. Inman Sealby.

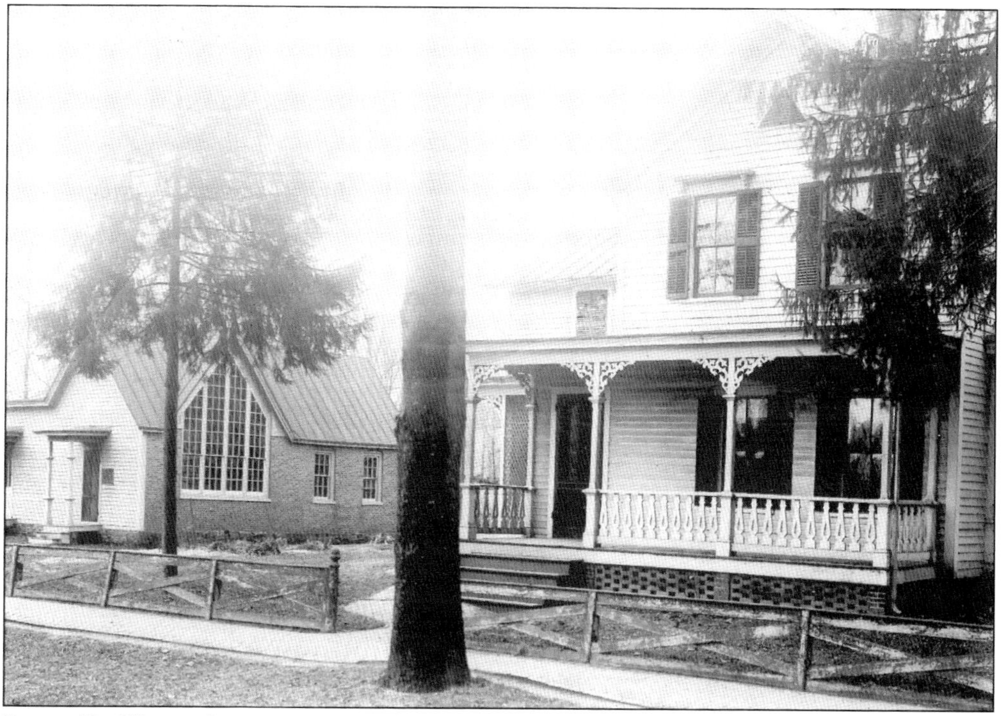

Frank De Wette Andrews, 1922. For 47 of the 49 years of his trusteeship, Frank D. Andrews served as secretary and treasurer of the board of trustees of the Vineland Historical and Antiquarian Society. His home was located on the lot directly next to the society, as shown in the picture above. His dedication to the society continues to be unrivaled by his successors. It is because of his work that the society's collections of the early history of Vineland are so great and varied. In 1916, he created the *Vineland Historical Magazine*, which the society has continuously published since then. The society's museum stands today as a memorial to Frank D. Andrews.

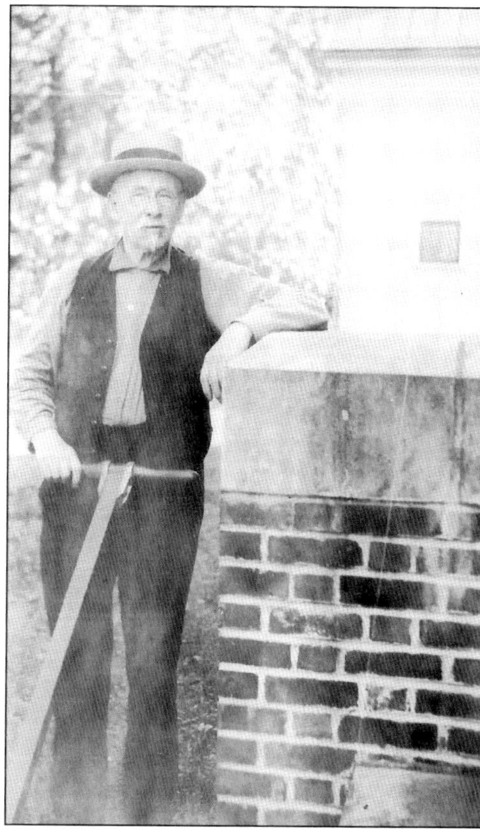